D0148964

SPACES FOR CONSUMPTION

PLEASURE AND PLACELESSNESS IN THE POST-INDUSTRIAL CITY

STEVEN MILES

Los Angeles | London | New Delhi
Singapore | Washington DC

'This is a great book. Powerfully written and lucid, it provides a thorough introduction to concepts of consumption as they relate to the spaces of cities. The spaces themselves the airports, the shopping malls, the museums and cultural quarters – are analysed in marvellous detail, and with a keen sense of historical precedent. And, refreshingly, Miles doesn't simply dismiss cultures of consumption out of hand, but shows how as consumers we are complicit in, and help define those cultures. His book makes a major contribution to our understanding of contemporary cities, but is accessible enough to appeal to any reader with an interest in this important area.'

Richard Williams, Edinburgh University

for Charlie
for Yanli Sun-Miles

© Steven Miles 2010

First published 2010

Apart from any fair dealing for the purposes of research or private study, or criticism or review, as permitted under the Copyright, Designs and Patents Act, 1988, this publication may be reproduced, stored or transmitted in any form, or by any means, only with the prior permission in writing of the publishers, or in the case of reprographic reproduction, in accordance with the terms of licences issued by the Copyright Licensing Agency. Enquiries concerning reproduction outside those terms should be sent to the publishers.

SAGE Publications Ltd
1 Oliver's Yard
55 City Road
London EC1Y 1SP

SAGE Publications Inc.
2455 Teller Road
Thousand Oaks, California 91320

SAGE Publications India Pvt Ltd
B 1/I 1 Mohan Cooperative Industrial Area
Mathura Road, Post Bag 7
New Delhi 110 044

SAGE Publications Asia-Pacific Pte Ltd
33 Pekin Street #02-01
Far East Square
Singapore 048763

Library of Congress Control Number 2009941474

British Library Cataloguing in Publication data

A catalogue record for this book is available from the British Library

ISBN 978-1-4129-4665-0
ISBN 978-1-4129-4666-7 (pbk)

Typeset by C&M Digitals (P) Ltd, Chennai, India
Printed in India by Replika Press Pvt. Ltd
Printed on paper from sustainable resources

CONTENTS

1

INTRODUCTION: THE CITY OF COMPLICITY

Our cities are what and where we consume. In essence, the city is in fact nothing more than a space for consumption in which we apparently express ourselves as citizens of a consumer society. Consumption lies at the ideological core of the contemporary city and, as such, consumption spaces lie at the very heart of what it means to be a citizen of the society in which we live. The contemporary city appears to be undergoing something of a transformation second only in scale to the onset of industrialisation. All around us are indications and representations of what has been labelled an 'urban renaissance', a period that promises good times ahead; times from which the city will emerge as *the* focal point for regenerative social change. Cities throughout Europe are being re-branded as places to be consumed; as tourist destinations, centres of culture and as places worthy of the 'cultured' middle classes. But are such changes any more than purely symbolic? Do they represent a substantive shift in how we as human beings relate to the cities around us? Is the soul of the contemporary city being sold to the consumerist paymaster and, if so, what does this mean for the long-term sustainability of our cities?

Spaces for Consumption is concerned with the contexts in which the omnipresent power of consumption is most powerfully expressed and, in turn, how the human condition is reflected in these spaces. The apparently revitalised nature of the urban condition may provide us with false promises. The transitory appeal of consumer-based landscapes offer us an instant high, but can such landscapes be maintained or are the dream worlds with which consumerism apparently placates us nothing more than a mirage on the commodified landscape? To paraphrase Horkheimer and Adorno (1973), does the diner simply have to be satisfied with the city booster's menu? Can our relationship with the city be sustained through the bricks and mortar that consumption bequeaths us? Is it possible to maintain a degree of place specificity in a global consumerist world?

It would not be an exaggeration to suggest that in its latest incarnation, the city is less a place for and of the people and more a unit for the efficient maximisation of consumption. Shopping malls, theme parks, art galleries, museums, cinema complexes, designer apartments, casinos, sports stadia and public spaces of consumption provide us with a mirror of ourselves or at least a mirror of a society that has apparently determined what it is we are. Perhaps more worryingly, the effect of consumption on the city is as much symbolic as it is real. Even if some of our cities are struggling to achieve the renaissance that is now considered to be the obligatory norm, they will at least pursue this renaissance at a symbolic level, not least in the hope that if the process of re-branding is believable enough, if you can get people to believe that there is an urban renaissance going on, then real change may follow. In Europe and especially in the UK prior to 2008, this process is no more graphically illustrated than in the example of the ultimate aspirational urban beauty contest, the annual competition to become European Capital of Culture. It is more important to be perceived to be undergoing a renaissance than to be seen not to aspire to the unbridled salvation that consumption can never, in actual fact, deliver. But this process brings with it an inherent danger because the very nature of capitalism and hence of consumption is such that it will always produce more losers than it will winners. In other words, whilst we can accept that consumption is more likely to divide than provide for the majority of individuals, on a macro-level, it is a non-sense to imagine that this inequality will not be reproduced in comparisons between one city and another. Wigan cannot be Liverpool, Liverpool cannot be Manchester and Manchester cannot be London. Or can they? Is the commodification of our cities robbing them of their very identities and turning them into clones that tell us something profound about the nature of 'consumerism as a way of life' (Miles, 1998)? Can cities be excluded along class lines in much the same way that groups of people are excluded within cities? *Spaces for Consumption* is concerned with addressing whether consumption is simply an expression of these processes or a key driver of them.

At one level, the city of consumption is of course a city of the built environment. In his Situationist treatise, Ivan Chtcheglov (2006) argued that a new architecture should express the very essence of a new civilisation, but that there was in fact no such thing as a capitalist architecture. In reality, an architecture of capitalism has emerged but it falls far short of what Chtcheglov envisaged a new architecture might achieve.

> Architecture is the simplest means of articulating time and space, of modulating reality and engendering dreams. It is a matter not only of plastic articulation and modulation expressing an ephemeral beauty, but of a modulation producing influences in accordance with the eternal spectrum of human desires and the progress in fulfilling them. (Chtcheglov, 2006)

This book will suggest that Chtcheglov's vision of the city of the future that he presented in 1953, a city of discovery and adventure, a sexy, pleasurable and exciting city, has never been realised. What has emerged in its place is a city that consumerism has deemed to be adventurous, exciting and pleasurable but only on its own terms. The city we live in is not a product of human desires, it is monument to the (alleged) failure of human progress but as such it is propped up by an architecture of capitalism. However, it is not argued here that this is a one-way street and that the cities in which we live are somehow foistered upon us by the ideological tentacles of consumer capitalism in which:

> The culture-ideology project of global capitalism is to persuade people to consume not simply to satisfy their biological and other modest needs but in response to artificially created desires in order to perpetuate the accumulation of capital for private profit, in other words, to ensure that the capitalist global system goes on forever. (Sklair, 2002: 62)

The ideological tentacles of consumer capitalism continue to exist but they are the product of a world that we brought upon ourselves and continue to pursue. Consumers are not victims of the consumer society, they are complicit in it. It is this complicity that lies at the very heart of the relationship between the individual and society and which defines the nature of the individual's relationship with that city: the contemporary city as a manifestation of the individual's struggle to be unique and yet simultaneously to be part of a group and demonstrate capitalism's predisposition to uphold this quandary.

In what is perhaps his seminal work, *The Metropolis and Mental Life*, Georg Simmel (1950) argues that the anonymity of relations in the metropolis are determined by the need for anonymous market relations. As the metropolis developed in the early twentieth century, it began to satisfy the psychological as well as the sociological needs of its inhabitants. It is in this sense that consumption plays the role of a mediating phenomena in determining the relationship between self and society. In his work on fashion, Simmel also argued that the whole history of society is about a compromise between adherence and absorption in a social group and the need for individuation and distinction at an individual level. Consumption is significant because it provides a bridge between the communal and the individual, and the city represents the most visible and revealing expression of this process.

The cities which we live in are the cities we want, but they are not the cities that we need. From this point of view, consumer spaces actively contribute to the nature of our experience of the social world around us. They help to make us what we are. For many of us, our experience of the city is defined by shopping. We experience shopping as freedom, as Zukin (2005) notes: we feel that it offers an arena within which we can exercise freedom of choice, of self-gratification and escape whilst simultaneously naturalising the market economy. For Zukin, shopping is the new class struggle – on the one hand, it offers freedom; with the other, it takes it away: 'Shopping is consuming our lives – but bringing us less satisfaction. More goods are for sale – but we can never find exactly what we want. Shopping is a deeply cultural experience and one that at an individual level feels creative. Around every city corner there is another unfulfilled promise of happiness and fulfilment and moreover because it is usually what we do when we "go out", shopping is how we satisfy our need to socialize – to feel we are part of a public life'. (Zukin, 2005: 7)

In effect then, urban expressions of consumption bind us to a dominant logic that necessarily undermines our creativity by containing it very deliberately within the confines of consumption. This is the premise that underlies the architecture of consumption. And yet, examples of consumption-led regeneration are given an unwarranted reverence because which policy-maker in his or her right mind could possibly stand up and say that their city is not world class? Spaces for consumption feed civic pride, but the degree of substance behind that pride remains a matter for considerable debate. In the past, civic pride was most readily expressed by the political and the private: town halls, parks and libraries (Satterthwaite, 2001). Consumption spaces used to be about as far away from civic pride as you could get. In recent years, urban planners and entrepreneurial urbanists have lauded the potential of the post-industrial city and the glorious possibilities of a world in which image is all. Richard Florida (2002) is an example of an urban evangelist who has valorised the role of the city as a productive unit but who does so in the context of consumption. It is in this way that urban planners and policy-makers are encouraged to enter a mindset in which consumption is all. But there is always the danger that this onus on consumption may actually take something away from the cities in which we live, so that they become nothing more than slight variations upon each other. Birmingham can be Edinburgh after all.

Our relationship with society is mediated by consumption and therefore consumption spaces provide a primary means of reasserting a particular vision of what our society is all about. But if that vision is ultimately unrealisable, the dangers for our urban environment are considerable and real. As consumers, we thirst after the sorts of escape that spaces of consumption appear to offer. We are seduced by the opportunity to consume and the sense of fulfilment and satisfaction that this implies but we do not do so in ignorance. We actively relish the sense of freedom that consumption implies whilst knowing full well that beneath the surface, it cannot produce on its promises.

At a time when the perceived risk of terror on our cities is at an all time high, the threat from within that consumption represents is more than ever accepted as the normal; as a natural state of affairs. The city of production is a city of the past. The city of consumption is an aspirational city: a city of the present and of the future. But it is within this assumption of triviality that the impact of consumption on our lives is potentially such a threat. Lipovetsky (2005) has described a state of hyperconsumption in which consumption absorbs and integrates more and more spheres of social life which thereby encourages individuals to consume for their own pleasure rather than to enhance their social status. A hypermodern society is a fluid society, but one characterised by tension, anxiety and a lack of tradition and above all one that privileges the pleasure of experience. Similarly, as Rifkin puts it:

> The changes taking place in the structuring of economic relationships are part of an even larger transformation occurring in the nature of the capitalist system ... Global travel and tourism, theme cities and parks, destination entertainment centers, wellness, fashion and cuisine, professional sports and games, gambling, music, film, television, the virtual worlds of cyberspace, and electronically

mediated entertainment of every kind are fast becoming the centre of a new hyper-capitalism that trades in access to cultural experiences. (Rifkin, 2000: 44)

Spaces for consumption provide a physical focal point for such transitions; they intensify a lack of tradition, and strip the city of its origins and throw it into the hands of the market so that any kind of recognition of our communal demise is washed away by the immediate gauging of the self; a sort of self-satisfying subjectivisation of space and place to the orthodoxy of consumption. But the very fact that it cannot deliver, and the fact continually returns in the hope that it will do so, is the very reason it is perpetuated. It is the very reason that, as consumers, we want the consumer society to do exactly what it does. We relish the freedoms that consumption appears to give us and we implicate ourselves in the process.

Consumption is ideological insofar as it is presented to us as the only solution to the traumatic consequences of a failed modernity and a failed industrialisation. The collapse of manufacture and distribution resulted in a desperate situation in which the very economic future of our cities was (and still is) utterly undermined. Cities in the UK and the so-called 'developed world' are having to deal with a long-term process of de-industrialisation. The weakening of the mass industrial culture that prevailed for the second half of the twentieth century, precipitated a political orthodoxy of privatisation and de-regulation and the fostering of a new 'entrepreneurial' style of local government (Hannigan, 2003). With nowhere to go and without the sense of pride engendered by industrial wealth and productivity, our cities have spiralled into decline; a pale reflection of themselves to the extent that even the grand buildings of great industrial cities such as Manchester and Liverpool appear to taunt their townspeople as to the inferior nature of the times. Throughout the world, cities are looking to iconic means of regeneration, known as the 'Bilbao-effect' (see Chapter 5), to provide the sort of instant chemical high intended to, artificially, bring them out of a slumber which simply cannot go on, or more accurately cannot *appear* to go on.

As cities struggle to construct an identity in a world of de-industrialised decay, the attractions of consumption (often masquerading as culture) have become too irresistible for policy-makers, commercial developers and planners to resist. The city has become a Mecca for the so-called creative individual, but in promoting this vision of creativity, we have by default created a model of the city that says more about the society in which we live than the people who belong to or more accurately are subjects of that society. From this point of view, the very process of creativity appears to be wed to the ideals of the marketplace so that any efforts to be an individual can only be resolved, albeit partially, through the marketplace.

The city is no longer simply an expression of who or what we are, but no more or less than a venue for consumption experiences; experiences that tie us to the capitalist priorities that underpin our social norms. As Craik (1997: 125) puts it, '... the spaces and places in which consumption occurs are as important as the products and services consumed ... Consumption occurs within, and is regulated by, purpose-built spaces for consumption characterised by the provisions of consumption-related services, visual consumption and cultural products. Circuits of cultural capital operate within broader financial parameters'. What we are dealing with here is what Zukin (1998) has referred to as a 'spatial embeddness', the way in which cultural capital is not just symbolic in nature but plays a key material role; it creates economic value in its own right. In this way, spaces for consumption constitute a physical manifestation of a lived ideology. As consumers who actively seek pleasure through spaces for consumption, we are effectively complicit in the ideologies by which we are implicated. As a venue for cultural experience, spaces for consumption naturalise the capitalist system so it appears to be the only possible alternative. We live and operate as consumers within the boundaries provided by spaces for consumption.

By focusing on the nature of these experiences and on the spaces that give life to these experiences, a key intention of this book is to highlight the ideological nature of the consumer city and the ways in which who we are and more specifically how we relate to the society in which we live is, at least in one sense, beyond our control. I am not wishing to present the image of an Orwellian society, but a society that is far more subtle in the way in which it imparts aspects of social control: a society that while promoting notions of specificity and diversity obliges us to behave in particular ways and to perceive of our cities in a particular way, for, if we were not to do so, we would undermine our very own conception of what our society is and the very nature of the citizenship it offers us.

Despite and because of the power of consumerism as a way of life, it is important to recognise that spaces for consumption are by definition paradoxical in nature. They offer the consumer a specific experience depending upon the immediate topography of the environment which they consume. They offer a degree of diversity and uniqueness that seduces the consumer into wholeheartedly embracing the opportunities that such spaces provide. The power of consumerism is indeed founded on this ability to seduce the consumer through specific variations of space and place. At one level, Canal Street in Manchester, for example, offers the novelty of gay culture, whilst NewcastleGateshead Quayside offers a diverse range of music, art and iconic architectural consumption. At another, these spaces operate ideologically: they define the city as a site of consumption. They celebrate difference, but they do so by imposing uniformity. To a citizen of a consumer society, to be part of the post-industrial future, you simply have to consume. This book will explore how far the individual is able to explore his or her own agency in a world in which everything seems possible, but in which satisfaction is never apparently achieved.

Spaces for Consumption aims to address what all this means for our actual experience of city life. Is it even possible to conceive of the contemporary as anything more than an adjunct to the world of consumption? It is for this reason that this book is entitled Spaces *for* Consumption, as opposed to Spaces *of* Consumption. The concern here is not with spaces in which consumption takes place, but rather the spaces in which consumption has an ideological cogence and how this creates a tension as the city and its people struggle to define what is genuinely unique about them. Consumption is not simply about the act of purchase but is rather a thoroughly cultural phenomenon that serves to legitimate capitalism on an everyday basis. In this sense, this is a book about consumerism and the ways in which consumerism is manifested and thus ideologically reproduced in the *physical–emotional* environment with which we engage. In effect then, this book is concerned with the ways in which consumption is choreographed in space and place.

Consumerism is generally regarded as being descriptive of a world which is overly preoccupied with consumption. But it would be misleading to suggest that this is necessarily a bad thing. *Spaces for Consumption* aims to highlight the contradictory nature of our relationship with consumer landscapes: the sense of satisfaction consumption can bring us alongside a nagging sense that a consumer's life is not quite as fulfilling as it perhaps purports to be. From this point of view, the relationship between the consumerist ideologies that underpin our society and the role these ideologies arguably play in constructing our identities are played out in the places which we inhabit and therefore reinvigorate. Places for consumption represent a meeting point between the society or structures that determine us, and the way we interpret them as individual agents.

The ideological impact of consumption is firmly rooted in the soul of the society in which we live. The urban renaissance that continues to go on in our cities and which will apparently ensure that all the cities in which we live can somehow be 'world-class' has created a situation where the impact of consumption on our cities and how we relate to our cities is especially fragile. As cities have become ever-more outward-looking, as they have sought to establish their role on the world stage, they have simultaneously been compelled to look within themselves. The topographic identity of the city is in a constant battle with the parameters that consumer society has laid down for it. Consumption represents a primary means by which our cities define themselves, but in doing so, a situation has been created in which uniformity and specificity are constantly in conflict, fighting each other for our attention. *Spaces for Consumption* will seek to describe and account for the nature of these tensions whilst ruminating about the long-term prospects for cities, world-class or otherwise, in a world which appears to be evermore superficial and yet, paradoxically, evermore ideologically profound.

Beyond what the emergence of spaces for consumption means for the contemporary city, this book is concerned with the reinvention of the public realm. Sze Tsung Leong (2001a: 129) has talked about how shopping in particular has emerged as a medium through which 'the market has solidified its grip on our spaces, buildings, cities, activities and lives. It is the material outcome of the degree to which the market economy has shaped our surroundings, and ultimately ourselves'. For Tze Tsung Leong, in the world of global capitalism, shopping is perhaps *the* defining activity of public life. The city is defined by the market. The dominance of the market has significant implications for the nature of selfhood in contemporary society. In *Spaces for Consumption*, I will argue that the changing nature of the self is manifested in the city through the destruction of the public realm. The dominance of consumption creates a situation in which the public realm is no longer viable. What emerges in its wake is a sort of public–private realm in which any communal existence is precluded by an individual one.

We live in a society where opportunities to commune are less visible than they were in the past. In effect, the public realm has become symbolic, virtual in nature. Any pretension towards a public life, as we might imagine it, is therefore illusory or beyond our reach because the exchange values upon which our society is based make it so. Perhaps the most graphic, some might say melodramatic, expression of this process is the recent trend toward mass expressions of public grief and mourning which was perhaps expressed most graphically in the public mourning for Princess Diana. Such a development represents a desperate attempt to regain a sense of the public in an individualistic culture that has arguably been robbed of a communal life. Much of the work that has sought to understand the changing nature of the city has done so without recourse to the changing nature of selfhood. To my mind, the two come hand-in-hand. The physical environment, the cityscapes increasingly dominated by spaces for consumption, constitute a graphic manifestation of the changing nature of selfhood and the changing ways in which the individual relates to society. Authors such as Kozinets et al. (2004) have pointed out that spectacular environments have important effects on consumer agency and that although such environments offer the consumer a degree of liberation, such liberation is instantly commodified. The consumer is certainly not entirely coerced by spaces for consumption, but the experiences that are framed for them *through* consumption inevitably limit the avenues though which individual agency is experienced and expressed.

The structure of the book

Spaces for Consumption is intended to address the impact of consumption upon how we imagine the city in a post-industrial world. The intention here is to critically consider the ways in which consumption is manifested in the lived environment and how the nature of both public space and the public realm is transformed as a result. Each chapter will consider a key dimension or aspect of the city as a space for consumption and in order to bring themes out of this discussion, chapters will conclude with a particular case study or case studies that demonstrate the impact of such processes upon space and place.

   In Chapter 2, I will begin to outline the significance of the process of individualisation and its relationship to consumption before moving on to discuss the implications for the city of the present and of the future. In doing so, I will develop the notion of 'complicit communality' in order to begin to sketch out how consumers, experience of social life and the pursuit of pleasure is transformed by the consumer ethic. The impact of this ethic is highlighted through a discussion of the archetypal non-space, namely the airport, which has emerged in recent years as a peculiarly urban space in which travellers are obliged to fulfil their role as consumers.

Chapter 3 considers the phenomenon of place-making as part of a broader process in which cities purport to be 'world-class'. Particular emphasis here is on how the city has become tied up with notions of creativity. The specific experiences of the city of Glasgow are then discussed as part of the broader discussion of the city as a 'sign' and hence whether or not the city belongs to the 'consumer' or to consumption itself.

Chapter 4 goes on to look at the role of culture in the reinvention of the city and its role as an arena for consumption. After discussing the nature of cultural tourism, the chapter goes on to consider the museum as a space for consumption before looking at the increasingly high profile of the cultural quarter as a focal point for the reinvention of the city. The chapter critically considers the extent to which culture is used in an instrumental fashion and whether or not the cultural sphere is fatally undermined as a result.

The next chapter focuses on the role of architecture in image-driven conceptions of the post-industrial city. By using Shanghai as a means of demonstrating this process, particular consideration is given to the key statements provided by iconic architecture and its relationship to the experience economy. The broader China experience and the iconic building of iconic buildings, the Guggenheim Bilbao, are also discussed in order to highlight the role of architecture in shaping the city of consumption, and in particular, in shaping an externally generated view of the cities in which we live.

Chapter 6 is concerned with what is probably the most physically graphic guise of a space for consumption, that of shopping. In describing the historical evolution of shopping, the chapter considers the way in which retail engages with the 'dream world' of the consumer. Focusing in particular on the shopping mall as a controlled public space, the extent to which such space can be appropriated by the consumer is considered. The emotional appeal of shopping spaces is further debated with discussion of Universal City Walk in Los Angeles.

Chapter 7 concentrates on the notion of the 'spectacular city' and in particular on the role of the mega-event in how cities have sought to portray themselves in a changing global economy. In discussing the role of the EXPO and of the Olympics, the intention of this chapter is to reinforce the contention that our understanding of the city is predicated on the construction of a particular image or rhetoric around that city, and the concern that the individual consumer may at least be constrained as to the degree to which he or she can interpret that environment as he or she sees fit.

Chapter 8 turns its attentions to the specific implications of a city that appears so dependent upon themed space. The powerful influence of the theme park and the broader impact of branded landscapes is thus debated with particular reference to how spatial theming has been appropriated in the urban landscape as a means of inscribing and legitimating a new set of social relationships. The particularly influential impact of Disneyland and, in turn, the Disney town of Celebration are discussed as examples of theming that constitute what Sharon Zukin (1993) has described as 'landscapes of power'. A key consideration of this chapter is how far the city can remain authentic in a situation in which there is so much pressure to package the wares of the city as part of a coherent theme.

In the final chapter, the book seeks to pull together the various threads that contribute to the construction of a city defined through spaces for consumption. The argument here and throughout the book is that consumption has a deeply profound impact on the city, so much so that the individual experience of that city is filtered through the processes implied by consumption. To this end, a key concern of the book is to resist the temptation to dismiss spaces for consumption merely as crass demonstration of the power imbalances that characterise contemporary urban life (although those imbalances are discussed throughout), in order to address the emotional implication of complicit communality and the extent to which the pleasures inherent in the consuming experience are sufficiently incorporated into academic critiques of the consumer society. Of course, it is important to be critical of the way in which spaces for consumption appear to determine our relationship to the city, but it is equally important to do so in a balanced way that takes account of the paradoxical nature of the consuming experience and, above all, the fact that the consumer is him or herself complicit in a process in which consumption appears to have such a profound hold on our everyday lives.

2

THE INDIVIDUALISED CITY?

Perhaps the defining characteristic of contemporary society is the shift towards a more individualistic, privatised society. In this chapter, I will suggest that processes of individualisation have had a key role to play in readjusting the relationship between the individual and society and thus in our relationship with the urban environment. Not only have the apparent freedoms that we like to feel we are able to explore through the opportunities consumption provides us redefined our relationship to the city, but they have fundamentally altered what it means to be a citizen of contemporary society. To belong is to be a consumer. It could therefore be argued that in a privatised world, our 'citizenship', so far as it exists, is manifested through our relationship to the public realm – a relationship defined by our interaction with spaces for consumption. In this chapter, I am therefore concerned with the extent to which consumption determines the nature of the individuality we experience, by tying that individuality to a broader process of sociation which is sculpted by the experiential nature of consumption.

Complicit communality

Zygmunt Bauman (2001) defines the historical process of individualisation as being the transformation of identity from a 'given' to a 'task'. In contemporary society, we are blessed with the freedom of experimentation whilst simultaneously being cursed by the fact we have to cope with the consequences of a world characterised by apparently constant experimentation. For Beck and Beck-Gernsheim (2001: xxi), 'it is not the freedom of choice, but insight into the fundamental incompleteness of the self, which is at the core of individual and political freedom in the second modernity'. Beck and Beck-Gernsheim identify a series of transformations that characterise the process of individu-alisation and not least the suggestion that the cultural and political dynamic of the individual's life, as opposed to class categories, is increasingly responsible for putting one's stamp on society. This new 'self-culture' effectively involves the individual making his or her life what he or she wants it to be as part of a broader lifestyle orienta-tion. In addition, any consciousness of freedom is internalised: we become self-authored. We are the products of a society that lauds the ethic of self-fulfilment and achievement: 'The choosing, decid-ing, shaping, human being who aspires to be the author of his or her own life, the creator of an individual identity, is the central character of our time' (p. 23). Living such a life or what we might usefully describe as an 'elective biography' means that questions of slippage and collapse are constant preoccupations of our existence, as Beck and Beck-Gernsheim (2001) suggest. Every failure is your failure and your failure alone. From this point of view, a more immediate rela-tionship between the individual and society is constituted, insofar as social crises are always interpreted or dealt with as individual crises. An individual's problems with the world well and truly sit upon his or her shoulders and, as such, life is forced to become a never-ending process of self-management. What is crucial about all this, as Beck and Beck-Gernsheim (2001) argue, is that whereas previously the self was always subordinated to the collectivity, thinking for oneself whilst living for others is no longer a contradiction, but a principle underpinning everyday existence (p. 28). We are dominated by our own lives which become our own personal projects: such an orien-tation that shapes the nature of our social interaction and thereby encourages a culture of other-directed homogeneity. As Sack puts it:

> The tensions in the structure of consumption point to a world that is becoming more homogenous overall, with fewer cultures, religions, languages, etc., but in which most individuals have far more variety at their fingertips. In other words, for the world, variety has diminished. For the individual, variety has increased. (Sack, 1988: 658)

Sack is a useful point of reference here insofar as the above sentiment demonstrates a key contradiction faced by the consumer experiencing the everyday world of consumption. What I want to suggest throughout this book is that such a situation does not merely promote a process of individualisation, but something a touch more multifarious. It is a process which at one level promotes an insular sort of selfhood which excludes pro-active social interaction (as demonstrated by the arguably individualising tendencies of new technologies such as video games, DVDs, iPods and the like) whilst at another level it promotes an alternative form of communal life, one in which you retain your individuality or at least your sense of that individuality, whilst exploring communal alternatives through the physical opportunities that consumption provides. This is not so much about sensory overload as about a context in which the individual garners control over the consumer images which he or she comes across in commodified space. Such space is not entirely communal but it offers a sense of communality that is deemed by the individual to be communal *enough*. To repeat, this is not merely a process of individualisation but one of **complicit communality**.

The above point brings to light an important issue highlighted by Brill (2001) who distinguishes between public life as sociability with a diverse range of strangers and community life as a sociability with people you know. It is my contention that we live in an age where the former is replacing the latter. In discussing public life, Brill reflects on the role of spectacle, entertainment and pleasure, notably for their high visual impact. What is interesting about the high profile of public life in a consumer society is that it ties the individual, at least at a superficial level, to strangers outside the home and the locale; by doing so, it provides an alternative venue for social learning, thus undermining the social control inherent in tight-knit social groups. This process means that public life becomes increasingly attractive, informative and indeed theatrical. Meanwhile:

> If Public life offers a freeing from control by the social structure of kin, neighbours, institutions and the state, it is also a social leveller, an equalizer of power inequities, at least temporarily and locationally, and because access is relatively free it is generally an accessible freedom … In Public life, we can even become the stranger to others. In public, there is anonymity and freedom to play act, to construct a personal mythos, to test what-if and engage in make-believe, all prerequisites to transformation testing. (Brill, 2001: 54)

To take the above one step further, complicit communality offers a degree of accessibility and comfort and the possibility of escape that offers an alternative, albeit in some respects, partial public life.

This brings us back to one of the most significant treatments of individualisation as discussed by Putnam (2001) in his book *Bowling Alone*, in which he laments the decline of American civil society. He does so not only in terms of political engagement but also insofar as Americans appear to be less likely to 'engage in the simplest act of citizenship' (p. 67) such as attending a public meeting. Putnam describes this as a psychological disengagement from politics and government. He recognises the fact that in the mid-1990s at least more Americans were bowling in the USA than ever before but that bowling in organised leagues has at the same time plummeted as further evidence of the decline of civic engagement and the vanishing form of social capital. In seeking to explain such developments, Putnam cites a variety of explanatory factors, but not least the technological transformation of leisure. He suggests that deep-seated technological trends are actively individualising the use of leisure time and opportunities for social-capital formation are threatened as a result. Television has had a big part to play in this process, according to Putnam, insofar as we find technology seductive and fulfilling, but we seek such fulfilment at the cost of more communal forms of engagement. The concern here is that there is a decline of social connectedness alongside a fall in civic engagement and trust. From this point of view, Americans relate to one another more as friends than they do as citizens: time is therefore organised towards ourselves and our immediate family and thus away from the wider community. There has been a 'silent withdrawal from social intercourse' (p. 115). This is indeed a disconnected world. Such disconnectedness has long been a preoccupation of social scientists, not least in the work of Richard Sennett (1970), who argues that the current bureaucratic organisation of cities actively cramps the development of human beings, suspending them in a perpetual adolescence. Sennett's thesis was that the urban family in the second half of the twentieth century was profoundly affected by the transfer of modern codes of contact from the work to home. Meanwhile, as work becomes increasingly time-demanding, adults are more and more likely to withdraw from civic participation in order to protect what it is they do have at home.

Many authors have attempted more broadly to describe the way in which city life debases human experience. Of these approaches, perhaps the work of Simmel (1950) is most important insofar as he describes the fact that the modern city is primarily designed to serve the calculative needs of money which thereby prioritises modes of interaction through exchange. Under such circumstances, social life becomes an increasingly calculable process. In discussing Simmel's work, Hubbard (2006) describes a situation in which 'the life of cities had become inconceivable without all of its relationships being organised and calculated within a firmly fixed framework of time (and space) which was designed to undermine individuality and spontaneity' (p. 19). Interestingly, Hubbard (2006) goes on to discuss the work of Simmel's pupil Siegfried Kracauer (1995) who when writing in the 1920s observed the rise of 'surface culture' in all facets of the city, but particularly through the development of a shop window culture in which shops distinguished themselves by the degree to which their exterior was more enticing than their competitors. As a means of demonstrating the ideological significance of everyday manifestations of the consumer ethic, we can quote Kracauer (1995: 75) directly: 'the position that an epoch occupies in the historical process can be determined more strikingly from an analysis of its inconspicuous surface-level expressions than from that epoch's judgments about itself ... The surface-level expressions ... by virtue of their unconscious nature, provide unmediated access to the fundamental substance of the state of things'. In his discussion of Las Vegas as the non-city or zeropolis that is neither here nor elsewhere, Begout (2003) suggests that this constitutes a course of action in which the mechanical process of society turns into a glamorous display of finery; a meaningless decorative flourish of urbanity. But for Begout, Las Vegas goes further insofar as he sees the consumption that characterises the city as a mindless form of consumption. Las Vegas is therefore deemed to be some kind of saccharine-fuelled refuge from the harshness of everyday life. The consumer is cretinised and small-minded by the pomp that surrounds him or her. Las Vegas is of course an extreme example of the impact of spaces of consumption and hence of the impact the ideology of consumption itself can have upon the urban fabric. Indeed, it could be said to be a space for consumption in its own right. But it is also very easy to dismiss Las Vegas out of hand as a space of consumerist excess. There are reasons that these spaces succeed and there are reasons why they attract consumers from the world over. Moreover, this isn't a one-way street insofar as the individual consumer isn't entirely controlled – spaces for consumption offer him or her a degree of control, however limited that control might be.

The argument here is that the decline of social connectedness and
the utter dominance of a consumer society are far from unrelated
phenomena; that, at least in part, social and civic disconnectedness
is a product of the consumer society. Where our cities are integrated,
they are usually integrated through retail and consumption. Where
they are designed, they are designed to maximise the opportunities
that consumption offers and thereby to intensify the superficial sense
that social engagement is possible in a world of shopping malls and
edutainment. The causal socialising to which Putnam aspires is, on
the one hand, so casual that it can almost be described as non-existent
and, on the other, constitutes a profound testament to the nature of the
consuming city. A knowing glance towards a fellow consumer eyeing a
particular branded product that you and she both admire is arguably
about as close as it gets but such fleetingness is a marker of significant
social change. Even the examples Putnam offers as proposed solutions
to these sorts of urban dilemmas – a town centre built to resemble a
converted train station in a town in which an actual train station had
never existed – is itself a partial solution; a solution built on the construction of spaces for consumption.

   In the above context, consumption does not provide some avenue
of escape as has been argued in the past but rather an ideological
space in which the norms of the consumer society are constantly
reinforced and legitimised. In order to understand the nature of the
relationship between spaces of consumption and the apparent decline
of the public realm, it is essential to clarify the role of consumption
as a means of determining who and what we are becoming, both as
individuals and as members of a consumer society. The world of consumption in which we are obliged to live is a contradictory one:

> On the surface, the world of consumption glitters with excite-
> ment and change … But not everything in the consumer's world
> is smooth, even on the surface. The threads which it interweaves
> threaten to unravel. This is a world without constraints and with-
> out responsibility. It makes each of us the arbiter of what is impor-
> tant and how much to consume. How do we choose one thing
> over another when there are no clear obligations and responsibilities
> and when there is no necessity? How do we form social relations
> and define ourselves when we have no particular projects or tasks?
> The unrestricted freedoms of the consumer's world could also
> create a weightless and disorienting world. (Sack, 1992: 199)

Sack's world of consumption is all about spaces such as shopping malls, tourist destinations and theme parks that are produced in order to maximise consumption. For Sack, such spaces function as disorienting settings for the display and production of commodities and, in doing so, they embody tensions that exist between reality and fantasy, authenticity and inauthenticity, as Mansvelt (2005) notes. In this context, consumption more than simply lays down the parameters within which we live – it has an active bearing on who and what we become in this context. It would be misleading to suggest that consumption straightforwardly constructs who it is we are – rather, what it does is interact with the sorts of tensions that characterise the contemporary life experience, and in one sense at least we are the product of such a process.

In one of the under-utilised contributions to discussions around the emergence of a consumer society, *The Minimal Self*, Christopher Lasch (1985) considers a pattern of social change that has transformed a handicraft-based production system into an interlocking technologically driven system of mass production and mass consumption that has assimilated all activities 'formerly assigned to private life' to the demand of the marketplace (Lasch, 1985: 52). Lasch describes a situation in which many critics have derided the emergence of an increasingly hedonistic selfhood. Lasch's position is that such an argument is misconceived. He talks about the emergence of a culture of narcissism but suggests that narcissism is not about selfishness. Rather, the self is threatened to the point of disintegration by its own emptiness. In this sense, the culture of narcissism is actually a culture of survivalism. In an increasingly bureaucratic society, the day-to-day existence of the individual is increasingly characterised by emotional disengagement and self-management. Indeed:

> The culture of narcissism is not necessarily a culture in which moral constraints on selfishness have collapsed or in which people released from the bonds of social obligation have lost themselves in a riot of hedonistic self-indulgence. What has weakened is not so much the structure of moral obligations and commandments as a belief in a world that survives its inhabitants. The fading of a durable, common, public world, we may conjecture, intensifies the fear of separation at the same time it weakens the psychological resources that make it possible to confront this fear realistically. It has freed the imagination from

external constraints but exposed it more directly than before to the tyranny of inner compulsions and anxieties. (Lasch, 1984: 193)

From the above point of view, the world of commodities in which we live fails us. It provides a dream world, a world that cannot hope to mediate between the tensions of our inner world and those of our outer world. We are overwhelmed by it. We are constantly confronted by the world of consumption offered to us. As such, 'the commodity world stands as something completely separate from the self; yet it simultaneously takes on the appearance of a mirror of the self, a dazzling array of images in which we can see anything we wish to see. Instead of bridging the gap between the self and its surroundings, it obliterates the difference between them' (pp. 195–6). In a culture which appears to exist for no other reason than to thwart our desires, we not only measure ourselves against others but we actively see ourselves through others' eyes. Thus, we live in a world in which public life has apparently collapsed and in which we as individuals are weak and dependent in a context over which we feel we have no control.

Some of the above ideas have resonance with broader debates associated with postmodernism. One such argument is that the essence of individualism is paradox. Although people are freer from rules and regulations than they were in the past, they are also more responsible for themselves (Lipovetsky, 2005). In effect, the individual has choice: the choice whether to accept their identity or not, whether to control themselves or to let themselves go. All this in a context in which, according to Lipovetsky, social life is more and more absorbed by a form of 'hyperconsumption' in which people primarily consume for themselves rather than as part of some kind of broader status game. But the world in which the individual lives is no longer one of emancipation, as Lasch also argues, but one of tension, and anxiety barely concealed by pleasure, or as Lipovetsky puts it, 'The consumerist fever for immediate satisfactions, the aspirations toward a playful and hedonistic lifestyle, have of course by no means disappeared – they are being unleashed more than ever: but they are enveloped in a halo of fear and anxieties' (Lipovetsky, 2005: 46). In a hypermodern world, the regulative power of collective institutions has weakened and the individual appears more socially independent as a result. This constitutes, as Lipovetsky puts it, a destabilised self rather than a pronounced state of self-mastery. Under these conditions, we can identify a decline on the value placed on 'abstract principles of citizenship' in favour of a world in which poles of identity are more immediate and particularist in their form. The fact that grand political principles are now so remote means that private happiness comes to the fore whilst unleashing an inner desire for an apparently unobtainable collectivity.

What emerges from the above process is a new kind of citizenship, where the extent to which you belong is defined by your ability to consume. As Bauman (1998: 1) puts it in his discussion of the 'flawed consumer':

> It is one thing to be poor in a society of producers and universal employment; it is quite a different thing to be poor in a society of consumers, in which life-projects are built around consumer choice rather than work, professional skills, or jobs. If 'being poor' once derived its meaning from the condition of being unemployed, today it draws its meaning primarily from the plight of a flawed consumer.

In this context, the collapse of the public takes on new meaning so that spaces for consumption appear to offer more opportunity for meaning-making than they can ever possibly fulfil. The public–private experience of the individual becomes defined by his or her ability to consume and his or her ability to see him- or herself as a consumer. The nature of citizenship becomes defined by the consumer's ability or otherwise to assert that citizenship though his or her experience as a consumer. As such, Saunders (1993) discusses the shift from socialised to privatised consumption. For Saunders, the privatisation of consumption is here to stay: it is a structural feature of mature capitalism and indeed could be said to underpin contemporary notions of citizenship. As such, as far as it exists, consumer choice is meaningless without the material resources that are necessary to attain it. The shift from socialised to privatised forms of consumption constitutes a genuine threat, according to Saunders, to a marginalised minority of households. For Saunders, markets enable self-interested behaviour but they do not directly cause such behaviour. From the above point of view, the more the state attempts to intervene in people's problems, the more voluntary forms of mutual sociation will decline and, ironically, the greater the need for state intervention. For Saunders, 'If our objective really is to sustain social cohesion, then it is to the private rather than the public realm that we need to look for a solution ... the privatized society which is slowly emerging out of the ruins of the collectivist welfare system holds out the prospect not of social and moral disintegration, but of new and active forms of citizenship based on individual competence and the development of genuinely collective forms of association and sociability springing up from below (pp. 85–8). Lash and Urry have similarly argued that a new form of consumer citizenship can be said to have emerged in which social agents constitute themselves as citizens through the goods and services they consume (Lash and Urry, 1994).

The key question here is whether or not such citizenship is illusory and whether it provides the sort of support that the individual requires or whether, alternatively, it simply ties that individual to a culture of consumption over which he or she effectively has no control. In debating the above approaches, Isin and Wood (1999) argue that under advanced liberalism, cultural citizenship emerges as a field in which the right to produce, distribute and consume culture becomes a key point of struggle. In defining liberalism, Isin and Wood point out that such an approach asserts the primacy of the individual against the claims of the collective. But the debate here centres on how much freedom the individual is able to explore through the arena of consumption. Notions of citizenship and their inherent focus on rights and obligations 'centred on social struggles' can, according to Isin and Wood, provide a counterweight to an overly simplistic reading of consumption as freedom.

Consumer citizenship

The argument being tentatively posited here is that perhaps consumption offers a new kind of citizenship, one that takes the individual out of the political realm and prioritises the private–public one instead. Isin and Wood point out that in an increasingly fragmented world in which identities are proliferated, there are profound implications for the nature of citizenship. The world appears less finite than it was in the past and the debate continues as to how schizophrenic identity becomes as a result. In a world in which signs are dominant and in which postmodern choices are knowing and ironic, there is apparently no possibility for any kind of genuine form of citizenship. The individual is freed from such shackles in a world in which meaning-making and consumer knowledge become key currencies (Isin and Wood, 1999). The world being described here is one in which the consumer is apparently subject to increasing opportunities and lifestyle spaces in which they can explore dimensions of freedom, but these freedoms, genuine or otherwise, are yet to be harnessed in the form of new political arrangements or rights.

My suggestion is that the above set of circumstances is so extreme that citizenship has been reinvented in a way that has long left politics behind. Another way in which citizenship can be conceived, given the role of the market in public services in particular, is in the realm of 'citizens as customers' but a key concern here is that consumer rights are more limited in the public than the private sector (Prior et al., 1995). It is deeply unlikely that the market can deliver the genuine degree of freedom and choice that authors such as Saunders (1993) ask of it. For many then, the freedom to choose is a matter of cultural capital. The ability of parents to successfully secure the best possible school for their children will be affected by their ability to manoeuvre themselves through the uncertainties of the educational system. Such a system is not about the freedom to choose, as some consumers are far more savvy as to the issues involved than others and moreover have access to economic resources that will further ensure they maximise the system. The practice of moving home to locate a child in a favoured catchment area is a case in point. The freedom to consume is a freedom that most so-called 'consumers' simply do not have.

To belong to contemporary society and to demonstrate our belonging to that society is to be a consumer: the political arena is rendered inadequate, wieldy and inconsequential when measured against the dazzling though partial freedoms offered by the consumer society. In this sense, the city operates as a focal point, or as Isin and Wood (1999) put it, a battleground, for the physical expression of globalised economic and social forces and their relationship to the local. It would be easy to dismiss outright any suggestion that local expressions of identity become impossible in such circumstances. This would be a simplification. However, the argument here is that the arena within which citizenship is constructed is now so prescribed that the impact of the local is inevitably only partial in nature.

Consuming the city

So what does all this mean for the city? Lofland (1998) talks about how technology has precipitated a participation in an apparent withdrawal from the public realm. At one level, the prevalence of the refrigerator means less trips to the supermarket and digital TV less visits to the cinema, perhaps. And, of course, even the car is primarily a private realm. The work of Sennett, as Lofland points out, is particularly significant in this regard insofar as he identifies the emergence of a more impersonal public: the decline of non-intimate relationships. To this end, Lofland (1998) quotes de Tocqueville:

> Individualism is a calm and considered feeling which disposes each citizen to isolate himself from the mass of his fellows and withdraw into the circle of family and friends; with this little society formed to his taste, he gladly leaves the greater society to look after itself ... I see an innumerable multititude of men (*sic*), alike and equal, constantly circling around in pursuit of the petty and banal pleasures with which they glut their souls. Each one of them, withdrawn into himself, is almost unaware of the fate of the rest. Mankind (*sic*), for him, consists of his children and his personal friends. As for the rest of his fellow citizens, they are near enough but he does not notice them. He touches them but feels nothing. (de Tocqueville, 1988: 691–2)

This book is premised on the suggestion that in one sense the city is not a place at all, but an historically specific 'way of seeing' (Donald, 1999). In many ways, the contemporary city is a product of the market system under which contemporary consumer capitalism operates. The significance of the market in the structure of contemporary society is well documented. Aldridge (2005) discusses the fact that the word 'market', or at least pro-market ideologies in their various guises, imply choice, consumer sovereignty, prosperity and freedom. On the other hand, critics of the market would argue that the market produces a dehumanised, unequal society 'obsessed with commodities and in thrall to transnational corporations' (Aldridge, 2005: 31). From a Marxist point of view then, the degree of choice provided by the free market is pathologised and has nothing to do with genuine human needs. Perhaps most importantly, the market appears to encourage a degree of personal autonomy, enterprise and self-reliance. But the difficulty here, as Aldridge goes on to argue, is that advocates of the free market tend to at least imply that the market is some kind of natural phenomena, that it can be left to itself and everybody will benefit as a result. Good or bad, is the market in some sense 'character-building'?

Despite and perhaps because of its impact upon individual lives, the market does have a fundamental role to play in individual character-building but also in terms of how it impacts upon the broader character of the places in which we live. The end result of this process is a more prescripted form of city identity than would otherwise have been the case. The suggestion here is that consumption, the physical manifestation of the market, actively predefines the parameters within which consumers relate to such modes of seeing. In other words, our sense of urban reality is governed by our relationship to consumption but this doesn't necessarily imply a loss of identity but rather an identity adjustment. Consumption defines the places in which we live in terms of their physical but also their emotional manifestation. If the city is a manifestation of social norms, behaviours and change, then it follows logically that the city is by implication an homogenous entity. The argument I want to present throughout the remainder of this book is that what is really interesting about the contemporary city is that the spaces of consumption that do exist are not accidental in nature. They are not simply a product of a planning process nor of a self-contained process of production–consumption. In effect, spaces for consumption offer consumers a degree of certainty in an uncertain world (Miles, 2000). Without any kind of a public realm to call upon, consumers rely on the next best things: a safe, highly surveilled and predictable world of consumption. As such, consumers are not the dupes of a productivist world of consumerist control. They are compliant (if unequal) partners in a pact where the so-called freedoms of consumption are readily embraced. A key issue in the above context is the question of pleasure which I will go on to discuss now.

Consumption as pleasure

The public appeal of consumption lies in its role as a realm of pleasure. At one level at least, the world of consumption is by its very definition a world of pleasure. Peter (2007) discusses the emergence of British pleasure architecture between 1925 and 1940. He does so in the context of an emerging city in which the city dweller is having to accommodate a kind of 'hyperstimulated' environment. Peter describes a situation in which leisure was expected to have an increasingly significant role to play in people's lives. Leisure effectively represented the promise of the future. To this end, Peter quotes George Orwell who wrote about leisure in the 1930s: 'The modern civilised man's idea of pleasure is already partly attained in the more magnificent dance halls, movie palaces, hotels, restaurants and luxury liners. On a pleasure cruise or in a Lyons Corner House, one already gets something more than a glimpse of the future paradise' (p. 30). Thus, in the context of industrialization, the architecture of pleasure, according to Peter, provided an environment in which the public could let off steam. But, on the other hand, these pleasures were always in danger of being frowned upon as such entertainment was deemed to be sinful and the spaces in which they took place were dismissed as dens of inequity (Peter, 2007).

But the ideological role of the city is no longer moral in nature or at least the discourse of consumption suggests it shouldn't be. Spaces of consumption are pleasurable but their pleasure is apparently short lived. More than anything else, such spaces serve a diversionary function. But it should not be concluded that this necessarily constitutes a fully fledged false consciousness in the Marxist sense, for consumers are nowadays savvy enough to realise that they are at least to an extent being controlled. What is interesting about an urban environment dominated by consumption is that consumers are aware of such limitations and are in effect happy to embrace them. Consumers at least appear to actively and consciously conspire in this process insofar as they are prepared to give up a notional degree of freedom in order to experience the partial freedoms and pleasures that consumerism has to offer. Spaces for consumption are not the direct product of one-way power relationships; they are the product of a negotiated nirvana in which the consumer consumes and in which the powerful structure the form that that consumption takes.

Airports, individualisation and pleasure

In contrast to the other chapters in this book, I want to bring my thoughts on the relationship between consumption and individualisation to a close by focusing on a generic example of a space for consumption that demonstrates many of the points made above to which I will return throughout the book. Lloyd (2003) considers the role of themed spaces in re-inscribing pleasure and desire in cities and relates such developments to the emergence of a new breed of airports which are no longer spaces through which people pass, but rather where it is they spend time: loitering as an economically useful activity. In effect, the mere act of consumption is an act of citizenship. In this context, Lloyd describes the experience of distraction as an end in itself – so that the traveller is immersed 'in the very surface of the travel experience' (p. 94).

The importance of travel demonstrates the increasingly deterritorialised nature of the world in which we live and the way in which any sense of citizenship is displaced from the places in which we live to broader notions of the consumer society. Before considering Lloyd's work more closely, it is worth considering in more depth the way in which the modern urban environment privileges representation over reality, thereby altering the relationship between the traveller and space. In his book, *The Image*, Daniel J. Boorstin (1987) talked about a new kind of synthetic novelty that dominated the American experience, namely the pseudo-event: a planned event for the immediate purpose of being reported or reproduced. For Boorstin (1987: 3), the progress that we have created has in turn spawned a 'thicket of unreality which stands between us and the facts of life'. From this point of views, we live in a world of unreasonable and extravagant expectations:

> Never have people been more the masters of their environment. Yet never has a people felt more deceived and disappointed. For never has a people expected so much more than the world can offer ... we have become so accustomed to our illusions that we mistake them for reality ... They are the world of our making: the world of the image. (pp. 4–6)

In a consumer society, imagery takes on the role of a new kind of social currency and means that we see our place in the world differently to how we may have done in the past. A key element of this process resides in our expectations of place as both near and far away; as exotic and yet understandable. Such a process creates a demand for illusion which we pay others to produce for us. And it is this demand for an illusory experience that for Boorstin became the business of America by the mid-twentieth century, so much so that the experience of travel is increasingly diluted and contrived: a product designed for the comforting, risk-free experience of thousands of apparently like-minded tourists.

The above issue has been taken up more directly in terms of the implications for space in the work of Augé (1995) who presents 'an anthropology of supermodernity'. Augé's argument is that supermodernity, 'a world thus surrendered to solitary individuality, to the fleeting, the temporary and the ephemeral' (p. 78) produces 'non-places': places which cannot be defined as relational, or historical or concerned with identity. The traveller's space is the archetypal non-place insofar as he or she engages with non-places in a partial way so that the traveller becomes the subject matter of his or her own spectacle: 'As if the position of spectator were the essence of the spectacle, as if basically the spectator in the position of a spectator were his own spectacle' (p. 86). The spectator then is the fabricated 'average man'. As far as the traveller, or indeed the flâneur, is concerned, once the individual has been through check-in and security, he or she is thrown into the pseudo-reality of duty-free shopping. Here the opportunity to purchase affordable luxury items is less important. For Augé then, the unchallengeable solitude and momentary experience of the departer for the reassurance and familiarity of the role itself is enough: 'Subjected to a gentle form of possession, to which he surrenders himself with more or less talent or conviction, he tastes for a while – like anyone who is possessed – the passive joys of identity-loss, and the more active pleasure of role-playing' (p. 103). The non-place is the opposite of a utopia; it exists and it does not contain any organic society, it is defined primarily economically and is defined by a lack of community, a lack of unpredictability and a lack of difference (Augé, 1995). In this sense, the airport is symbolic of the broader processes of individualisation going on in a consumer society and how they are manifested in an environment characterised by contrived communality.

The airport is in many ways the exemplar of the non-place. It is not surprising in this context that, as Lloyd (2003) notes, the figure of the global traveller is allied to that of the global consumer. The airport is then a kind of hyperspace that offers a stop gap between national territory and globality. For Iyer (2001), the airport is based on the underlying presumption that everybody comes from somewhere else and thus everybody is in need of something to make him or her feel at home. For this reason, the airport becomes an anthology of generic spaces.

> Part of the pathos and stress of the airport is that lives are being changed irreversibly, and people have nothing to steady themselves with but a Coffee People outlet, a Sky Plaza, and a Smarte Carte that (in Los Angeles at least) speaks seven different languages. All the comfort of home; made impersonal. (p. 44)

Image 2.1 Beijing 2008 Olympics new airport terminal by Norman Foster
(Photo Andy Miah)

Iyer argues that the whole process of flying leaves us floating in a
state of temporary intimacy with anonymous space, a sort of out-
of-body state of suspended animation and spaced-out dreaminess.
Consumption provides the resource that feeds this state insofar as it
presents the traveller with a form of individualised 'pleasurable waiting'. Thus, in recent years, the airport has been repositioned as a fun
place to be and retail lies at the heart of this development. In this context, Omar and Kent (2002) point out that, above all, airport travellers constitute a captive retail audience. Relieved at having arrived
on time and free of the constraints of everyday life, travellers find
themselves in a state of relaxed limbo in which 'spontaneous consumption behaviours' are self-consciously encouraged. Such spaces
are often marketed to local residents as well as travellers, London's
Gatwick Airport being a good example. As Thomas (1997) argues,
however, the main property for marketers in an airport environment
is to take advantage of dropping stress levels and the growing levels of
excitement, the period Thomas labels as the 'happy hour'.

In trying to explain this unique urban form, Fuller and Harley (2005) describe the airport as signifying the rise of a new 'metastable' urban form which is constantly changing and yet which appears stable. For Fuller and Harley, the airport is a type of city designed to facilitate massive global movement as efficiently as possible (p. 11). In doing so, the airport inevitably cuts away difference and promotes sterile conformity. What is interesting about the airport as a space is that 'Old distinctions between private and public, leisure and work, open and closed, global and local, complete and incomplete, fold in on each other to create spaces of multiple reactions' (p. 105). From this point of view, the airport is more of an 'other space' than a non-place: a real, transgressionary space linked to numerous other types of space and potentially contradicting those spaces as it does so. In one instance of such a transgression, Pimlott (2007) describes the increasing mallification of airports from the 1980s and argues that there are clear sympathies between the airport and the shopping mall as building types. In short, both offer the spectacle of 'continuous experience' in order to control the patterns of consumption and movement of a large number of consumers.

> As adjuncts, if not centres of this environment, the interiors of airports have been surrendered to consumption, and like the malls that they increasingly resemble, they offer freedom – confirmed through broad social agreement, effected through deeply ingrained ideological lessons – for the masses that move through them. (Pimlott, 2007: 293)

For Pimlott, airports promote a kind of flânerie which involves the pacification of the consumer. The airport is a phantasmagoric interior that isolates the individual from the external world and surrenders the individual to the signals, signs and representations of the immediate environment. Retail space is crucial for airports, economically of course, but also as a means of sustaining the entire organism of the airport. This process, as far as Pimlott is concerned, works insofar as the traveller associates the freedoms of mobility and consumption with the freedoms they are about to experience through travel itself. The airport environment thereby naturalises consumption and obliges the consumer to be part of that environment's consuming life. Another way of interpreting the contemporary airport is therefore as a themed environment (see Chapter 8 for a more detailed discussion of this phenomenon) and, in this respect, Gottdiener (2001) argues that airport terminals are very much reminiscent of the massive interiors we associate with shopping malls and their primary characteristic is an over-endowment with sign systems. Above and beyond the signs used to move travellers along their way, an altogether different level of signs operates in order to ensure that the traveller's role as a consumer remains paramount during their time in deterritorialised space.

In his cultural history of the airport, Gordon (2008) talks about how the theories of commercial developers such as Victor Gruen became more important than those of Gropius or Le Corbusier in influencing the work of airport architects in the late-twentieth century. Important in this regard was the fact that, by the mid-1990s, the average wait for an international flight was two hours and twenty-three minutes, a period of time that could only increase with the more stringent security measures put in place in airports across the world post 9/11. The atmosphere of airport terminals is as much about retail provision (which has moved in an increasingly high-end direction) as business class waiting rooms. But the more comprehensive reinvention of the airport as a space for consumption is perhaps best demonstrated by Idlewild/Kennedy Airport in New York which by the mid-1960s was providing employment for over 19,000 people. Idlewild was designed as a flamboyant tourist attraction in its own right: an advertisement not only for New York and for the wonders of jet flight, but as an advertisement for the American way of life (Gordon, 2008), so much so that the central area was called 'Liberty Plaza' described in the publicity as being intended to 'relax the tensions of travel by enchanting the eye'. The gardens of Versailles provided a model for the central plaza of Terminal City as it became known. The aim here, as Gordon (2008) suggests, was to imply a sense of limitless possibility. Gordon describes the terminal as 'the ultimate consumer state' and as new terminals emerged in the second half of the twentieth century, high-profile retail provision increasingly became the case. There is certainly a case for arguing that the airport is a place which plays out the underlying forces and anxieties of modern society. Indeed, for Gordon (2008), although the airport continues to be at the threshold of change, it no longer holds out the hope of a utopian future, not least in the context of a world at least apparently ridden by terror. Perhaps this is best demonstrated by a state of the art example of airport development, namely Heathrow's Terminal 5 which was officially opened in March 2008. Built at a cost of £4.3 billion and designed by the Richard Rogers Partnership, Terminal 5 has the capacity for thirty million passengers annually and offers over a hundred shops and restaurants. The new terminal has in one fowl swoop managed to provide half again the amount of Heathrow's retail provision. Aimed at the luxurious end of the market, Terminal 5 represents an ambitious effort and one that looks increasingly risky during a period of crippling economic downturn. One of the most notable features of the new terminal is its lack of seating which some critics have described as a cynical design strategy (Gordon, 2008). But, of course, like the majority of its European rivals, Heathrow Airport must operate along strictly commercial lines: it is effectively a gigantic shopping mall. Although the biggest income for American airports is through car hire in Europe and Asia, retail is all.

In the above context, Sze Tsung Leong (2001b) has described airport shopping as 'the next major step in the evolution of shopping'. From this point of view, airport retail is the new department store or shopping mall of its time insofar as it constitutes a captive space in which the experience of the consumer can be synthetically induced. Cynics might also argue that the above also constitutes a reasonable definition of the contemporary city. Rather than easing a traveller's transit, the argument here is that the labyrinth-like airport of today works insofar as it slows the traveller down and creates a situation where shopping is all. For Sze Tsung Leong, airport shopping is shopping in its perfect state, mainly because its controlled, laboratory-like spaces for consumption have saved the airport as a workable economic entity. In this light, BAA, the world's largest commercial operator of airports which runs seven British airports including Heathrow as well as many others overseas, generates 60 per cent of its profits from retail outlets. For Sze Tsung Leong, airport shopping is the current panacea for the survival of the consumer-driven society, the only question being, how long can it last?

Conclusion

A more important consideration and a key concern for this book is what can the above panacea tell us about where the world has been and where it might be going? The process is undoubtedly under-pinned by the role of the consumer in the reinvention of notions of citizenship. Consumer society is constantly reinventing notions of citizenship on its own terms. The relationship between the individual and consumption is similarly a product of the individual's relationship with society as defined by his or her role as a consumer. Spaces for consumption isolate us as consumers in a cocoon through which we appear obliged to define freedom through the consumptions that consumption can allegedly provide. Perhaps it is worth returning to the words of Siegfried Kracauer who, in what follows, is talking about the hotel lobby of the 1920s, but in some ways could just as easily be talking about the spaces for consumption found in today's airports:

> Removed from the hustle and bustle, one does gain some distance from the distinctions of 'actual' life?, but without being subjected to a new determination that would circumscribe from above the sphere of validity for these determinations. And it is in this way that a person can vanish into an undetermined void, helplessly reduced to a 'member of society as such' who stands superfluously off to the side and, when playing intoxicates himself. This invalidation of togetherness, itself already unreal, thus does not lead up toward reality but is more of a sliding down into the doubly unreal mixture of the undifferentiated atoms from which the world of appearance is constructed. (p. 179)

For Kracauer, a world of surfaces, although betraying a world lacking a degree of depth, also offers hidden potential. The 'mass ornament' is potentially progressive in that it represents as new kind of collectivity 'organized not according to the natural bonds of community but a social mass of functionally linked individuals' (Levin, 1995). In this sense, it seems apt to leave the last word to Kracauer himself as quoted by Levin (1995). Kracauer's discussion of unemployment offices demonstrates the role of physical space in the reproduction of society. But in a society and thus in a public realm that is now more fundamentally defined by consumption, his thoughts on such matters are evermore prescient. Throughout the remainder of this book, I will consider the role of consumption as an arbiter of social relations: in effect, I will consider the role of consumption in constructing and curtailing our dreams in an urban context. The individualisation of the city from one point of view at least, is no kind of individualisation at all.

Every typical space is created by typical social relations which are expressed in such a space without the disturbing intervention of consciousness. Everything that consciousness ignores, everything that it usually just overlooks, is involved in the construction of such spaces. Spatial structures are the dreams of society. Whenever the hieroglyph of any such spatial structure is decoded, the foundation of the social reality is revealed. (Kracauer, 1994: 37)

The foundations of a post-industrial society are perhaps best understood as being constructed through a model in which the dreams of the individual are filtrated though the market and in doing so become by default the dream of both the people whilst playing out those dreams through the spaces of consumption which they occupy. In the next chapter, I will turn my attention to why it is that the city has evolved as a focal point for such developments.

3

CREATING CITIES

The final 20 years of the twentieth century saw the emergence of a new kind of city: an apparently revitalised post-industrial city, a city of surfaces and of dreams in which anything appeared and apparently now appears possible. As well as looking different and feeling different, the post-industrial city is run differently and at its core lays an entrepreneurial stance that is all about creating the appropriate conditions conducive to capital accumulation (Hubbard and Hall, 1998). Such developments lay the groundwork on which the consuming city and indeed spaces for consumption became so fundamental to the experience of urban life in the twenty-first century. In this chapter, I will consider the development of the post-industrial, entrepreneurial city and raise the question as to whether what that city offers on the surface can actually be realised in reality.

The emergence of spaces for consumption as a key marker of the changing nature of the consuming experience and indeed the changing nature of the consumer's experience of the city can only be understood in the context of the broader economic processes that appear to be underpinning the emergence of what many commentators have called an 'entrepreneurial' city (Hannigan, 2005). In this chapter, I will consider what it is that constitutes the entrepreneurial city, and what the implications of such a conception of city life might have for the longer-term future of the city as a space for consumption. Focusing in particular on the lessons to be learnt from the city of Glasgow, the intention of this chapter is to develop an insight into the sorts of urban governance questions that have resulted in something of a fission between the symbolic city and the city as experienced on the ground; a state of affairs in which 'Places are now commodities to be produced and to be consumed' (Hall, 1997: 65) or in which as Kotler

(1993: 11) puts it, 'places are, indeed, products, whose identities and values must be designed and marketed'.

A post-industrial Future

The re-envisioning of the city as a site of consumption is directly related to the need for an economic reinvention in light of the collapse of the industrial city and indeed the emergence of global economies. What has thus emerged can be described as a new urban consensus or what Arantes et al. (2000) call the 'city of single thought'. A key issue here, certainly as far as the UK is concerned, is the decline of the city as a centre of manufacture. As Ward (1998) notes, between the 1970s, and 1990s, Britain lost 45 per cent of its manufacturing jobs and that gap had to be filled. Meanwhile, globalisation brought with it new pressures, not least the shift of manufacturing industries to South East Asia. The deindustrialisation of British cities was also accompanied, as Jones and Evans (2008) point out, by a particularly damaging trend of urban population loss with cities such as Liverpool and Manchester feeling the worst of its effects. Under these conditions, the entrepreneurial city offered a means of generating employment, most notably in the service industries; the intention being that cities might compete with one another to sell themselves as desirable locations within the new economy of services, communication, media and biotechnologies which can more broadly be defined as information or knowledge intensive (Jones and Evans, 2008). In this context, competitiveness can be said to be about transforming the city into a place in which it is cheap to do business. The new service-based city offers a mix of other attributes that makes that city attractive to key industries, although it should be said, as Jones and Evans (2008) and Krugman (1996) point out, that many economists have questioned the extent to which it is possible for territorial units such as cities to actually be competitive.

For authors such as Savitch and Kantor (2002) and Short and Kim (1999), the city is the embodiment of globalisation in the sense that global processes lead to changes in the city and cities are constantly reworking and situating in this context. In effect, the city becomes the spatial expression of globalisation. A knowledge-based economy accelerates the need for face-to-face contact and for a situation in which professional services are concentrated in a common locale, making trade as easy as possible so that cities become the productive hubs of the post-industrial era. The city is the world's incubator of innovation, whilst its role as a hub of transportation means it lies at the geographical heart of such changes (Savitch and Kantor, 2002). Whether one of the great core cities such as New York or London, a secondary city providing a hub for industry such as Glasgow or Lille or a port city having to recover from a situation where their mode of transportation is effectively redundant, all cities have had to adapt:

> This reshuffling of the urban hierarchy has brought old and new cities into a competitive scramble to secure their economic well-being. As old industries decline and new investment patterns emerge, citizens and politicians are drawn into finding a niche for their communities in the new economic order. In the process, cities may be gripped by a certain angst – internal conflicts over means and ends, a belief that if a community does not grow it will surely die, and a rush to move faster. (Savitch and Kantor, 2002: 8)

The latter has created a situation in which cities are having to compete for their economic survival with other cities and regions on a global scale (Hall, 1997). Thus, Yeoh (2005) discusses the impact of globalisation on cities in South East Asia. She argues that territorial reconfigurations of capitalism have led to a reassessment of the ways in which a city relates to the outside world. In this context, many South East Asian cities have sought to present themselves as truly global mega-developed cities, fit to compete with their European competitors (see also Broudehoux, 2004). This process creates particular problems for South East Asia. The re-imagining of the global city tends to be even more spatially concentrated here than it is in the West and as such a massive gap is created between the mega-cities of the region and their Fourth World counterparts, raising the broad question of 'cultural justice', a key issue for all cities partaking in the global economic arena (Yeoh, 2005).

What is certain is that the international restructuring of capitalist economies has created a situation in which cities are having to think more and more like businesses determined to maximise the benefits to be gained from investment culture (Short and Kim, 1999). The mobility of capital has created a situation in which regions and cities have become increasingly autonomous as competitive, economic entities; the more global a city, the more economic independence it has (Stevenson, 2003). The result of this process is an aspirational context within which cities are fighting to establish for themselves a coherent role or niche. Industrial cities find themselves in a particularly difficult situation, given the fact that the industrial infrastructures of their past are simply not suited to a post-industrial future. Consumption offers a way out, providing the terrain within which the competitive city seeks to establish its global credentials (Stevenson, 2003).

In attempting to clarify what constitutes the emergence of an entrepreneurial city, the work of David Harvey (1989) is especially informative. Harvey laments a situation in which the study of urbanisation has become separated from that of social change and economic development when in actual fact urbanisation lies at the very core of such changes. On the other hand, Harvey warns against the temptation to reify cities so they are deemed to be active agents rather than mere 'things'. Bearing this point in mind, there are three main characteristics of the entrepreneurial city (Harvey, 1989):

(1) An emphasis on public–private partnerships in which a key priority is to develop structures which attract external sources of funding and which therefore include a key role for elements of local boosterism.
(2) An entrepreneurial city that is by definition speculative in nature and is therefore subject to the uncertainties unfamiliar to an environment that would previously have been rationally planned.
(3) An emphasis on the construction of place rather than with the construction of territory. In other words, Harvey argues, there is investment beyond the desire to improve conditions in specific territories, through housing and education for instance, to a broader (more speculative) commitment to the image of place which, it is hoped, will have a trickle-down effect for the city as a whole.

The intention is to create the conditions in which the city becomes an exciting place to live and visit, and above all, in which to consume: 'The task of urban governance is, in short, to lure highly mobile and flexible production, financial, and consumption flows into its space' (Harvey, 1989: 11). Moreover, the pursuit of strong economic growth creates something of a tension for local government which is inevitably implicated in aspects of private enterprise. According to Harvey, urban entrepreneurialism also inevitably contributes to increasing disparities in wealth and income. The ultimate irony here is that this model of urban investment has become so popular and is reproduced so readily that any competitive advantage is soon lost.

The move towards an entrepreneurial city constitutes a move away from urban planning, 'for ephemerality and eclecticism of fashion and style rather than the search for enduring values, for quotation and fiction rather than invention and function, and, finally, for medium over message and image over substance' (Harvey, 1989: 13). The situation which we are seeking to understand here is all about the presentation of self and as such perception is all. What is most important is that the image of prosperity must win out, regardless of the less palatable truths that may lay underneath. The entrepreneurial city is grounded in a sense of place built upon image rather than what is likely to be the more uncomfortable reality that lies beneath. Such an approach will often have a political pay-off insofar as the image constructed around the entrepreneurial city is likely to rub off in some shape or form on the resident of that city who basks in the glory of the feel-good factor that results.

Given the above contradictions, what is the post-industrial city? Some authors, such as Ward (1998), have described a situation in which the post-industrial city has effectively become a caricature of itself. But in understanding how this is so, it is important to consider the actual constituent parts of such a city. The post-industrial city is dominated by employment in the service sector. It also often boasts a thriving and distinctive retail offer and in presenting itself to the outside world, its relationship with tourism is key. In this respect, the post-industrial city is prepared to place considerable investment in its cultural capital, both high and low-brow (Ward, 1998). Museums, galleries and historic buildings are especially important in this regard, as are modern well-designed venues, restaurants, nightclubs and entertainment opportunities. These spaces for consumption are likely to be found in the city centre or typically in former industrial and/or waterfront districts which seek to maximise the city's geographical and historical location. Ward describes this as the construction of an, 'animated' urban landscape or at least of an urban landscape that appears animated as compared to the bland functionality of the suburban mall.

Marketing the post-industrial city

So how does the post-industrial city go about marketing itself in this global, symbolic landscape in a situation in which every other comparable city appears to be pursuing the same ambitions? The point of a marketing approach is that it emphasises the positives and ignores the negatives (Paddison, 1993). As such, place marketing is inevitably a reductionist practice that simplifies and reduces the city in such a way that the experiential range that underpins the deeper identity of a place is almost entirely neglected (Murray, 2001). The marketing of place is all about presenting that place as a commodity to be consumed in a unified form where unity did not necessarily sit before (Philo and Kearns, 1993). In many respects, this process is about manipulation. Most often, the past is manipulated in order to create an image of the present to be consumed by both external consumers and local residents. As Hall (1997) notes, this can in turn lead to a situation in which cities effectively exploit their own past, through a spurious exploitation of nostalgia and display the end result of which is 'the city as a theme park'. This is a situation in which cities would actually benefit from their promotion as a living, evolving entity in which the ingenuity and creativity of local people can be mobilised in a locally distinctive fashion (Murray, 2001).

The term city marketing first came into prominence in Europe in the 1980s where it has been characterised by a self-conscious emphasis on economic objectives. Thus, as Paddison (1993) suggests, city marketing objectives in the UK have rarely been incorporated within the physical planning of the city as a whole, unlike in the case of the USA, which has meant that broader issues of social planning and welfare have tended to be neglected in this context. For Kavaratzis (2004), marketing represents more than just a means of helping to solve the problems of an emerging postindustrial city but not least given Firat and Venkatesh's (1993: 246) proclamation that a postmodern world in fact constitutes 'the conscious and planned practice of signification and representation'. From this point of view, place marketing constitutes an actual philosophy of place management. In this context, marketers present the city as imaginary. They do so through three main techniques: 'personality branding' (e.g. the promotion of Barcelona through the Gaudi effect), 'flagship construction' and 'events branding' (Kavaratzis, 2004), For Graham (2002), the aim here is to conceive of the city as a commodity not least through the guise of the 'external city' which can be represented to the outside world through one or two key landmarks or buildings. Graham contrasts the external city with that of the internal city, the city of the mind, a more subjective experience of complex and ambiguous meanings invested in the city experience: an experience which one might argue is all too often neglected by marketers. As Kavaratzis (2004) points out, all encounters with the city take place through perceptions and images so that effective city branding needs to focus on the intersection of the internal and external city if it is to succeed.

Local authorities and other organisations spend considerable sums on promoting place imagery. In this context, Young and Lever (1997) quote Millington's work (1995) which indicates that in 1995–96, 93 per cent of local authorities engaged in promotional activity with an average budget of £279, 600. The problem here as far as Young and Lever (1997) and Millington (1995) are concerned is that there is little evidence as to the effectiveness of place marketing, particularly given the fact that the examination of the success of marketing by outputs is not in itself sufficient. There is indeed very little attention paid to the ways in which images of place are consumed, so there is a genuine gap between the meaning produced by producers and the meanings constructed by the consumers in receipt of those images. In considering the marketing of the city of Manchester by the Central Manchester Development Corporation, however, Young and Lever (1997) argue that the image presented in this case is one of a city with good communication links, and aesthetic and architectural appeal. In effect then, Manchester is marketed as a 24-hour city of consumption. This is reflected in the actual images used which are constituted by photographs of Manchester resplendent in bright sunshine, an orange glow presenting the redeveloped buildings of the city in a positive light. Such images, according to Young and Lever (1997), tend to be devoid of cars and people, most notably the sorts of social groups, such as the homeless, that do not fit in to the vision of Manchester that has to be presented as part of 'the city of single thought' (Arantes et al., 2000).

Philo and Kearns (1993) discuss place selling from a particularly critical perspective. They see the process of place selling as being all about the packaging of place to ensure two main prerogatives: to encourage geographically flexible or footloose economic enterprises to locate in a specific place and to encourage tourists to visit in large numbers, whilst convincing local people that they are an important part of this process and that 'good things' are being done on their behalf. In this context, culture is primarily a means to an economic end; a resource for economic gain so that history itself is manipulated in order that the past provides a source of pride and inspiration for the present (see Chapter 4). An important element of this process for Philo and Kearns (1993) is the selling of place as an exertion of power by the urban elite over the peoples of surrounding territories as well as those within the city. From this point of view, urban culture is the active project of the urban bourgeoisie and the city is a key instrument in ensuring their dominance as a social group.

But despite the implications of place selling for power relation-ships, it is important not to imply that those in control of that power do not have the best interest of place at heart, as Philo and Kearns (1993) suggest; though of course their actions may not actually be in the best interests of those places in the longer term. Nonetheless, by extolling the unique qualities of a place, place marketers often end up using a universal vocabulary that robs a place of its individuality. Such processes can potentially drain identity politics out of the area being marketed, depleting it of its meaning in the process:

> A nineteenth century quayside where casual dockworkers laboured in appalling conditions for ridiculously low wages was a context rich in meaning and political satire, for instance, but such a quayside done up as the backdrop for postmodern ware-house-turned-into-apartments occupied by a mobile new middle class has been stripped of its original meanings and political resonances. (Philo and Kearns, 1993: 24)

The concern here is that a manipulation of place may result in a range of conflicts because such manipulations run counter to the mean-ings invested in place by local peoples. This is especially so given the fact that one particular version of place and indeed of the memory of that place, namely that of the bourgeoisie, will usually become the officially sanctioned version of that place so that the act of sell-ing places conflates history and meaning in the name of economic gain (Philo and Kearns, 1993). For Goodwin (1997), the creation of 'city myths' is part of a broader process of commodification in which images and myths are relentlessly packaged until they become more real than reality itself. As Scott Lash (1990) puts it, there is, in effect, no such thing as a reality as such – only representations of reality in its various guises. The end result of all this is a kind of cultural speculation in which mythical landscapes and images are created with the prime motivation being to build speculative confidence in the city as a fully functional economic organism in its own right.

The creative city

The suggestion here is that the post-industrial is in many ways more inherently divisive than even its industrial predecessor. In order to further demonstrate this proposition, I want at this stage to briefly consider the work of a key contributor to current debates around the future of the city, namely Richard Florida (2002), the implication of whose work I will consider in more depth in Chapter 4. As I have already noted, the evolution of the post-industrial chapter has meant that the city has had to find new ways of reinventing itself. At the core of Florida's argument is the suggestion that creativity lies at the heart of such a transformation. Florida argues that the creative ethos is increasingly dominant in our society and that cities need to exploit this dominance in the best interests of their own economic futures to the extent that, 'regional economic growth is driven by the location choices of creative people – the holders of creative capital – who prefer places that are diverse, tolerant, and open to new ideas' (Florida, 2002: 223). The core concern of a post-industrial city from this point of view is how best to ensure that that city attracts what Florida calls 'the creative classes'. Florida's thesis is that it is not the case that such people move simply for jobs – they have a broader range of cultural and place-specific demands to which cities must respond.

> The Creative Centers are not thriving for such traditional economic reasons as access to natural resources or transportation routes. Nor are they thriving because their local governments have given away the store through tax breaks and other incentives to lure business. They are succeeding because creative people want to live there. The companies then follow the people – or, in many cases, are started by them. Creative centers provide the integrated eco-system or habitat where all forms of creativity – artistic and cultural, technological and economic – can take root and flourish. (Florida, 2002: 218)

A successful post-industrial city is one that offers a diversity of amenities and experiences, an openness to diversity and the freedom for creative people to validate their creative identities. Florida therefore presents a 'human capital' theory of regional development that is underpinned by the suggestion that creative people require 'quasi-anonymity'; in other words, they prefer the flexibility of weak community ties as opposed to the constraints imposed by strong community ties. For Florida, quality of place is more important than quality of life and the job of an effective post-industrial city is to create the conditions in which the creative classes can feel at home. This can be achieved by offering an appropriate built environment; by a city offering a diverse population and by implication, by vibrant social interaction and an animated street life. As Florida (2002: 284) puts it, 'The bottom line is that cities need *a people climate* even more than they need a business climate. This means supporting creativity across the board in all its various facets and dimensions – and building a community that is attractive to creative people, not just high-tech companies'.

There is no doubt that this approach has had a major impact on the thinking of policy-makers. At the heart of Florida's approach is a Creativity Index, a composite measure based on indicators of innovation (measured by patented innovation), high-tech industry (measured by high-tech industrial output), creativity and a gay index – the fraction of gay people living in a city. By creating a pecking order of urban creativity, Florida has produced a measurement which has an inherent appeal for those decision-makers looking to pursue an alternative economic future. It offers a reassuring vision of such a future underpinned by a sense of hope and possibility. From a more critical point of view, there is a concern that such an approach simply lays too much at the door of creativity. Moreover, an approach which purports to be about creativity is actually, it could be argued, underpinned by notions of consumption in the sense that any ambition to make a city more appealing to the creative classes is inevitably bound up with a reinvention of the city through the opportunities for consumption which that city provides. To this end, McGuigan (1996) quotes Robins (1993: 321–3) who argues:

> With its emphasis on art, culture, consumption and a cappuccino lifestyle, the fashionable new urbanity seems to be shaped in the image of exactly the same social group that stands behind

the wider political programme of post-Fordism ... [It] is only about revitalizing fragments of the city. It is about insulating the consumption of living spaces of the postmodern flâneur from the 'have-nots' in the abandoned zones of the city.

Florida's approach tends to imply by default that culture-led regeneration is any easy option when it is of course nothing of the sort. Moreover, as Peck (2005) has argued in his critique of Florida, it is simply not feasible to produce authentic neighbourhood cultures through deliberate public or, for that matter, private interventions. Such interventions constantly run the risk of creating a self-consciously 'funky' city where the authentic, if such a thing exists, is nothing but an after-thought. Although the divisive nature of consumption remains unexplored in Florida's work, it is clearly the case that the sort of vision of the post-industrial city that Florida presents is an inherently divisive one.

The above process is inevitably intensified by the vision that Florida presents. His approach to city-making is driven by an economic imperative that has little if any time for the disparities that such a city will create. The transformation of the post-industrial city could thus be said to, potentially at least, actively exacerbate aspects of social polarisation, an argument expressed in Castells' (1994) concept of the dual city: a city divided between the cosmopolitanism of the elite and the tribalism of local communities. It is in this context that there has been a more recent move towards understanding the role of diversity in understanding and promoting the development of our cities. The work of Charles Landry (2006), for example, has tried to focus on the way in which difference can be celebrated and utilised in a more vibrant city and which thereby moves beyond reductionist views of culture. The work of authors such as Florida which exists outside of an academic paradigm and constitutes in itself an economic contribution to a reinvented entrepreneurial city is nonetheless interesting, as it highlights the emergence of a particular way of thinking about the city that is essentially rhetorical in nature. Perhaps then our cities or at least the rhetoric that surrounds our cities are in this sense unreal: more the creation of an idealised bourgeois image of what a cultural city might be than a genuine expression of what it means to live in a place. In the current climate, it appears that cities no longer have any kind of a genuine choice. They have to compete as part of the symbolic landscape discussed in this chapter because that is the only show in town. To opt out of this civic boosterism is to deny the dreams and the aspirational possibilities that are inherent in the vision of a post-industrial city. The dangers of thinking in this way are no better expressed than in Broudehoux's (2004) work on the redevelopment of Beijing:

> The image of the city that is constructed and promoted in the process of selling places is often based not on the local reality but on stereotyped notions and exaggerated representations, which seek to enhance the marketability of the locale. The ready-made identities assigned by city boosters and disseminated through the mass media often reduce several different visions of local culture into a single vision that reflects the aspirations of a powerful elite and the values, lifestyles, and expectations of potential investors and tourists. These practices are thus highly elitist and exclusionary, and often signify to more disadvantaged segments of the population that they have no place in this revitalized and gentrified urban spectacle. (Broudehoux, 2004: 26)

Urban regeneration fails to come to terms with the emotional dimensions of urban culture. Cities are reduced to an idealised vision of a prosperous future that has scant regard for who might be the losers in such an equation. In what follows, I will consider the reimagineering of Glasgow as a competitive city as a practical means of coming to terms with some of the limitations of a place marketing approach.

Glasgow's Miles Better campaign

In many senses and more so than many other cities, Glasgow can be described as both the product and the victim of industrial decline. In a previous life, it was the second city in the British Empire and it provided that Empire with a hub for shipbuilding and heavy industry (Jones and Evans, 2008). By the 1970s, Glasgow was officially the most deprived locality in Britain and was in dire need of a reversal in economic fortune. Glasgow, as Paddison (1993) notes, does indeed offer one of the more extreme examples of an industrial city in decline as demonstrated, for example, by its startling demographic decline from being a city of 1.1 million residents in 1961 to one of 662, 000 in 1991. The fact that Glasgow's employment base contracted by over one quarter between 1960 and 1980 is equally troubling and reflects broader trends occuring in developed cities worldwide.

A key dimension of this intended reversal of the above trends was the celebrated 1988 Glasgow's Miles Better campaign, alongside a range of other activities and policies that sought to attract private resources, most notably to the city centre; examples including new retail developments at Princess Square and the Italian Centre as well as the gentrification of the Merchant City (Jones and Evans, 2006). This market-driven conception of the city centre was intended to complement a broader emphasis on the development of the culture of Glasgow, although it remains unclear whether or not the increased onus on the service sector reflected an actual strategic decision as such (Gomez, 1998; Savitch and Kantor, 2002). Thus, MacLeod (2002) refers to the creation of a new business-led quango, Glasgow Action, in the 1990s, whose aim was 'to make the city more attractive to work in, to live in and to play in; to recreate Glasgow's entrepreneurial spirit; to communicate the new reality of Glasgow to its citizens and to the world' (MacLeod, 2002: 611).

As far as Glasgow's Miles Better campaign is concerned, the intention here was to help to put the brakes on Glasgow's downward spiral (Paddison, 1993) by offering a new version of Glasgow to be consumed both by audiences in the south of England and internationally who had been brought up on images of Glasgow as a city defined by its poverty and crime. Moreover, the aim was to boost locale morale so that the people of Glasgow themselves felt good about their city (Paddison, 1993). As a first step in urban renewal, the campaign was a great success insofar as it played a strategic role in attracting new tourists to Glasgow (Wishart, 1991). Glasgow was entering a stage of image reconstruction (Paddison, 1993). The evidence that the campaign alongside broader infrastructural improvements in the city centre were working is compelling: in 1982, some 700,000 visitors came to the city as compared with three million in 1990, 600,000 of which could be attributed to the designation of European Capital of Culture status in 1990 (Paddison, 1993).

The award of the title 'British City of Architecture' in 1999 provided the city with a further impetus in presenting a particular image of Glasgow to the outside world. Thus, the campaign 'There's a lot Glasgowing on in 1990' and later 'Glasgow's Alive' tried to further correct some of the extreme visions of Glasgow that had predominated during the 1980s (Mitchell, 2000). Commentators such as Gomez (1998) and Damer (1990: 1) describe a situation in which the media image of Glasgow was, as late as the 1980s, still 'of a filthy, slum-ridden, poverty stricken, gang-infested city whose population consisted of undersized, incomprehensible, drunken, foul-mouthed, sectarian lumpen proletrians who were prone to hit each other with broken bottles and razors without warning'. But as Mitchell (2000) points out, the Glasgow of the 1990s was a different proposition and the nature of this proposition was very much determined by how images were used to help people to re-evaluate their perceptions of the city. To this end, Mitchell compares photographic representations of the city in the 1960s with those in the 1980s and in doing so highlights a key transition between a city defined by its people and their activities to one focused on the urban landscape:

> The transition, one could say, is from a city of public spaces, a city of people at home in the city, not wealthy, but not abject either, to a city as landscape, a place devoid of residents, a landscape in which people are only visitors and welcome mostly as consumers (especially of imagery). The city-as-landscape does not encourage the formation of community or of urbanism as a way of life; rather it encourages the maintenance of surfaces, the promotion of order at the expense of lived social relations, and the ability to look past distress, destruction, and marginalization to see only the good life (for some) and turn a blind eye towards what life is constructed out of. (Mitchell, 2000: 8)

Clearly, as Mitchell goes on to argue, the people of Glasgow are entitled to enjoy the many improvements in the physical and cultural infrastructure of their city, but the fact is that 'Glasgow's Miles Better' for some residents more so than it is for others: inadequate public transport creates a core/periphery effect in which only the core is deemed a legitimate representation of the city at large (see Jones and Wilks-Heeg, 2004 for a discussion of Liverpool in this context). As Savitch and Kantor (2002) also point out, Glasgow is very much a dual city and the city continues to struggle with the realities of industrial obsolescence – the sparkling city centre sits in stark contrast to the realities of poverty and decay in the 'real' city. For MacLeod (2002), Glasgow's city centre is simply mutating into 'a plethora of interdictory landscapes contrived in the image of fictitious capital and consumerist citizenship' (p. 615). As far as Mitchell is concerned, the increasing emphasis on the image and the cultural offer of the city has much broader implications and reflects the process of globalisation to which I referred above. The more the economy globalises and the more it goes down a route of constant revolution and reinvention, the more any kind of identity stability, established over centuries, is undermined. To extend Mitchell's argument, the very foundations of place upon which a city is founded is threatened by the very process that purports to offer it a sustainable future.

Various authors have questioned who it is that benefits from the regenerated city, as Jones and Evans (2008) suggest. Any assumption that in the regenerated city wealth is likely to trickle down appears unfounded. Indeed, there is a concern that the regenerating city becomes a patchwork of spaces, some of which have been regenerated and others which have not. Jones and Evans (2008) go on to quote the work of MacLeod (2002) who argues that the splintering of space in the city is often accompanied by social splintering so that certain social groups are excluded from regenerated spaces. This process is again all about image: in order to sustain the image of a revitalized regenerated space, logic has it that such space must be 'purified'. Social groups such as the homeless whose faces do not fit into the image of the new city, primarily because they simply do not have the resources to partake in the newly commodified landscape, are not only policed but actively excluded from the spaces of consumption that a place marketing model of the city implies.

Of particular interest for MacLeod (2002) in this regard is the fact that this kind of exclusivity discourse is often normalised through the popular press who are liable to feed into a way of thinking about the city that purports that the image of the city holds precedence over the rights of its citizens. For Jones and Evans (2008), this reinforces a situation in which a neo-liberal logic, demonstrated here in a cultural as well as an economic context, is so dominant that private wealth generation becomes a far more important 'public' priority than welfare and wealth distribution. This constitutes what MacLeod (2002) describes as a distressing geography of exclusion; a geography of exclusion represented in the actual architecture of new retail developments which, for example, serve to 'appease the pleasures and fantasies of consumerist citizenship, and was not to be extended to those without a home' (MacLeod, 2002: 613). Paddison (1993) meanwhile points out that the use of 'hallmark' events such as the European City of Culture simply serve to compartmentalise success. What benefits one part of the city may have limited effect on the rest, pushing the problems of urban decline out of sight and out of mind. The truth is that the projected image of the new Glasgow has little in common with the lived realities of deprivation as they continue to be felt by a high proportion of the city's population (Paddison, 1993). To this end, Tucker (2008) quotes Laurier (1993: 13): 'Glasgow's extravagant year of culture in 1990 was not about focusing on rich and vibrant cultural milieu, but was about hiding grim "working class" history from tourists and captains of industry'.

Despite the limitation inherent in an image-driven model of regeneration as demonstrated in the Glasgow case, there is, however, no doubt that Glasgow has benefited in many ways from the process of repackaging. In their discussion of six UK's cities' efforts to attract the meetings market, for example, Bradley et al. (2002) note that meeting organisers had positive perceptions of the city in light of its year as European City of Culture and expressed the thought that the city felt culturally vibrant as a result. Many of the meeting organisers described Glasgow as 'cultured', 'trendy' and 'cool', providing a further indication that the re-imaging of Glasgow was having some positive long-term effects. Garcia (2005), meanwhile, acknowledges the fact that 1990 has resulted in a genuine cultural legacy for the city, an issue I will consider in more depth in the next chapter.

Even though there is evidence to suggest that the image of Glasgow has altered the picture, it is not an entirely rosy one given that a genuine economic recovery has failed to materialise (particularly as far as employment figures are concerned). And, yet, the city's reputation as a hotbed of regeneration and revitalization continues unabated. Rightly or wrongly, Glasgow has become something of a model for other cities seeking a more prosperous industrial future, as Gomez's (1998) comparison between Glasgow and Bilbao illustrates. But the perceived success of the Glasgow approach perhaps tells us something more about the limited ability of the local council to intervene effectively in a way that they could have a genuine effect on local factors of production (Gomez, 1998). The image of regeneration that emanates from the Glasgow experience is ultimately a very limited formula that revitalises the surface of the city but not the city within. The truth is that Glasgow failed in its ambitions for employment recovery, even if its central area did provide the consolation of a core of commerce, education, culture and tourism (Gomez, 1998). In the end, the *appearance* of regeneration is not in itself enough.

Bringing the situation more up to date, in some senses, Glasgow's future is bright. The city won the right to host the Commonwealth Games in 2014 at an estimated cost of £288 million alongside a £50 million influx through sponsorship, broadcasting and ticket sales. Tucker (2008) goes as far as to suggest that Glasgow 2014 will put the Scottish city among the global elite of urban, economic power-houses. More importantly, Glasgow has secured yet another mecha-nism to further regenerate and sustain the city's physical and social fabric' (p. 22). The primary beneficiary of such developments is likely to be Dalmarnock in the East End of Glasgow, home to the new athletes' village in what was traditionally a very deprived area of the city (Tucker, 2008). Tucker sees Glasgow as something of a success story and argues that European Capital of Culture status was key in creating a 'cultural mindscape' for the city whilst energising the city economically. To this end, Tucker (2008) quotes Ward (1998) who argues that 'Culture was the "icing on the cake": today it has become part of the cake itself'. The key question is whether that cake tastes as good as it looks and whether it can provide sufficient sustenance to the communities of Glasgow.

Conclusion

The above discussion raises some key issues for the long-term sustain-ability of the city and how the role of the city has changed given its reinvention or at least a perception of its reinvention around notions of entrepreneurialism. In this context, Blum (2003) discusses the city as an imaginative structure in which the city becomes nothing more than a sign. Thus, from the point of view of our discussion around con-sumption, if we compare one city with another, we compare the way in which one city discriminates goods as compared to another. By using consumption as a means of comparison, we render, according to Blum, the city subject to an artificially designed and abstract language that relinquishes real differences, insofar as the appearance of that city is privileged ahead of what lies beneath. For Blum then, the city is actually an object of desire that comes in and out of view through the course of everyday life.

> The proposition that the city is nothing but a sign is an irony
> inspired by a vision of the end of transcendence that, in its way,
> is designed to challenge and, so open up the question of the link
> between territorial and discursive spaces. That is, if culture is
> a symbolic order, then 'it' is not located in any space, because
> culturally it appears to exist placelessly. (p. 48)

In considering Blum's ideas in the context of a debate around spaces
for consumption, his contention that the bourgeoisie are intent not
on attaining the desirable object but rather the look of the desire
is particularly prescient. What is important is that the city looks
contemporaneous; that it looks of the moment. Moreover, as Blum
points out, the look of desire is not equally obtainable by all. If the
city teaches us one thing, then it teaches us that the pursuit of freedom and opportunity is inevitably limited at least to some extent by
the spectre of class. One of the consequences of the entrepreneurial
city is that the city spectacle comes increasingly to the forefront. The
version of the city presented to its residents and its visitors presents
the spectacle as a source of fascination. The city provides promise
and a profound lack of fulfilment at one and the same time (Blum,
2003). We appear to be seduced by it. Thus, for Blum, the diversity
inherent in the city presents us with a superficial spectacle that cam-
ouflages the class distinctions that lie beneath, so that city life is all
about the loss of individuality through the detachment implied by
consumption. The capitalist, entrepreneurial city could then be said
to offer a city a kind of brilliance that is more apparent than real.
Given the power of capital to emancipate desire in the contemporary,
such a city is inevitably 'skin deep'. It empowers an imaginary world
in which life is full of possibilities whilst concealing the powers that
are concealed by this arrangement.

> Thus, we note again how the city which is at the centre of a
> civilisation is the capital precisely because it can make the
> dissemination of worldly desire its capital concern, a concern
> of such capital importance that it can be theatricalised as an
> expanded public stage in which all participants are reciprocally
> performers and audience, two-in-one, seeing each other and
> being seen in an environment enlarged to illuminate its varied
> choices and restricted to keep dark the possibility that those
> differences make no real difference. (Blum, 2003: 231)

In further discussing the way in which the contemporary city creates an environment of spectacular consumption, Blum considers the instructive example of the cineplex experience. In watching a film in such an environment, the experience is not so much about the film but the experience more broadly. 'Such "built environments" create and sustain desire for objects by using the primary antiquated action (film, groceries, books) as a pretext for stimulating congregation. In this way, they are often praised as new public spaces. In displaying diverse arrangements of functions, they not only offer something for everyone but succeed in affirming their own concentration of functions as a spectacle that enhances collective power' (p. 257). By catering for a diverse range of interests under one roof, the desire for quality and discrimination that may have prevented people from engaging in such activities in the past has, according to Blum, been undercut. As far as marketing is concerned, the vision in which such spaces of consumption have such a key role is in danger of achieving what Graham (2002) has described as the Laura Ashleyisation of the high street.

The notion of the city as a spectacle is something I will return to in Chapter 7. At this stage, it is worthwhile reiterating a theme that has emerged again and again throughout this chapter, namely that of the way in which a spectacular vision of the city creates a particular vision of space and place in which popular participation is less than a priority. As Harvey (1989: 14) puts it, 'The image of prosperity ... masks the underlying difficulties and projects an imagery of success that spreads internationally'. This is an issue taken up by Vaz and Jacques (2006) who point out that the withdrawal of the state and the increasing role of the market in urban planning has led to an increasing mercantilisation of the city that is replicated the world over. Such efforts produce 'a multiplicity of standardized attractions that reduce the uniqueness of urban identities, even while claims of uniqueness grow more intense' (Zukin, 1998: 837). In an increasingly homogenised urban landscape, the tourist does not appropriate space but simply crosses it. The citizen therefore has no more status than an extra on a stage set (Vaz and Jacques, 2006). The priority here then is not just the city's image: but its brand image: 'In a word, this brand synthesizes an object of desire and connects the consumer to it' (Vaz and Jacques, 2006: 249).

The consensus around the contemporary consumer city creates a situation in which many of the 'actors' that make the city what it is are excluded from the processes that are deemed valid in a move towards a post-industrial economy. Meanwhile, as consumers retreat into their own private worlds and self-authored existences, their ability to influence the public realm appears compromised. The more pleasure is found in or through consumption, the less, arguably, that pleasure is shared. The process of spectacularisation legislates against the very urban revitalisation to which it aspires, given the fact that those people who bring places to life are excluded from such a process. The end result is a deeply predictable, clinical kind of a city, and one that is intentionally so because the alternative is apparently not economically viable. In order to compete, the city is obliged to play by the rules of the game. It is simply not feasible to reject this vision of an entrepreneurial city or indeed those determined by the market. Vaz and Jacques, perhaps optimistically, call for a situation in which the city ceases being a stage set and becomes a stage *floor* for its citizens. The city should in effect be an experiential entity, a place for exchange, conflict and meaning rather than an object of action deliberately stripped clean of the physicality of the human body (Vaz and Jacques, 2006). Whether or not such a vision is possible in a consumer society remains debatable. As Harvey (2008) notes, the notion of human rights that dominates in contemporary society does not in any way challenge the dominance of the market. In this sense, the city 'belongs' to private and quasi-private interests. It belongs to an ideology of consumption and not to the consumer. Lived social relations are not a priority in an entrepreneurial city in which image perception is the primary indicator of quality. The extent to which the individual is still able to forge a path of his or her own making, despite such constraints, is a key issue and one to which I will return.

4

CONSUMING CULTURE

One of the key characteristics of the emergence of the entrepreneurial city as discussed in Chapter 3 has been an increasingly co-dependent and pragmatic relationship between the economy and culture to the extent that art and culture are an integral part of urban economic development (see Scott, 2000; Evans, 2001). In this context:

> It is becoming more and more difficult to determine where the cultural economy begins and the rest of the capitalist economic order ends, for just as culture is increasingly subject to commodification, so one of the prevalent features of contemporary capitalism is its tendency to infuse an ever widening range of outputs with aesthetic and semiotic and above all symbolic, as opposed to material, content. (Scott, 2000: x)

For Lash and Urry (1994), this reflects a process of de-differentiation in which the distinctiveness of cultural spheres is increasingly undermined so that there is a shift from contemplation to consumption and an apparent privileging of choice. In this context and in a process in which sign values become evermore prevalent, the consumer becomes an agent of aestheticisation or branding. Thus, the touristic experience is consumed in the sense that the consumer transforms service and experiences into signs (Lash and Urry, 1994). The argument here is that such developments are physically, and by implication emotionally, manifested in the form of spaces for consumption.

What we can identify here is a process in which the built environment is revalorised around cultural consumption (Zukin, 1995; Short, 2006). In this context, culture has become more than the sum of its parts, in the sense that the role culture plays in the consumer's relationship to the city is less about the straightforward consumption of cultural forms and more about the consumption of an ideology transmitted through culture (an ideology at that which potentially undermines the meaning which underpins that cultural form in the first place). This chapter is therefore concerned with the impact of cultural tourism on the construction of the post-industrial city and whether the commodification of culture can ever fulfil the ambitions that policy-makers apparently invest in it. Culture and the arts constitute a prime weapon in cities' efforts to compete on the global stage, as I pointed out in Chapter 3. Culture offers a graphic demonstration of a city's ability to compete through the enhancement of image and prestige and to associate the brand of that city with cultural sophistication (Landry, 2006). Meanwhile, the cultural economy and in particular the creative industries has provided, rhetorically at least, a positive outlet for local and national politicians to talk up the role of the local in broader processes of global economic change (Evans, 2001). Such developments can clearly be related to notions of the experience economy (Pine and Gilmore, 1999) which is itself reproduced through the increasingly blurred boundaries between shopping, learning and the experience of culture. This:

> ... involves creating settings and using every trick in the book, where customers and visitors participate in all-embracing sensory events, whether for shopping, visiting a museum, eating at a restaurant, conducting business-to-business activities or providing any personalized service from haircutting to arranging travel. In this process, shops can develop museum-like features, such as the Discovery Store or Hard Rock café, with its display of original artefacts. Vice versa, museums can become more like extensions of entertainment venues.... . (Landry, 2006 152)

Cultural tourism

As Meethan (2001) suggests, the notion of cultural tourism is very difficult to pin down but can perhaps be considered as a form of tourism that is about more than the aimless pleasures of mass tourism. Cultural tourism is more serious in intent so that:

> To be a cultural tourist is to attempt ... to go beyond idle leisure and to return enriched with knowledge of other places and other people, even if this involves 'gazing' at, or collecting in some way, the commodified essences of otherness. (Meethan, 2001: 128)

Image 4.1 City marketing through culture: MTV Europe Music Awards, Liverpool 2008
(Photo Andy Miah)

In many ways, the reinvention of the post-industrial city is about presenting the city as a place in which the opportunities to consume culture in this way are prevalent. However, the high profile of tourism as symbolic currency has effectively, as Craik (1997: 135) suggests, put too many grand expectations at its door:

> Tourism has been promoted as the answer to economic decline, providing cultural industries with the opportunity to develop as industries with export potential, as well as a vehicle to cultivate the cultural life of visitors, locals and the public sphere. These are lofty ideals and, from the point of view of government, highly attractive: the crass overtones of tourism can be reframed; economic ills addressed; training schemes in creative and service jobs promoted; and cultural identity fostered. The tourism industry itself, after some initial hesitation, has pounced on the cultivation of tourism as cultural commodity and phenomenon with considerable enthusiasm, prompted by

new opportunities to package and market its product and to entice new markets.

Interestingly, as Craik goes on to argue, there remains a lack of unanimity, at least within the arts and cultural communities, as to the benefits of marketing culture as a product to be consumed. The contention here is that the economic processes that I have identified as emerging throughout this book have been interpreted in such a way that any form of culture is deemed fair game in an effort to carve out some kind of a new economic future for the city. For Meethan, processes of de-differentiation and the blurring of high and low cultural forms are not however creating a situation in which places are becoming more and more like each other, but rather imply a complex situation in which global forms of culture and their consumption are less constrained by old rules, so that 'globalization does not itself lead to cultural homogeneity, rather it seems to be generating more differences than similarities' (2001: 137). It is on this point that I depart from Meethan who argues that it is something of an oversimplification to describe such process as being determined by commodification and that we should in fact be focusing on the way in which such processes impinge on the cultural norms of host societies in complex ways. I would argue, in contrast, that however much we interrogate the way in which the cultural economy is deployed locally, the process of commodification operates in such a normalising fashion that there is very little room to negotiate any kind of an alternative to its orthodoxy. The individual consumer may negotiate his or her own place within the boundaries defined for him or her by consumption, but he or she is ultimately subject to the structures determined for him or her by the consumer society.

Of course, there are local variations, but those variations are most likely to be determined by a model of the city produced for consumers and for the act of consumption so that 'localised identities' are almost inevitably compromised as a result. What is certain is that the way in which places are evoked through advertising has in recent decades taken on an increasingly emotional and sensory tone. Thus, Prentice (2001: 6) quotes claims made on behalf of Berwick-upon-Tweed which can apparently offer landscape that is 'a personal revelation every time you visit it ... there is an immense feeling of space, otherworldliness, and of having discovered something special for the first time' and in doing so argues that this constitutes a new kind of media-driven Romanticism. Such Romanticism is all about the construction of expectation and daydreaming about the possibilities of place and thus echoes some of Campbell's (1987) work on the desirous daydreaming nature of the consumer experience. But the irony here is that although the above construction of place is founded upon a notion of the individual's personal interaction with place, that place is inevitably packaged in order to appeal to as many consumers as possible. As such, it is essentially depersonalised. In discussing the nature of experiential cultural tourism, Prentice (2001) goes on to argue that cultural tourism is all about the marketing of cultural products as cultural experiences. This onus on the experiential is about providing a cultural offer that appears at least to be non-packaged and individualised – a kind of post-Fordist tourism.

One of the most important exemplars of how cities can be renewed through their cultural 'offer' in such a way as to revitalise place is undoubtedly Baltimore (Ward, 2006). Ward describes the extraordinary transformation that has occurred in the Inner Harbor area of Baltimore over the last 30 years or so. Baltimore offers something of a model in demonstrating how to replace industrial jobs with a service economy based on leisure and how best to exploit cultural tourism through the harnessing of private capital to public money. This process constitutes the physical manifestation of the more rhetorical symbolic processes underpinning place-making as discussed in Chapter 3. The city of Baltimore began promoting its Inner Harbor as a tourist destination from around the early 1970s. Such developments included the opening of the Maryland Science Center in 1976, the marina in 1978 and crucially the Harborplace festival market in 1980 and, sure enough, Baltimore soon became internationally renowned as a case study in post-industrial redevelopment (Ward, 2006).

The key to the revitalisation of the city of Boston was similarly the festival marketplace, developed by the well-known Baltimore developer James Rouse. Working alongside the Boston architect Ben Thompson, Rouse redeveloped the historic but derelict Faneuil Hall market area of the city. The aim here was to focus on the notion of the distinctive characteristics of a market location as opposed to the imposition of a shopping mall template on the area. The great success of the redevelopment was at least partly due to effective marketing as demonstrated particularly well by Rouse's slogan 'Cities are fun!'. Moreover, it is worth noting Ward's point that what is interesting about the Baltimore model is the fact that it actually involved less private capital than may have appeared to have been the case on the surface. This development was effectively defining a new avenue of exploration for cities, that of cultural urbanism (Ward, 2006):

> In a broader sense Rouse realised that many Americans yearned for a romanticised notion of a vibrant traditional city. In reality this was a place that had never been, a scene of happy animation where people might safely gather in large numbers. It was a scene untroubled by all the competing and troubling realities of the industrial past or the post-industrial present. Here was a carefully managed enclave from which all the many problems of urban decay, crime, social and racial tension had been banished. (Ward, 2006: 277)

For Ward then, Baltimore's Harborplace constitutes a form of sanitised cultural entertainment whilst providing a model for other cities including Boston (which often employed Rouse himself) to replicate what was achieved in Baltimore in other cities such as Boston as well as Sydney, Barcelona and Tokyo, each of which displays many of the key characteristics associated with Baltimore's revitalisation (Ward, 2006). The Baltimore experience became a global model for cultural-tourism-led regeneration, the irony being that although the redevelopment of such places depended upon the place distinctiveness of a particular physical setting, the popularity of such a model has meant that the character of such places is increasingly *less* particular. Meanwhile, the economic impacts of the Baltimore approach are highly questionable (Ward, 2006). Ward goes as far as to suggest that in Baltimore itself, the model of cultural tourism once characterised by the city has moved on and is 'detached from the place itself' (p. 284). More importantly for the evolution of the post-industrial city, the Baltimore vision has inadvertently spawned an urban culture of emulation so that the notion of 'cities are fun' has become an urban orthodoxy in which to be 'fun' is no less than the norm.

Judd (2003) describes the enormous political and physical impact on the character or at least the personality of cities in the United States and elsewhere. Judd and Fainstein (1999) thus identify three kinds of tourist cities: resort cities built for consumers, tourist-historical cities that seek to maximise historic reference for the good of the tourist economy and converted cities that have been reinvented for tourists in light of post-industrial decline. Of particular concern for Judd is the way in which tourism has acted as an island of renewal in 'seas of decay' (p. 6). A key characteristic of the converted tourist city is the carving out of defended entertainment zones or 'tourist bubbles' for middle-class consumers looking to escape the problems of urban blight. In this situation, argues Judd, the city becomes a simulacrum, a stage-set that idealises the less desirable city that sits beyond.

A key element of the emergence of the tourist city is the development of a privatising discourse of public infrastructure as discussed by Perry (2003). The private sector fills in the gaps that cannot be filled by the state as Ward (2006) also demonstrates in his discussion of Baltimore, and in doing so creates an infrastructure of performance venues, galleries, convention centres and, of course, hotels. The concern for Perry is that in this situation the financial markets effectively operate as a *de facto* outer boundary for the political choices that underpin the development of the tourist city so that the control of that city is, potentially at least, increasingly in the hands of the market. This has arguably had a negative impact on the character of the city, given that profit and not authenticity is the primary motivation of private business (Frieden and Sagalyn, 1990). Thus, Evans (2002) highlights the dangers inherent in commodifying public cultural spaces by revenue-led initiatives such as, for example, museum retailing operations.

A question that arises from the Baltimore model of cultural tourism is how genuinely creative the cultural consumer can be under such conditions. This is an issue discussed by Richards and Wilson (2006) who discuss the role of culture and tourism in the aestheticisation of the urban landscape. From this point of view, culture is a theme from which the narratives of place-making are derived. But as I demonstrate elsewhere in this book, this inevitably implies a process of commodification that in turn creates an inherent tension in which distinction becomes harder and harder to achieve. Moreover, as Richards and Wilson (2006) point out, the number of cultural projects in search of visitors is increasing faster than demand. Many projects of this kind are unable to fulfil their ambitions due to factors such as a lack of sufficient finance, plans that are by necessity over-ambitious in order to secure funding in the first place and local political hurdles that prove insurmountable as Jones (2009) highlights in his discussion of the ill-fated Fourth Grace in Liverpool (which was eventually superseded on the Liverpool waterfront by the more anodyne Liverpool Museum). As a result, 'The effect is to produce a growing series of relatively sterile, inflexible cultural tourism spaces, dominated by passive consumption and the use of familiar historical references' (Richards and Wilson, 2006: 1212).

The above raises the question of authenticity which Shoval (2000) discusses in the context of the tourism of holy places. He points out that religious sites have long been the object of commodification; Orthodox and Catholic churches effectively being themed environments with a religious ambition as opposed to a commercial one. And although Shoval argues that many pilgrims are in search of the authentic experience when it comes to their visit to the Holy Land, that quest for authenticity is inevitably compromised by an environment that has become increasingly susceptible to multimedia extravaganzas and simulations. The argument here is that the meaning people invest in the culture of the pilgrimage is under threat by the packaging of that experience so that the inherent meaning is in increasing danger of being trivialised. The implication here is that meaning is effectively given to rather than constructed by the individual. In effect, tourism is about 'communicative staging'. It is all about persuading tourists that they are having an authentic experience as opposed to actually providing them with one (Cohen, 1989).

The question of passivity is crucial. For Richards and Wilson, the tourist city demonstrates significant creative potential. Creative tourists are in the habit of seeking the sorts of creative opportunities that also appeal to the creative classes I referred to in Chapter 3. From such a perspective, consumers are not passively consuming the city but actively engaging with it so that they are able to produce their own experiences, regardless of how uniform and globalised the tourism spaces they occupy may be. But of course the onus is on those responsible for producing the tourist city to create a situation in which the active involvement of the tourist is encouraged, so that at the present creative tourism is more of an aspiration than a reality. As Richards and Wilson put it, 'the important point in developing creative tourism is to provide a context in which the experience not only becomes a framework for learning, but also for transformation of the self' (2006: 1220).

Consuming the museum

The process of commodification has significant implications for the consumer at a number of levels. The issue here is concerned with how culture is packaged, how we engage with that package and what it tells us about what it means to be a citizen in a consumer society. The changing experience of museum attendance provides a useful illustration of what I mean. Prentice (2001) describes the way in which in recent years museums have had to adapt largely as a result of the sorts of market pressures that have been brought to bear on them. Prentice discusses the massive expansion of the sheer numbers of museums in Europe and their recent efforts to offer the consumer an authentic experience which delights and provokes. The need to present the 'authentic' is of course not new for museums, but the pressures for museums to compete with other organisations presenting the authentic *is* new to the extent that 'Museums are today immersed in a wider commodification of culture: the extensive proffering of place as a means of attaining the "real"' (p. 7). Thus, the museum experience is increasingly associated with the themed and the interactive. Moreover, there has been a popularistaion of heritage in recent decades which some authors have attributed to a crisis of post-modernity (Laenen, 1989; Goulding, 1999) which has produced something of an apparently depthless society that is apparently defined by its surface reality. Thus, for Goulding (1999), heritage tourism offers a means of searching for meaning in a society in which meaning is otherwise bereft. In effect, heritage sites act as an emotional stimulus for people's nostalgic thirst for the past. Museums sell that experience and the apparent fulfilment of that emotion to the individual consumer.

Let me illustrate what I mean further with a brief consideration of the notion of edutainment as discussed in the work of Podesta and Addis (2007). 'Edutainment' basically refers to the convergence of learning and entertainment, not least through multi-media technologies which enable consumers to become active participants in virtual environments. Thus, Podesta and Addis talk about the Rose Center for Earth and Space, a branch of the American Museum of Natural History which opened in New York in 2000 and which provides a home for the world's most advanced virtual reality simulator. The Ross Centre houses the Hayden Planetarium which in turn includes the high-tech Space Theater which utilises the world's most high-tech visual technologies. Some commentators have gone as far as to argue that the Centre has transcended the world of the planetarium and should instead be referred to as a 'future theatre' or a 'cyberdrome' (Podesta and Addis, 2007):

The museum's new positioning is based on a real visitor orientation strategy which considers the visitor as the customer, the starting point of its marketing approach. Every component of the services offered, including virtual reality, is utilized to create the experience of the visit. This approach leads to the convergence between education and entertainment, and between high art and popular art. (p. 146)

For Podesta and Addis, entertainment is a vehicle through which consumers' learning is maximised and the point of this process is that it involves the consumer in the product more extensively and deeply than would have previously been possible. From this point of view, edutainment empowers the consumer whilst simultaneously allowing producers to revitalise their 'product range'. In this context, McCracken (2005) suggests that a preferment model of the museum, in which the role of the museum is to advance and civilise the individual through culture, has gradually been superseded. Interestingly, McCracken argues that what lies at the heart of this transition and other broader social and cultural transitions is a shift towards a consumer society. This shift brought about a situation in which the consumer became the arbiter of what counted and in which institutions such as museums became obliged to accommodate themselves to the needs of the individual. As McCracken puts it:

The consumer society has changed the expectations visitors have of the museum ... The new visitor comes looking ... for experiences that do not pull them upward in the hierarchy but outwards into a world of experience. They come looking for engagements not with status mobility but with a kind of existential mobility. Visitors come looking for new experiences, emotions and participations. These experiences are still transforming, but they are transforming in new modalities according to different cultural logics. (p. 143)

In effect then and as a direct result of the above processes, museums, much like other cultural institutions, appear to be modelling themselves on tourism (Kirshenblatt-Gimblett, 1998) and as such are moving away from their image of dusty, quiet places for contemplation to be reinvented as venues engaging in senses, emotions and imagination. To put what McCracken says above in a different way, museums are no longer defined by their relationship to objects but rather by their relationship to their visitors (Kirshenblatt-Gimblett, 1998).

Goulding argues that the above transition should not lead us to conclude that the consumers of heritage are somehow manipulated. Consumers do not automatically consume museums in the way museum professionals may expect them to. For example, many of the museum visitors that Goulding interviewed expressed a dissatisfaction with the intrusive nature of historical reconstructions and said that they would have preferred the contemporary museum experience to provide more opportunity for solitude and imagination. Thus, Prentice (2001) quotes the example of *Eureka!* in Halifax in the UK, a museum that emphasises touch, smell, hearing and speaking so that the experience of consumption is designed to be an involved rather than a passive one. It is about 'the search for thought-provoking stimuli to effect mindful experience' (Goulding, 1999). The point here is that however active the consumer may or may not be in this context, there is no escaping the fact that such mindful experiences are made possible within the parameters laid down for the individual by the space for consumption in which he or she consumes.

Many authors have recognised that modern tourism is effectively defined by the process of commodification (Richards, 1996; Watson and Kopachevsky, 1994). From this point of view, tourism involves the emptying out of places through the superficial consumption of those places. Nonetheless, as Richards (1996) notes, influential authors such as Boorstin (1987) and MacCannell (1976) have debated the extent to which tourism can be actively imbued with meaning through the act of consumption. One thing is for sure: the cultural and symbolic capital attached to specific places must be utilised effectively to ensure that tourism continues to tick over as a key consumption practice in the maintenance of the contemporary landscape of production (Richards, 1996).

Watson and Kopachevsky's (1994) argument is that to argue that the modern tourist is a metaphor for the shallow and inauthentic nature of the commoditised nature of contemporary life is misleading and yet 'with the growing commodification of symbolic forms, and their virtual incorporation into, and monopolization by, mass communication, tourism as a social behaviour becomes more and more dislodged from the spontaneity and free choice that is regularly to define the tourist and tourism experience' (Watson and Kopachevsky, 1994: 645). This point is crucial insofar as if tourism is a metaphor for anything, it's a metaphor for the way in which the contemporary life experience appears to be founded on ideals of free choice when that choice is actually at least to some extent ideologically prescribed.

In defining commodification as the process by which objects and activities come to be primarily evaluated in terms of their exchange value, given the high profile of the spectacle in contemporary society, Watson and Kopachevsky (1994) also recognise the need to bear in mind the significance of sign value. Tourism is effectively packaged for exchange and in doing so implies to the consumer that only through consumption can they find the happiness to which they aspire. The argument here is that the consumer is alienated by the way in which tourism, through the package tour for example, restricts choice whilst purporting to extend it as I suggested above. In other words, tourism does not provide any kind of escape from the logic of capitalism – it is simply an extension of it. Spaces for touristic consumption are often subject to a highly staged experience which appears to be free of external control insofar as you can escape into the experience, but in fact by the very prefabricated nature of this so-called escape, the tourist loses control over how his or her non-work time is activated. In other words, '... consumer culture proceeds through people's obliviousness to the reality that it privatizes the many social experiences of daily life, so that they are never perceived as *social*' (Watson and Kopachevsky, 1994: 648).

The cultural quarter

The impact of cultural tourism on the city is clearly bound up with a range of complex processes. At the very least, this chapter has begun to demonstrate the inherent difficulties involved in trying to make sense of culture in all its diverse forms. The culture we might associate with a visit to a contemporary art gallery, for example, is something very different to that we might associate with the culture being sought out by a tourist in the Outer-Mongolian countryside. Nonetheless, all forms of culture are increasingly subject to structural interventions that frame the nature of that experience. To illustrate this point further, I would like to consider an example of a particular way in which culture has been appropriated within the broader reinvention of the post-industrial economy, namely through so-called 'cultural quarters'. It is no surprise to suggest that as places of concentrated cultural activity, cultural quarters can actually take on many forms and as such might include: museum districts, an institutional, cultural district incorporating museums and performing arts institutions, metropolitan cultural districts in which such venues are part of a broader and dynamic urban mix and industrial, cultural districts characterised by the production of the creative and design industries (Montgomery, 2007). But as Montgomery points out, cultural quarters cannot succeed in pure isolation. Their public popularity and economic success depends on people's engagement with the aura or buzz of an area and through the consumption opportunities it provides, most notably perhaps in the form of the evening economy. Cultural quarters are attractive to consumers insofar as they merge the formal and the informal.

In their book, *City of Quarters*, Bell and Jayne (2004a) refer to Hall and Hubbard's (1998) suggestion that urban villages have emerged as 'shop windows' created through the enhancement of historically distinctive areas or by generating signatures for 'previously economically, culturally or spatially ambiguous' (p. 1) areas for the promotion of conspicuous consumption. Bell and Jayne argue that cultural quarters or 'urban villages' are characterised by the gentrification of residential city enclaves but their character can vary immensely, say in the form of gay villages, ethnic quarters, ghettos, red-light zones or creative quarters. Tied to the initiative to promote a 'creative city' which we discussed in Chapter 3, these spaces are designed to re-enliven the city through culture and through the supposed inherent vitality of a variety of social groups including lesbians and gays, youth and ethnic social groups:

> This is an urban renaissance based on wealth creation associated with consumption (and the production of consumption). The cultural and service industries, with a focus on visual attractions which encourage people to spend money – including an array of consumption spaces from restaurants, museums, casinos, sports stadia and specialist and designer stores (and not traditional industry and manufacturing). This is a post-industrial economy based on the interrelated production of such economic and cultural symbols and the spaces in which they are created and consumed. (pp. 3–4)

Although looked at from one angle cultural quarters offer a critical mass of urban-based, culture-related activity (McCarthy, 2006a), the basis on which those spaces appeal is largely to do with the fact that they offer a carnivalesque space for private consumption whilst simultaneously creating a sense of belonging in a common enterprise but only amongst those who have sufficient cultural and economic capital to join in (Bell and Jayne, 2004a).

What is interesting about cultural quarters, as Montgomery (2003) suggests, is that whereas previously they would evolve as an accident of history or as part of the gradual development of the city, nowadays they offer a very deliberate strategic means of regenerating inner urban areas so that many cities big and small are putting their hat in the cultural quarter ring. This civic aspiration for a cultural quarter reflects the broader point made throughout this book, namely that the future of the post-industrial city is increasingly dependent upon both symbolic representations of the city and a rhetorical investment in the notion that every city can aspire to the sorts of dynamic and culturally productive heights implied by a culture-led regeneration of the city.

The most oft-quoted example of a cultural quarter is undoubtedly Temple Bar in Dublin. One of the oldest parts of Dublin, given its dockside location, the area has a long tradition of buying and selling, but by the end of the twentieth century it had become something of a backwater (Montgomery, 2004). Despite its reputation as a place of vitality, by 1990 Temple Bar was in something of a dilapidated state and the decision was taken to regenerate the area as a cultural quarter. A property renewal scheme was enforced and cultural projects were cross-subsidised. The total public funding for Temple Bar was IR£40.6 million, £37 million of which was spent on the Cultural Development Programme between 1991 and 2001. This process included a revitalisation of the urban fabric and investment in the tourist infrastructure so that there was a significant increase in shops and restaurants and, by 1996, twelve cultural centres had been established. The final major development was the new retail and residential cluster in the western end of Temple Bar. It is important not to forget, as McCarthy (1998) notes, that the Temple Bar initiative has a considerable number of achievements to its name, not least the physical regeneration of the site, the modest scale of which allowed for a critical mass of initiatives to be carried out in a concentrated fashion. But what is perhaps most interesting about the development of Temple Bar other than that it has been lauded by none other than Richard Florida (2002: 302) for its 'clever and far-reaching strategy of levering authentic cultural assets to attract people and spur economic revitalisation' is how it has been received since its regeneration. As Montgomery (2004) notes, chief amongst those criticisms is the suggestion that the area has ironically become too popular and too facile as a direct result of being taken over by the 'Stag and Hen' market and by the sheer overload of licensed premises (McCarthy, 1998) which drove other Dublin residents and visitors away, so much so that in 1998 Temple Bar publications issued a ban on British stag parties (Rains, 1999).

The apparently trivial example above demonstrates a broader problem of regeneration of this kind, namely the way in which a formulaic conception of culture and regeneration defined largely through consumption fails to take into account the diversity of parties likely to engage with consumption opportunities (Rains, 1999). Many cities have struggled to satisfy the conflicting demands of one form of culture as against another and the night-time economy is often a focus of such tension. Newcastle is a good example of a city that has had to face a delicate balancing act between presenting itself to the world as a hotbed of culture (given its relationship to the cultural venues the BALTIC and the Sage Gateshead just across the water) whilst maximising revenue from working-class drinking cultures on the Bigg Market, the area primarily responsible for Newcastle's tag as a 'party city'. In describing the way in which nightlife in Newcastle reverses social norms and transgresses normative behaviour, Chatterton and Hollands (2003: 207) argue that young people in particular invert the 'selfish individualism of modern consumer culture' to create their own mini-communities or 'cultures of resistance'. As such, regardless of the tensions on the surface, the reality is that as Hobbs et al. (2000) argue a city's pleasure zones and entertainment quarters are deliberately designed to function as 'zones of patterned liminality'. As Hobbs et al. (2000) put it, 'for the most part liminal zones thrive on the promise rather than the deliverance of communitas' (p. 712). In other words, any sense of a unique communal experience that contributes to a sustainable sense of identity is, as is the case in all forms of consumption, likely to be partial in nature. In whatever form culture is corralled it is corralled for an economic purpose.

As far as the development of Temple Bar is concerned and however illusory the freedoms associated with a public drinking culture may be, there is parallel concern that the area is suffering from the negative consequences of gentrification. The impact of gentrification on a sense of place is always a matter for considerable concern, but should not, according to Montgomery (1995), be assumed to be a social evil, 'The question, then, is to gauge when a healthy bout of gentrification or area revitalisation, one which adds to the vitality and diversity of place, tips over and becomes unhealthy gentrification where rather than diversity the move is towards sameness' (p. 168). Indeed.

The truth is that many of Temple Bar's original practitioner population, local businesses as well as residents, have been forced to leave, unable to cope with rising capital values and rents arising from the improved physical infrastructure. Meanwhile, estimates as to the number of residents originally expected to move into the area have not been realised in a context in which 'much of the original "bohemia" ambience seems to have been lost because of the raising of property values and rents, the displacement of many original residents and the in-migration of more affluent residents' (McCarthy 1998: 280). These concerns reflect McCarthy's contention (2006a) that the development of cultural quarters is potentially and by its very nature an exclusive enterprise, purely because the people attracted to these areas are most likely to be from higher-income sectors of society. This in itself creates genuine social tensions, including what Miles (2004) describes as 'variable voluntariness': a situation in which residents of the gentrified city actively choose to be there whilst others do not.

From the above point of view, the cultural quarter provides another example of a culture-driven form of regeneration that appears to be for the common good of the city but which ultimately serves some residents of that city better than it does others. Moreover, culture as represented by the cultural quarter has become an all too easy symbolic solution to the problems of post-industrial decline, to the extent that Dungey (2004) has noted that 'No major town or city's plan is now complete without a designated cultural quarter, seeking to attract and develop knowledge economy industries in entertainment, arts, media and design' (Dungey, 2004: 411).

In referring to the role of public art in the development of cultural quarters, a key concern here for McCarthy (2006a) is the suggestion that the need to use public art to reinforce local identity lies in direct conflict with the desire to promote the image of such space beyond the local context. Other criticisms of the cultural quarter approach to regeneration include the suggestion that the promotion of a unified collective identity as designated in the urban village or quarter may actually work against broader efforts to promote the cosmopolitanism and difference that cities otherwise seek to promote (McCarthy, 2006b). Montgomery (1995) is convinced about the dynamic and cultured feel of Temple Bar and suggests that at the time of his writing it was too early to judge if it constituted a success, but a visit to the area today does seem to suggest that the primary success lay with Temple Bar's drinking culture which is now at the very heart of the buzz of the area.

So can cultural quarters really deliver what it is they promise? Jayne's (2004) assessment of the role of culture in the reinvention of Stoke-on-Trent, a former ceramics town in the West Midlands of England, is further testament to the contrast between the unbridled belief in the potential of culture and the more prosaic reality. Jayne presents a rather sober analysis of attempts to use notions of the cultural quarter for urban regeneration in Stoke-on-Trent. Critiquing the suggestion that cultural investment, notably in the creative industries, can attract post-industrial jobs, whilst encouraging people to live in city centres, and generally improving the urban quality of life, Jayne argues that it is important that critical rigour is applied to the ways in which creative industries development has become aligned with regeneration in our cities:

> Unlike many other Western cities, Stoke-on-Trent remains overly dominated by working-class production and consumption cultures. The city is thus, in a sense, rendered illegible to post-industrial businesses, tourists and to the many young people who leave the city in search of the more dynamic economic and cultural opportunities offered in other cities. (Jayne, 2004: 208)

In other words, the combination of a flawed cultural strategy and a bigger economic picture in which Stoke-on-Trent simply cannot compete meant that any aspirations for a fully fledged cultural quarter in the city were doomed to failure. The problem here is that cities are obliged to opt-in to an orthodox vision of a post-industrial future, apparently regardless of what it is they can genuinely offer to the outside world purely because it appears to be the only playing field available to them. In order to be even vaguely competitive, such cities appear to have little choice but to set forth on a fundamentally unequal playing field (see Bell and Jayne, 2004a).

Conclusion

For some authors, tourism equates to a learnt set of styles or performances. It is in itself a performance and as such tourists may even go as far as to collude with tourism providers in achieving self-deception (Prentice, 2001). Touristic consumers are prepared, pre-programmed if you like, to be impressed by the 'authentic' fare presented to them for and by the experience economy. The point of cultural tourism is not however to present authenticity but rather to invoke it (Prentice, 2001). In this context, touristic consumers, as Rojek (2000) notes, are well aware of the limitations of the tourist sites they consume. They embrace the artificial, stimulated environments that confront them and they actively seek out the experience implied by a world in which artificiality and 'super-simulation' are the norm. As such, Rojek questions the wisdom of an entirely negative view of cultural tourism and thus of a condemnation of culture as a means of urban revitalisation. For Rojek, contemporary tourism is inherently plea-surable and offers significant opportunities for re-enchantment as a result. Yes, tourism is about consumption; but it is actually primarily about the consumption of difference insofar as however sanitised the cultures we consume and however homogenised the physical setting in which cultural tourism takes place, whether it be visiting the Sydney waterfront or Stoke's cultural quarter, the experience itself is in at least some sense unique and place-specific in nature (Rojek, 2000).

> The industrialization of tourism has displaced one form of enchanted relationship in tourist experience based upon a quest for authenticity. However, at the same time, in producing new types of urban-industrial superartificiality and in drastically increasing the velocity of movement it has re-enchanted many aspects of urban-industrial life. The movement between disenchantment and re-enchantment is a continuous one, and tourism will remain caught up in twin tendencies for the foreseeable future. (Rojek, 2000: 67)

Perhaps what is going on here is that rather than many tourists looking at places with a tourist gaze intent on finding something distinct (Urry, 2002), many tourists can actually be said to be intent on fitting in with the environment and do so in a performative fashion (Maitland and

Newman, 2009). From this point of view, the passive experience of other cultures is far from the be all and end all of cultural tourism. One of the most important considerations of authenticity in tourism can be found in the work of Cohen (1988) who argues that authenticity is actually a negotiable entity, depending upon the aspirations of the consumer concerned. Cohen thus dismisses the idea that the consumer society changes the meaning of cultural products, particularly given the fact that many of such products are presented in a spectacular staging of that culture. Cohen considers the suggestion that although the consumer may feel his or her experience is authentic, in actual fact what is presented to him or her is no more than a front stage, 'a staged tourist space, from which there is no escape' (p. 373). He argues that the fact that the tourist accepts the cultural product on his or her own terms, insofar as some of its traits are deemed by that individual to be 'authentic', is in itself enough. In other words, the consumer's conception of authenticity is a relatively loose one and constitutes one dimension of that individual's experience of tourism as 'play'. A degree of make-believe, a suspension of belief is crucial, argues Cohen, if the tourist's experience is to be maximised. Moreover, the commodification of culture can also help to preserve what may otherwise have been a cultural tradition destined to be lost:

> While to the external observer, commoditization may appear to involve a complete transformation of meaning as a cultural product [it] is being reoriented to a new, external audience … Local people frequently interpret novel situations in traditional terms, and thus perceive of a continuity of cultural meaning which may escape the observer. (pp. 382–3)

In terms of our broader discussion of the relationship between cultural tourism and spaces for consumption, the problem with Cohen's interpretation appears to be his assumption that the playful experience of cultural tourism is in itself enough to counterbalance the notion that the consumer is somehow 'deceived'. The degree of deception involved in consuming tourism is not indeed the point. What is interesting about a world in which spaces for consumption play such a key role in attaching us to our role as consumers is that we are actually complicit with the values espoused by the consumer society. Yes, we accept the fact that our experience as tourists is at least partially inauthentic. We are complicit with the pleasure that this self-deception allows us. The question remains whether the freedom to experience pleasure as defined through consumption which serves to tie our emotional engagement with our physical surroundings so closely to a particular orthodoxy is any kind of a freedom at all.

As Bell and Jayne (2004b) have argued, in a regime of flexible accumulation, landscapes of consumption and devastation inevitably co-exist. Moreover, inequalities between cities are compounded in a narrative that claims every city is equal when it simply cannot be so. Efforts to construct a vision of the cultural city are inevitably formulaic as Gibson and Klocker (2005: 100) point out. The city of culture is a mythical construct and can never fulfil the demands that policy-makers have of it. McGuigan (1996: 95–9) therefore considers whether any:

> amount of public investment in culture can ever satisfactorily ameliorate the devastating consequences of de-industrialisation ... Such urban regeneration, in effect, articulates the interests and tastes of the postmodern professional and managerial class without solving the problems of a diminishing production base, growing disparities of wealth and opportunity, and the multiple forms of social exclusion.

A key concern for McGuigan is the apparent way in which commerce has been victorious over culture insofar as the needs of capital dominate the public interest so that culture has effectively been reassigned from its original guise as a public sphere resource to an exclusively marketable commodity. As Sklair (2002) suggests, above and beyond the fact that consumerism is ecologically unsustainable, it is also a primary cause of class polarisation. Moreover, as McGuigan (2004) points out, we can identify a genuine shift in the nature of capitalism to an era of 'cultural capitalism' (Rifkin, 2000) and what Hochschild (2003) has described as a 'commercialization of intimate life'. Such processes involve the economy and culture coming closer and closer together. Rifkin offers a stark warning as regards the colonising powers of capitalism and argues that capitalism is actually enclosing literal space. In a situation in which culture is effectively being mined to exhaustion, Rifkin argues that hope lies in civil society, 'the third sector' where ordinary sociality can help trust and meaning to prosper.

The immediate concern here, as Rifkin suggests, is that the cultural sector is shunted from pillar to post in a kind of no-man's land between the market and government; its actual practice being constantly undermined in the process. Culture is not something we 'possess'. Rather, we should look to share and celebrate our humanity through culture. And yet the instrumental way in which culture is being used has created what appears to be a less optimistic future.

> Cultural rituals, community events, social gatherings, the arts, sports and games, social movements and civic engagements are all being encroached upon by the commercial sphere. The great issue at hand, in the coming years, is whether civilization can survive with a greatly reduced government and cultural sphere, and only the commercial sphere is left as the primary mediator of human life. (Rifkin, 2000: 10)

Spaces for consumption play a key role in framing an individual's relationship to both the city and to the cultures of that city. The key nature of this relationship reflects the inability of elites to control the evolution of post-industrial economies and indeed to control what Zukin (1995) describes as 'the chaos of urban life'. To this end, Zukin's somewhat sombre conclusion is that 'if entire cities, led by their downtowns, continue to be ghettoized by public rhetoric and private investment, the dream of a common public culture will fall victim to an empty vision' (Zukin, 1995: 265). From this point of view, the deliberate cultural logic that has infiltrated our cities serves to reduce multiple dimensions of culture into a single coherent visual representation, a representation founded primarily upon an ideology of consumerism.

5

ARCHITECTURES OF CONSUMPTION

It could be argued that architecture plays more of a key role in the symbolic reproduction of the consuming city at this point in history than it has ever done before. But the symbolic power of the city of consumption, as demonstrated by a supposedly revitalised post-industrial cityscape, is by no means a recent phenomenon. Nor is the strategic value of culturally driven building projects. From the Crystal Palace in 1851 to the Eiffel Tower in 1859, from the museum quarter in Kensington in 1851 and The Kelvingrove Museum in Glasgow in 1901, from the Festival Hall to the South Bank Complex in 1951, the role of iconic architecture in perceptions of space has had a long history (Evans, 2003). Architecture clearly plays a key role in navigating the consumer's relationship to the city and in determining the degree to which the consumer is able to actively negotiate that space. More importantly perhaps, architecture fulfils a key role as the propaganda of the post-industrial. It is assigned the task of presenting cutting-edge urbanism to the outside world and of graphically representing how the city sees itself. In an age in which iconic architecture and regenerated public and private spaces have become so fundamental to how a city relates to both itself and its external audience, the nature of that relationship is, however, uncertain. This chapter is concerned with the role of architecture in providing a physical, ideological context within which spaces for consumption can thrive and hence with some of the specific places in which such a process is manifested.

For authors such as Crilley (1993a: 231), the architecture of redevelopment is a key component of place marketing 'playing a major role in mediating perceptions of urban change and persuading "us" of the virtues and cultural benefits of speculative investments'. From this point of view, architecture is actively mobilised in order to reproduce a myth of urban vitality. This serves the function of implying a degree of geographical urban prosperity that simply does not exist; a feel good factor that deflects attention from the social problems that exist beyond the shadows of the buildings concerned. Moreover, such a process serves to legitimise a notion of the public founded upon the private so that the way in which an individual should engage with the contemporary city is through the proclamations that city makes about its place in the world; proclamations that are founded upon symbolic notions of the city as a space for individual exploration; a city where the individual is self-authored but in which the individual narrative of such authorship is defined through the parameters laid down by consumption. In effect, post-industrial architecture constitutes a marketing tool, but its impact is more profound than that insofar as the messages it sends amount to an unchallengeable construction of what constitutes the orthodoxy of the contemporary city: it pronounces the ideological power of consumption and leaves no room for anything else.

In considering the above concerns, it is of course important not to over-generalise about the impact of architecture per se, for of course architecture takes many forms. For the purposes of this chapter, my understanding of architecture is as a practice that embodies and projects key symbolic messages about the status of the consuming city. The architecture to which I refer here then is a particular kind of architecture implicated in key power relations that constitutes a physical support to a particular ideological view of what the post-industrial city is all about (see Jones, 2009). In the last chapter, I talked about the role of marketing and the selling of place in the construction of the post-industrial city. Architecture is a key, if not the key constituent element in this process.

The Shanghai exemplar

In trying to understand the role of the construction of the city of buildings as a manifesto for the contemporary city, an understanding of the places in which such manifestos are constructed is vital. To this end, Shanghai offers a particularly graphic demonstration of ideological intent. Indeed, China as a whole will provide vivid illustrations of how important outside perception is to economic aspirations of a rapidly urbanising society throughout the remainder of this book. The construction of a futuristic, post-industrial, urban fabric creates a way of thinking about place that cuts off any alternatives. As such, the city of Shanghai can only be understood as a city intent on presenting its forward-looking face to the outside world. It is no exaggeration to suggest that the physical and economic transformation of Shanghai from the 1990s is unparalleled in urban history. The new Shanghai makes a significant statement about the aspirational modernity inherent in a new China. But as I will continue to point out throughout this book, the dangers of a so-called revitalised city of whatever description are immense.

Shanghai is a city of gleaming dream worlds, characterised above all by the Pudong district of the city, an area of 350 square kilometres of land that is located on the east bank of the Huangpu River and which was once the home to run-down houses and farms and which now presents Shanghai's capitalist face to the rest of the world. A location for two of the tallest buildings in the world and some of the best retail opportunities in China, the tourist can even access Pudong through the ultimate consumer experience, that of the slightly camp, underwater Sightseeing Tunnel. In the above context, architecture operates as a means to an end, the end being to provide a stage upon which the prerogatives of market capitalism can be played out. Architecture actively endorses spaces for consumption as the shop window for the consumer society: the orthodox paradigm by which the post-industrial society presents itself to the outside world. Such a process has serious consequences in undermining the coherence of the city and in this case Shanghai. As Wang Anyi puts it:

> In a nutshell, Shanghai is not sensual any more. New buildings construct a new cover for it, which separates the city from the physical senses of its inhabitants. Such a fancy cover, however, does not fit perfectly. There is always empty space between the exterior and the real thing. Or maybe it is because it is due to the fact that we are too close to the city and it happens to undergo drastic changes. All the visions are blurred. (quoted in Huang, 2004: 100)

Such a process subsumes the interests of the population to the assumed interests of the economic majority. Thus, the imaginary city is all, and the role of architecture, ideologically at least, is to provide a graphic physical manifestation of a market-driven philosophy. In his epilogue to a book on Shanghai as a world city, Alan Balfour (2004) suggests that the realities of commercialism have overwhelmed, even vulgarised, Shanghai and that what has emerged from this process is a new kind of ideology in which the propaganda tools of consumerism place a veneer over the realities of dictatorship. From such a perspective, the real Shanghai, as represented by its old streets, has effectively been destroyed in favour of a city devoid of community or place.

> Shanghai is a city out of balance. The most ancient pursuit of the Chinese – continually adjusting forces to find a sympathetic relationship between the yin and the yang – is so far unresolved as the country transforms. One might claim that the male element is far too prevalent, because of the testosterone of … consumerism, and some profound adjustment in the culture is urgently needed to resurrect the feminine in the fabric of the city. (Balfour and Shiling, 2002: 362)

Shanghai in fact is a city determined by its capitalist aspirations and unable to see itself beyond the realities defined for it by those aspirations. Authors such as Short (2006) and Wu (2000) have therefore described Shanghai as a sort of urban statement of global intent: a self-conscious global city, whose relationship to the outside world is demonstrated through its architecture. As Short (2006) argues, the architectural is a key priority for a city that aspires to reach the top of the urban hierarchy. The question here is whether the city which Shanghai, or at least the decision-makers behind Shanghai (and cities aspiring to be like it), aims to be is one that is compatible with the city recognised or at least remembered by its inhabitants.

Architectural identities

Shanghai is perhaps somewhat of an extreme example of how buildings provide an outward-looking face to be observed from beyond the city walls. But such an example should make us think more carefully about the broader relationship between architecture and place making. Perhaps the most comprehensive treatment of the relationship between architecture and consumption, at least from an architectural point of view, is Klingmann's (2007) discussion of 'brandscapes' in which she argues that the function of architecture has moved further and further away from the function of objects and their ability to incite symbolic meaning to act as a catalyst as part of an experiential transformation. A key debate here is concerned with the degree to which an individual is able to explore his or her self and build their own customised lifestyles within the constraints provided by a highly designed consumer-driven space and in a context in which architects put professional agendas ahead of the requirements of their customers. In fact, argues Klingmann, architects have largely turned their back on the experiential component of architecture and the day-to-day effects of architecture that this implies. In a market-driven environment in which consumers, at least on the surface, appear to have a degree of choice, it could indeed be argued that architecture has manifestly struggled to offer a suitable and evolving product that delivers the needs of the consumer (Benedikt, 2007).

The modern day architect's relationship (Herman, 2001a, 2001b) with consumption is an ambiguous one. In the specific context of retail (discussed in more detail in Chapter 6), architects traditionally denied its very existence. Indeed, as Herman (2001b: 738) points out, 'Architecture, as a whole, has nothing but contempt for shopping' (p. 738) and, as a result, architects' ability to positively affect what has emerged as probably the key factor in the evolution of twentieth-century urbanism has been partially hamstrung. More recently, architects appear to have embraced the principles of commercialism whilst simultaneously, it would seem, withdrawing wholesale from any genuine notion of their social role as architects. Perhaps the problem here is that architects are unable to pursue a social purpose in a world that is so fundamentally commodified.

> The 'proper' calling to architecture is taken to be working towards some utopian ideal to do with achieving a harmonious existence in quality, well-designed surroundings for everyone. Any hint of consumerism would taint this idyll, detracting from its main underlying purpose: to free society from the structures of desire. This unwritten contract of modernity contains within it the seeds of its own failure: it privileges progress, yet progress needs a motivating force, and in the 20th century consumption has been its most effective impetus. (Chaplin and Holding, 1998: 7–9)

In the architectural profession itself, there exists an implicit and often explicit hierarchy in which those firms that build for profit are deemed less worthy and more populist than their design-driven colleagues (see the discussion of Jon Jerde, also in Chapter 6). This, in a world in which peer acceptance is more important than public approval (Chaplin and Holding, 1998). In discussing the role of the architect in the changing post-industrial landscape, Rem Koolhaas argues that the architecture profession is constituted in such a way that it can do little more than remove authenticity. For Koolhaas (2001: 408), we live in a world dominated by 'junkspace': the fallout from modernisation; the human debris that modernisation left behind so that, at least as we knew it, 'architecture disappeared in the 20th century'. The end result of this is a process in which architects apparently working individually are in fact implicated by the same inescapably coherent junkspace. Junkspace colonises the aura of the past to infuse it with new commercial lustre so that the architectural masterpiece becomes 'a semantic space that saves the object from criticism' (p. 414). In this context, entertainment is dictatorial insofar as it is inherently exclusive and concentrated to the extent that the world becomes public space for the very purpose of entertainment or it at least masquerades as such. Koolhaas (2008) also discusses some of the thoughtless ways in which a vision of the city is imposed through the market. As he puts it in his discussion of public space, '... we allow ourselves to be lulled into a false privacy. In which privacy is in fact traded for security, where we become willing participants in a regime of constant surveillance. We live on a curious diet of harmlessness alternating with catastrophe' (Koolhaas, 2008: 323). Koolhaas goes on to discuss a situation in which a 'systematic laundering' of authentic conditions in urban life are enforced in the name of gentrification which, according to his argument, has been effectively reduced to four key categories: film screenings, music, fashion and shopping. The result is that public space becomes a nostalgic celebration – in effect, a celebration of the absence of public space. Under these conditions, the civility of the past is celebrated whilst meanwhile we drown in a world of depthless infotainment. Interestingly, Koolhaas extends this discussion to the development of the new era of tropical, mega-architectural cities such as Dubai and Abu Dhabi, and argues that in such necessarily air-conditioned environments, the outside is actually evacuated and by implication the public become an entirely captive audience. They are the property of the consumer society.

The concern here is that the world presented to us through spaces for consumption offers a particular kind of orthodoxy that is more accessible to some groups than to others. Davis and Monk (2007) recognise this in their discussion of the architectural dream worlds of neo-liberalism, in which they argue that the 'the spatial-logic of neoliberalism revives the most extreme colonial patterns of residential segregation and zoned consumption. These dream worlds, often founded on the notion of architectural monumentality enflame desires that they go as far as to argue are incompatible with both the "ecological and moral survival of humanity"' (p. xv). Thus, Mike Davis (2007) goes on to discuss the emergence of Dubai and iconic developments such as the artificial 'Island World', an underwater luxury hotel and Dubailand, the theme park of theme parks (Davis, 2007), key components of the vision of Sheikh Mohammed al-Maktoum, effectively the CEO of Dubai, and his consuming passion for monumental architecture. But, for Davis, the end product of such a vision is little more than an overblown pastiche. In building the biggest theme park, the tallest building, the biggest mall, and the biggest artificial island, Dubai becomes a laboratory in the urban extreme that simply demonstrates processes going on throughout the world, albeit in diluted form. The point is that it is the branding that such building programmes bring that makes the city what it is. Dubai is an oasis of consumer freedom (or at least presents itself to the outside world as such) and the state of Dubai in this context has become indistinguishable from private enterprise insofar as the need for enterprise is of a higher order and thereby trumps the need for consumer freedom (Davis, 2007). Meanwhile, the physical demonstration of the power of free enterprise is entirely dependent upon an army of 'super-exploited' South Asian labourers who are themselves banned from the new spaces of consumption. As Davis notes, hundreds of construction workers are killed on the job annually, whilst thousands of workers have demonstrated against unpaid wages and poor working conditions. The fantasy world of consumption is a fantasy world in the truest sense of the phrase.

The divisive nature of contemporary architecture has long been the concern of the architectural critic. Huxtable (1997), for example, suggests that such division is the inevitable product of an unbridled desire for short-term profit. He criticises the role of architecture in the process of constructing a very real 'unreal' world bereft of value judgement. This is a world in which instant gratification is apparently all. For architects, the challenge is to produce buildings that do more than cheapen and diminish the world in which we live through the profit motive. In this context, it is argued, architects need to regain interest in their public role and social responsibility. Such spaces will often attempt to attract as many customers as possible by combining the core business of the operation with a range of complementary activities. A typical example might be the hosting of a large multiplex cinema within a themed shopping mall. But as Gottdiener (2001) warns, the way in which such cross-fertilisation makes spaces for consumption so irresistible to the consumer may in turn contribute to the decline of the city centre, so that any notion of what a city is really all about is lost along the way.

Iconic architecture and the soul of the city

Perhaps the single most graphic demonstration of the symbolic power of architecture as a means of transmitting a kind of manifest credibility onto the post-industrial city project is the iconic building. Charles Jencks (2006) describes iconic buildings as 'enigmatic signifiers' in a world in which differences and distinctions have been broken down so that any building can effectively be iconic. The iconic building is, from this point of view, the product of a number of processes: the decline in belief and the eclipse of the monument as well as the demand for a 'wow factor' in new buildings and the concomitant impact of 'the Bilbao effect' (which I shall discuss in greater depth later on in the chapter). The iconic building is primarily motivated by the need for economic development and the determination to attract tourists. It is often therefore the result of a city planning strategy. In discussing the impact of the iconic upon the city of Vancouver, Toderian (2008) argues that iconic buildings are about attention-seeking so that iconic architecture becomes a proxy for revitalisation. There is an inherent and real danger that by setting out to design an iconic building, the excellence of the broader architectural environment and the risk-taking which that environment demands are neglected as a result.

Architects would not be human if some part of them did not aspire to belong to the elite of architects deemed capable of producing such buildings and thus on maintaining their gloss in a media-driven world. In a sense then, the architect behind the building is more important than the building itself. Museums and galleries are today's public

Image 5.1 The archetypally iconic Walt Disney Concert Hall, Los Angeles
(Photo Andy Miah)

monuments. But their function at least in terms of the presentation of art
is questionable. Evans (2003), for instance, argues that the Pompidou
Centre in Paris has emerged from its second £55 million refurbish-
ment as a culturally legitimated 'amusement park' in which less than
20 per cent of its daily 25,000 visitors actually come to see art. They
prefer instead to hang-out, walk through and consume. But this is
precisely the point. The role of the 'starchitect' is to produce buildings that take on a more important role than what goes on within
them and which thus offer an aspirational experience that may never
actually be fulfilled. Such buildings will succeed not because people come
to view the art therein, but because they spend money in the café, restaurant and bookshop. Cultural buildings of this kind, the archetypal
form of iconic architecture, offer an exterior architectural statement
that says less about the art and more about the opportunities to consume
that such iconic imagery inevitably implies.

This 'experience is everything' philosophy is graphically demonstrated by the Imperial War Museum of the North located in Trafford,

Greater Manchester which was self-consciously designed by the architect Daniel Libeskind to disorient the visitor in order to mirror the disorienting experience of war. More worrying is the fact that many iconic cultural buildings, as Evans (2003) notes, struggle to establish a coherent sense of their own identity and have no clear idea of what their practical role may be beyond the need to simply be iconic. Critics have argued that Manchester's museum of the urban, Urbis, for example, which is soon to close, has been in a constant battle with itself, unsure whether its purpose is for education or entertainment. Such a dilemma is the product of a world in which architecture is more about a physical statement than the realisation of functional intent. For Hetherington (2007a), Urbis is all about the consumer. It is a space defined by the practice of consumption: the visual consumption of what lies within the museum pales into insignificance compared to the experience of the whole, so that visiting a museum such as Urbis becomes a lifestyle experience in its own right (Hetherington, 2007a).

The power of iconic architecture is perhaps above all a reflection of the wholly uninspiring urban landscape that surrounds it. This is an issue taken up by Kunstler (1993) who argues that architects have to take some of the responsibility for a state of affairs in which they no longer appear to be able to distinguish between good or bad nor between human and antihuman. For Kunstler, who discusses the development of modern America, the consequence is a monotonous and soulless urban environment and a world that has lost its connectedness beyond that determined by cars and telecommunication. Similarly, in calling for radical change, Huxtable does not go as far as to predict the demise of capitalism but he does call for a sustainable economy (as opposed to an exhaustive one); a particularly prescient comment as the author writes during the global recession of 2009. The suggestion here is that the places we build are simply not serving a social purpose. They are not equipped to house the sustainable economy to which Huxtable aspires. This is arguably particularly evident in the case of isolated residential developments that mirror Rem Koolhaas' vision of junkspace in the United States of America but with, apparently, even scarier consequences:

> So much of the nations' wealth is tied up in badly designed communities, inhuman buildings, and commercial highway crud that we cannot bring ourselves to imagine changing it. But time and circumstances will change our ability to use these things,

whether we choose to think about it or not. What will become of all the junk that litters our landscape? (414)

In developing an analogous theme, the architectural critic Martin Pawley (1998) presents a thesis that the real value of buildings today lies not in their aesthetic value but in their role as terminals for communication. From this point of view, we live in a world of misplaced urbanism in which the places we designed simply do not work in the sort of synthetic, technologically driven society in which we find ourselves. Intriguingly, Pawley describes a situation in which the streets of the old producer cities have been rebuilt in the form of 'consumer envelopes' despite the fact that they visibly do not reflect such a change, so that urban architecture is increasingly nothing more than a 'fictional' construct. Pawley thus describes the emergence of 'stealth architecture', a variant on post-modern architecture which is self-consciously designed to reassuringly retain the historical facades of the past. What is going on here then is allegedly an 'architectural deception' that reflects a concomitant process in which tourism becomes increasingly crucial to the future of the city. We are therefore residents of cities characterised by commercial buildings that have effectively been robotised by cutting-edge information technology.

> The result of such heroic surgery, which eagerly collaborates with the force of electronically annihilated distance, is that all formerly real places and all formerly recognizable categories of building are disappearing. Their 'historical strata' have been compressed like computer files. By such means the contemporary city conceals the manner in which urban real estate is already fighting for its life. (Pawley, 1998: 171)

The processes of globalisation have thus constructed a new form of connection in which all cities are linked but in essentially non-human ways, so that what results is a 'sand-heap' urbanism in which the settlement pattern is one without heritage, history or difference (Pawley, 1998). For Pawley, urban populations are increasingly fragmented and are less and less like residents and more and more like visitors fulfilling the role of touristical consumers. This transition from a producer-based urbanism to a consumer-based one represents a shift from place to space in which the individual experiences the primary architectural constructs of the city, alongside the secondary reality of TV, cinema, MP3 players and the like. The argument here then is that the consumerisation of the city leads to the breakdown of traditional 'factual' relationships so that 'every link dependent on interdependence and place will give way to an equivalent time-based "fictional" consumer relationship. Reflecting and conforming to this change, the very architecture of the city will be compelled to lose its factual producer identity and dissolve into discontinuous hotel-style, time-based consumer accommodation' (p. 176). This is a landscape in which production becomes invisible; an invisible global city of ephemeral architecture where what *seems to be* is more important than what actually is.

China as a laboratory of architectural change

In coming to terms with the role of architecture and indeed architectures in constructing spaces for consumption and therefore in reinforcing the ideologies of the consumer society, for the purposes of this chapter, I would like to consider two case studies that offer different perspectives on the same issue. First, and bearing in mind my earlier reference to Shanghai as a demonstration of the value of architecture as a statement of how a city sees its place in the world, I will look at the role of architecture in the reinvention of China as an urban entity. I will then look specifically at an example of a single building, namely the Guggenheim Bilbao which is often fêted as the archetypal example of iconic architecture, a guise in which it may tell us something about the role of symbolic meaning in the construction of the consumer society.

In her discussion of Chinese architecture, Nancy Lin (2001) discusses the commodification of architecture and the accelerating changes associated with the changing real estate market and the phenomenal rise of pre-sales. In terms of the development of residential buildings, such processes have created a situation in which 'architectural recipes' are implemented so that existing or previous projects can be recycled with minimum fuss and maximum speed (Lin, 2001). In this context, architectural drawings fulfil the role of commodities insofar as developers will purchase those drawings prior to a project being designed for a specific place. Such practices reflect a pragmatic environment in which buildings appear almost overnight, but they also demonstrate a move towards a more global and indeed homogenised conception of architecture in which the dominant market-driven orthodoxy is apparently the only alternative. The construction of commercial buildings in China is also inevitably beset with problems. The speedy construction of public buildings, even shopping centres, means that access, for example, has not always been sufficiently thought through. For example, Lin refers to the Luohou Commercial City in Shenzen which at one level has obvious locational advantages given that it sits beside a train station. Yet, such apparently prime spaces, bearing in mind the sheer numbers of people and traffic on Chinese streets, create 'urban islands' where the mere act of entering such a space of consumption becomes a death-defying act. In this context, the production of the finished building as an isolated end-product is more important than a broader conception of how that building fits into place. This is a space for consumption for the sake of consumption.

The above sorts of issues are discussed in depth in the work of Mars and Hornsby (2008) who argue that architecture is becoming an increasingly industrialised process in China so that the architect is less an artist and more a prefabricator. Chinese cities are now symbols of the dominance of mass-producing, high-density, urban lifestyles and all the negativities that this entails. These cities are epicentres of a consumer boom; spaces for consumption in their own right: the very essence of the Chinese economic miracle being based on the principle that cities have to be transformed from industrial bases into sites of bourgeois consumption (Mars and Hornsby, 2008). Such processes create an incredibly divided society: one divided between rural and urban and between urban dweller and migrant. The latter is encouraged, symbolically at least, to seek out the benefits of this consumer society, but the reality is somewhat different. This is a world in which the migrant cannot depend on any of the social support mechanisms that will allow him or her to become even a partially fledged member of the consumer society or at least a citizen able to access some of the social supports associated with being an urban resident.

So China's economy is simultaneously dependant on, and hindered by, its corollaries: cheap labor keeps production costs low enough to swipe foreign markets, but also means workers are not becoming consumers within China itself. Urban growth from migration is not consumurbation [the conflation of consumerization and urbanization]: it just puts peasants in cities. It helps the local economy to produce but not consume. This is the incomplete promise of Consumerbation: millions of low-wage migrants are needed to facilitate it for others, but can engage only in a very thin version of it themselves. (Mars and Hornsby, 2008: 446)

The above is a scenario that is not limited to the experience of Chinese migrants. The consumer society is inevitably divided and architects (as well as planners) have a role in exacerbating such division. But returning specifically to the question of architecture in the construction of spaces for consumption, Mars and Hornsby make the interesting point that China seems to be a country in which aesthetics are actually irrelevant and in which architecture has no obligation beyond that to the consumer society. Thus, the cities of China are built upon a kind of imitation modernity which awaits its own demolition to the extent that 'Architecture seems to be squirted against the facades like sauce from a squeeze pack' (Mars and Hornsby, 2008: 534). The process that these authors describe is a process based upon the dream of a wealthy, comfortable lifestyle in a modern cosmopolitan metropolis: a vision that has captured the imagination of hundreds of millions of aspirational Chinese who aspire to a sense of freedom through consumption that, for cultural reasons, cannot be obtained through politics. Architecture, and in China's case more than anywhere else, the reinvention and revitalisation of the city as retail creates the physical boundaries within which this process takes place, but in doing so it reproduces and privileges a notion of freedom that constitutes a diversion more than a truth.

Of course, China's relationship with consumption is not just about the construction of new buildings. Thus, Broudehoux (2004) discusses the commodification of history and specifically Yuanmingyuan, the Old Summer Palace of Beijing. In an increasingly nationalistic period in Chinese history after the uproar of Tiananmen Square in 1989, the Chinese authorities went through a period of rediscovering and restoring historical sites that in turn offered new spaces for public entertainment and consumption. Broudehoux argues that by transforming this particular site into 'national heritage', the Chinese authorities effectively imposed one set of meanings and denied the role of hundreds of other people in determining what those meanings might be. Yuanmingyuan served a very important function in its new guise to help foster patriotism and to reinvigorate anti-imperialist sentiment. The reconstruction of the ruined site was an expensive business as a lack of state subsidy meant that the park was forced to explore its own ways of ensuring profitability. To this end, the park administration went about turning the imperial grounds into what Broudehoux describes as a 'Chinese Disneyworld' in which private entrepreneurs rent out space to run commercial franchises and provide spaces of consumption for tourists. As such, various islands around the park have been turned into mini theme parks while the lakes themselves are now festooned with pedal boats reflecting, according to Broudehoux, a broader situation in which the hegemony of the consumer culture has led to the commercialisation of preservation. In this context, the need to educate is always tempered by the need to entertain (Broudehoux, 2004). And yet this site is deemed as an important propaganda tool and a privileged site for holding political and patriotic rituals. For example, the Chinese capital's celebrations commemorating the handover of Hong Kong to China in 1997 were held here, whilst it is an important place for teaching students about the evils of imperialism given the gardens' destruction, by Anglo-French troops at the end of the Second Opium War in 1860. The heavy commercialisation of the site has indeed been heavily condemned in many quarters insofar as:

> Chinese scholars claim that entertainment activities clash with the park's memorial role and should not be allowed to co-exist with the ruins. Commercial transactions trivialize the site's heritage value and belittle the past grandeur of Yuanmingyuan, thereby obfuscating the park's historical message and the significance of its downfall. As a result, critics claim, Yuanmingyuan has become a site of consumption rather than reflection, where ruins and landscapes compete for people's attention with papier mache animals, trinket vendors and carnival stands. (Broudehoux, 2004: 78)

Broudehoux points out that elitist criticisms of the park are deeply ironic given that it was originally, in effect, an imperial pleasure ground. But of particular interest is the suggestion here that dominant meanings attached to the new Yuanmingyuan as a place for anti-imperialist discourse are actually subverted by those who visit the gardens, and whose own meanings are more concerned with romantic notions of ruined space as a marker of the durability of time and identity alongside notions of personal vulnerability. From this point of view and given Broudehoux's observational work at the site, her argument is that the facilities provided at Yuanmingyuan bring its history alive through the opportunities for hedonistic pleasure that they provide. The entertainment is indeed the attraction, but once there visitors are compelled to 'consume' the ruins around them, with limited reference to the anti-imperialist message that the Chinese authorities would have them retain. Consumers of the site can therefore be said to subvert and rework dominant readings. The opportunity to consume thus constructed offers a different kind of freedom, further illustrating the complex nature of the relationship between the consumer and spaces for consumption. Ultimately, it seems to be the case that people primarily come to the park to see and be seen – it is a means of displaying oneself through the tableaux of the new consumer society in which state-sanctioned patriotism is far from the priority, as Broudehoux suggests. This reflects a situation in which heritage is easily manipulated to fit different agendas. What is interesting in this regard is the fact that the agenda of those people who are actually resident on the site are the least visible, the eviction of peasant residents being an accepted norm as part of a broader process of producing a reinvented Chinese nation in which members of society are expected to show their patriotism by sacrificing their homes for the common good (Broudehoux, 2004).

Involuntary residential relocation was particularly in evidence in the context of build-up to the Olympic Games in Beijing in 2008 (see also Chapter 7). The Games themselves were undoubtedly a massive success in terms of the unlimited opportunity they provided the Chinese authorities in remarketing China to the rest of the world (an estimated 1 billion people or 15 per cent of the earth's population are said to have watched the opening ceremony alone). But of equal and in fact more interest is the process by which the city of Beijing was re-imagined prior to the Games themselves, an issue discussed by Broudehoux in some depth (see the discussion of her work in the context of the Olympics in Chapter 7). The demolition of swathes of traditional hutong houses and the relocation of thousands of Beijing residents is now a familiar story, not least in the context of the Olympic Park. As a site of consumption, the Olympic Park is indeed an architectural wonder. The National Stadium, known as the Bird's Nest and costing US$501 million to construct, is an icon in its own right. A monument to the thousands of migrant workers that constructed it, the Bird's Nest is no doubt architecturally significant in terms of establishing China as a player on the global architectural stage whilst being one of the most extraordinary sports stadia in the world. However, its future is deeply uncertain. Plans to house a football club in the stadium were shelved following the realisation that the stadium was simply too large for such a purpose given the limited fan base commanded by the potential tenants, the Beijing Guo'an Club. One strong possibility announced by the venue's owners in January 2009 is, ironically, that the site be turned into a shopping and entertainment complex.

The Bird's Nest does not of course exist in iconic isolation. It sits beside the Beijing National Aquatic Center – 'The Water Cube' – which is equally architecturally striking. The up-keep of such buildings is excessively expensive whilst the long-term use of facilities is questionable. For example, there appears to be limited need for a public swimming facility of this kind and it is more likely to be used in the long term as a venue for elite aquatic sports. Some of the other facilities available in the Olympic Park will no doubt in time be demolished. What remains is most likely to offer some kind of a private haven: a space of elite consumption founded upon the memories of three weeks in the summer of 2008.

The Guggenheim Bilbao

I will return to the implications of the above in the context of my discussion of the Olympic Games as a form of spectacular consumption in Chapter 7. But, at this stage, I want to reinforce a discussion of the role of architecture in the construction of the symbolic landscape of the consuming city with a look at the impact of the Guggenheim Museum. I talked a lot in the last chapter about the role of culture in the construction of place-making. In the context of the Guggenheim, I am interested in the role of architecture in constructing a particular aura around place through spaces for consumption. In this respect, the Guggenheim Museum in Bilbao is archetypal. For decades, arts projects have been amongst the most prestigious commissions for architects (Pryce, 2007). It seems that arts buildings provide architects with more scope for challenging the creative spectrum than any other kind of building. Technological advances and the branding of architects through the 'starchitect' phenomenon have created an elite architectural playground in which the imagination can apparently run free. Add commercial pressures to the mix and in many senses these iconic cultural venues are the most prominent examples of spaces for consumption on the urban landscape. The Guggenheim Bilbao, as Pryce (2007) suggests, is the most successful example of this phenomenon insofar as a marriage between a global arts brand and a previously unglamorous city in the Basque region of Spain has demonstrated the symbolic and practical value of iconic cultural architecture.

Effectively a franchising arrangement, the Guggenheim Museum would provide the focal point or what Pryce (2007) describes as a 'honey pot' at the centre of a much broader regenerative building programme in the city. Designed by Frank Gehry, the building is self-consciously iconic, a perplexing artefact of wave-like titanium shapes: a bright dream world in stark contrast with its drab industrial surroundings (Pryce, 2007). Costing £100 million (as well as $20 million for the use of the Guggenheim name over 20 years), the Museum attracted an estimated 1.3 million visitors in its first year, and 3 million in the next two years. However, by 2001, a decline in local interest meant that total attendance had decline to 760,000 whilst within three years of opening, the Guggenheim Bilbao had generated growth of 0.47 per cent to the Basque GNP in 1997. What is interesting here is that the director of the Guggenheim, Thomas Krens, as Pryce (2007) notes, actually defined the art museum as 'a theme park with four attractions: good architecture, a good permanent collection, primary and secondary art exhibitions, and amenities such as shops and restaurants' (quoted in Pryce, 2007: 221) – in effect, the archetypal space for consumption: a philosophy further reinforced by the fact that Krens also hosted a Giorgio Armani dress show in the Guggenheim Bilbao in 2001 (in addition to another in New York) in exchange for $12 million. Moreover, it has been suggested that as a self-consciously architectural space, the Guggenheim Bilbao is deeply dysfunctional, almost intimidatory in nature, at least as far as the presentation of art is concerned: a space which actively overshadows the very art it is supposed to enhance. In discussing this issue, Evans (2003) suggests that modern cathedrals of art such as the Tate Modern in London and the Baltic in Gateshead outshine the canvas within and are by implication compromised by the limited range of art they are able to display. However much designed for the specific requirements of contemporary art, such renovated spaces are perhaps on the one hand very different to that of the Guggenheim Bilbao, but on the other they constitute post-industrial spectacles in their own right.

A criticism of the Bilbao example, certainly from the local artistic fraternity, is that such a model is unsustainable beyond the initial impact of the museum as 'event'. To this end, Evans (2002) quotes Robins (1993) who argues that such spaces are primarily about insulating the residencies of the middle-class consumer from the unsightly realities of the inner city. Many cities have flirted with the possibility of repeating Bilbao's apparent success over the years (for many more cities, such plans have fallen through); the latest incarnation being the Gehry- designed Guggenheim in Abu Dhabi which will be located on Saadiyat, the 'Island of Happiness', the ultimate space for and statement of consumption that will include a gigantic culture-led development project with global pretensions, incorporating a new location for the Louvre.

The above developments reflect an underlying rationale that taking the name of an established cultural institution (the role of the Tate in Britain offers a comparator on a somewhat smaller scale) offers a short-cut towards credibility: a marker of a world-class cultural offer (Landry, 2006). The intention here is to maximise international exposure. The 'Bilbao' or 'Guggenheim' effect has indeed become such a hackneyed regeneration cliché that there is significant doubt that such a vision exists other than as hyperbole destined to pale in comparison to what happened, at least for a time, in Bilbao. In its early days, the Guggenheim Bilbao was far from free of controversy: many commentators felt the large sums involved, for instance, should have been spent on more self-evident socially and economically beneficial initiatives such as the opening of new factories. But, more generally, the success of the Guggenheim is remarkable not for the achievements of a single architectural vision but because of the communal vision and strength of conviction that this implies (Marshall, 2001). Unfortunately, it simultaneously implies that an architectural vision can be imposed without the appropriate communal and indeed historical and geographical foundations to support it in the longer term.

Klingmann (2007) considers the above developments from an architectural point of view and argues that the key achievement of the Guggenheim Bilbao was its role in redefining the city so that a more comprehensive urban renewal process involving many of the world's greatest architects could be made real. From this point of view, the Guggenheim Bilbao isn't merely a museum – it is primarily a marketing tool that presents Bilbao to the rest of the world as a city on the cutting edge. But the key here, as far as Klingmann (2007: 251) is concerned, is that the Bilbao effect cannot be applied unilaterally:

> The challenge lies in using architecture strategically as part of a local condition, rejecting aesthetic notions that are inherently disconnected from the particularities of place ... If we view architecture as a catalyst for realizing a city's shifting aspirations tied to a contemporary expression of its local identity, we need to separate architecture's strategic potential to act as an engine for urban renewal from its formal expression as spectacle.

The use of iconic cultural venues in reinvention is not of course a fail-safe option. The closure of the Guggenheim Las Vegas in 2002 after a mere 15 months in business (although the Guggenheim Hermitage museum did last for seven years) could be seen to offer a case in point. Spectacular art, architecture and financial investment is perhaps not enough to sustain the city of entertainment and as such raises the question of whether entertainment is enough (Ryan, 2007). The architecture of consumption offers a symbolic solution to the dilemmas of a post-industrial city, but if the role of architecture is to prop up a city founded upon the transitory nature of experience, the question is whether framing an individual's relationship with the city through the transitory can ever suffice.

Conclusion

This chapter has tried to make some sense of the relationship between architecture and spaces for consumption. In many senses, architecture is an agent of the consumer society: it appears to act on that society's behalf in reinforcing the orthodoxy of the market. In this context, Jones (2010) has argued that iconic buildings are inherently politicised projects. Each iconic building finds itself in a situation where it is obliged to eclipse the last so that such buildings become nothing more than objectified commodities. For Jones then, the iconic building operates as a site of contestation founded in a rhetoric that claims that such buildings are more important as signifiers than they are as physical structures that fit comfortably into the urban landscape. Iconic buildings can from this point of view be best understood as materialisations of power which tell a highly partial story about where the city is and most importantly about where the city is going. In this situation, the public are no more than passive consumers of visual imagery, the meaning of which has been pre-established (Crilley,1993; Jones, 2009). The problem with Jones' analysis is that it ties any understanding of the role of architecture very closely to that of a neo-liberal version of the city and in doing so cuts off any genuine debate as to whether consumption offers any room for negotiation, however partial. Bearing this point in mind, the underlying intention of *Spaces for Consumption* is to highlight the paradoxical nature of the consuming experience as manifested through, in this case, architectural practice, which offers us a moment of freedom just as that freedom is apparently taken from our grasp.

Klingmann (2007) argues that architects should engage with consumerism not as an impoverishing process but as an inspirational and excitingly creative opportunity. Perhaps the problem here then is that architects perceive of consumers as passive entities who effectively get the sorts of top-down consumer landscapes that architects imagine they deserve. Of course, things are more complicated than such a version of events would suggest. Human beings do of course read and use buildings as individual agents. But the problem here is that such agency can only ever go so far when the environment in which it takes place is so clearly the product of such a deeply ingrained way of thinking about the world – a view of the world that we as consumers so readily embrace.

The reality is that the architect plays an important strategic role in the construction of a city that speaks of consumer freedom. Architecture provides an arena of immense promise. It offers a sense of liberation and a fresh start for the city of consumption. New buildings constitute an ideological commitment to a sociability defined through consumption but also to a world that is inherently fragile and impermanent (Blum, 2003). What is interesting here is not that such freedoms are false but that they create all sorts of tensions and compromises for the consumer (as demonstrated, for example, by Broudehoux's (2004) discussion of the Old Beijing Summer Palace) which he or she appears able and willing to endure and possibly even savour.

Of course, we need to ask whether civil relationships can genuinely be promoted around notions of the city as a space for exploration and commodified adventure, and whether the market is sufficiently flexible in this regard. But this is not so much a political question, a matter for disgust and outrage, as a situation in which the supposed freedoms of consumption are determined contextually, suggesting that we should therefore move away from a critique of culture in the neo-liberal context to an understanding of culture as an arena for freedom and choice (however flawed that freedom and choice might be). As a realm that materialises power, as Jones (2009) suggests, architecture clearly constrains choice but the more interesting question centres on how the sense of freedom and choice that consumers garner from their interaction with spaces for consumption is played out in every-day relationships with the consumer city.

Perhaps, despite everything, in some small way, the consuming city actually fulfils at least some of the sort of enabling possibilities that are implied by the rhetoric that underpins it. The role of architecture is nonetheless to actively legitimate a particular conception of what the post-industrial city is all about and in so doing, as Pawley (1998) suggests, it engages in a particular kind of public deception. The architecture of consumption provides the consumer society, in the form of the clean, clinical lines of the post-industrial landscape with a powerful front stage in which notions of freedom and choice are made explicit. To put this another way: spaces of consumption, much like any other form of advertising, have social power but what they do not have is social responsibility (see Leiss et al., 1990).

6

SHOPPING FOR DREAMS

Architect Rem Koolhaas (2001) argues that shopping has come to colonise, even replace, almost every aspect of urban life; even more so in an era of place marketing in which the revitalised urban realm has become synonymous with the provision of retail (McMorrough, 2001). The shopping mall is indeed living testament to the physical domination of consumption upon the urban fabric. At one level of course, shopping spaces fulfil a functional role insofar as they provide the spaces within which commodities are purchased. They offer a convenient means of commodity exchange, but both their physical presence and the way we engage with that presence as consumers also tell us something important about the nature of the society in which we live. In this chapter, I want to consider the status of shopping in contemporary consumer society and how the experiential nature of consumption through shopping may be fundamentally altering our relationship with the city insomuch as the city becomes 'framed' by the consumer ethic. As early as 1961, Jane Jacobs recognised the way in which monopolistic shopping centres abstracted culture and commerce from the intimate relations of everyday life in the city. As Zukin (2005: 7) puts it, 'Shopping is consuming our lives – but bringing us less satisfaction. More goods are for sale – but we can never find exactly what we want. Each store promises us happiness, every label guarantees high quality – but we're still dreaming of the virtuous ideal: Truth. Beauty. Value.' Shopping spaces play a crucial role in this process. This chapter is therefore concerned with the emotional pull of the shopping experience; the sense that regardless of the above that experience is special to the consumer and allows him or her some kind of a sense of partial satisfaction that he or she cannot apparently find elsewhere.

As a means of beginning this discussion and of highlighting the sheer physical influence of shopping, and in particular shopping malls on our lives, I want to briefly consider an architectural account of the issues and challenges facing shopping centres at the turn of the century. In his book, *Shopping Environments: Evolution, Planning and Design*, the architect Peter Coleman (2004) argues that retail has a fundamental impact on the social and cultural make-up of a country, accounting for 20 per cent of the workforce. Meanwhile, he quotes pre-recession figures that indicate plans to meet a demand for 11 million square metres of new floor space in the UK by 2012. Shops then lie at the very heart of our towns and cities. For Coleman, one of the greatest challenges to the world of retail is the need to re-invent itself in an increasingly visually oriented world alongside a more challenging and discerning shopping public. This issue is manifested in the public's desire for natural, often external, shopping environments as opposed to the internal ones served up for them by developers. But perhaps of most interest to this chapter is Coleman's contention that in a world where people's attention spans are shorter and shorter, shopping has to compete in an increasingly visual context. It has to be exciting so that the images it deploys stand out from the crowd. This reflects, according to Coleman, an increasingly discerning consumer who refuses to be patronised and whose needs need to be accurately reflected in the construction of new shopping facilities.

Whether or not the consumer has much say over the physical manifestation of the city as space for shopping, the notion that shopping is less a functional activity and more and more about the experience is an important one in helping us to understand the broader evolution of the city. In recent years, there has been a mini-boom in retail projects that claim to have the consumer's interests at heart and which like to make the case for retail provision that is beyond the norm. Such projects include Westfield London, Bristol's Cabot Circus and Liverpool One, the latter claiming its mix of architecture and inclusion of a public park demonstrate the way forward for a more consumer-sensitive and satisfying retail provision. The question is whether the above focus on the visual really does constitute recognition that the public no longer trusts institutions and that they require a more pro-active relationship with their shopping environments and, more importantly, whether the apparent recognition that this is the case is reasserting power in favour of the consumer. To

Coleman (2004), shopping is all about mental well-being: 'Shopping expeditions are continuing to progress from providing experiences to transformations, for instance, by incorporating opportunities for the visitor to participate in a civic or cultural activity' (p. 5). From this point of view, shopping centre design is all about making a shopping environment a memorable experience that incorporates a sense of place – 'an issue we will consider in more depth at the end of the chapter in the form of a case study that looks specifically at Universal CityWalk, Los Angeles. In a sense, the sense of place engendered in the shopping experience means that the shopping trip becomes more important than the actual purchase. Spaces of consumption take on a purpose beyond that of their mere function. If the marketing of the above new developments is to be believed, shopping centres are apparently in the process of reinventing themselves as civic destinations. But is this really the case? Are our shopping environments really as responsive to the needs of consumers as Coleman suggests or are they simply the product of the competitive model of the city I outlined in Chapter 3? And perhaps most importantly, is the civic society implied by consumer space any kind of a civic society at all?

The historical development of shopping and the shopping mall

In order to frame the above debates and to provide a degree of historical context, it is important to highlight the circumstances under which shopping malls emerged as a primary focus of the urban environment. An understanding of the emergence of spaces for consumption cannot, of course, be understood without a broader understanding of the historical development of consumption. And the first point to make in this regard is that there is considerable debate as to whether the impact of consumption on society is best described as a recent phenomenon or a long-term, historical one. Is consumption a child of the modern era or has it been part and parcel of social change for centuries gone by? In their book, *The Birth of a Consumer Society*, McKendrick, et al. (1984) identify a consumer revolution in eighteenth-century England where for the first time it was possible to identify a society where material possessions were prized less and less for their durability and more and more for their fashionability. McKendrick et al's (1984) argument was not that the desire to consume was an eighteenth-century novelty but that the *ability* to consume was new, certainly by the nineteenth century, when many of the foundations of modern consumption practices had been established. Similarly, Braudel (1974) suggests that the emergence of consumption is not tied up with modernity nor with the process of industrialisation. Exchange relations had in fact developed in a sophisticated manner even before industrialisation, notably in the guise of seventeenth-century French markets which provided a focal point for the development of urban centres. Fairs and carnivals also offered spaces for consumption, demonstrating the way in which the roots of modern consumerism were undoubtedly found in trade. Indeed, Braudel goes as far as to argue that trade had an important social function from early feudalism, and that from this period a sophisticated system of exchange has always been in place, thereby reinforcing the suggestion that consumerism and the spaces of consumption that promoted it have long been an historical fixture.

A key reference point for understanding the role of spaces for consumption as a key player in the construction of city places is undoubtedly Walter Benjamin's (1970, 2002) work on arcades. As Paterson (2006) points out, Benjamin saw the arcades of Paris, small shops with plate-glass windows and glass-covered streets offering protection from the elements, as the defining buildings of the nineteenth century. The arcades offered the consumer a city in its own right, a world in which everything is accessible. As authors such as Buck-Morris (1989) have pointed out, Benjamin (1970, 2002) regarded arcades as 'dream worlds' in which middle-class women could engage with the symbolic dimensions of consumerism. Key in this regard was Benjamin's discussion of the flâneur, an iconic figure who strolled through public spaces in order to see and be seen. From this point of view, spaces for consumption offer the consumer a site of individual and collective dreaming where the spectacle of the space itself can be consumed (Mansvelt, 2005). Dovey (1999) identifies the Galleria Vittorio built in 1867 as a prototype for the mall insofar as it offered a permeability that had not previously been available to the consumer: such arcades offered a dream world of seduction out of which '... emerged a spatial milieu which was social but not communal, a zone of "public life" that privileged the individual over the group. The arcades privatized the public imagination' (p. 125).

The above ideas are also played out through discussions of another particularly significant moment in the evolution of shopping, namely the development of the department store in the nineteenth century (Corrigan, 1997). For Corrigan, the department store was a visible manifestation of the formalisation of consumption in which prices became fixed, entry was free and in which no one was obliged to buy anything. Crucially, from this point of view, the department store also made the consumer more passive than he or she had been previously insofar as regardless of the temptation that surrounded him or her, he or she was obliged to accept the prices on offer. Corrigan argues that department stores allowed shoppers to exist in a dreamlike state, entranced by the alluring wares that surrounded them. This was indeed 'the democratization of luxury'. The development of the department store was also very much bound up with the development of transportation infrastructure and by changes in the layout of cities in the nineteenth century that meant it became easier to move goods and consumers alike across the city. Transport often tied itself to shops by using advertising that offered the best possible means of accessing such stores. As Corrigan points out, perhaps the most impressive characteristic of the emerging department store was its sheer size and the fact that it appeared to offer the consumer everything they wanted under one roof. This in itself is an interesting ideological notion: the claim to be able to provide everything, putting the consumer into the debt of those who make that provision. The daunting size of the department store is, from this point of view, intended to intimidate. The consumer is intended to be in awe. Meanwhile, such stores promoted the value of luxury. Although department stores were dependent upon the supply of cheap goods in high volume and at a low mark-up, cheap products are not in themselves enough – department stores needed to attach themselves to notions of luxury in order that they could offer the degree of prestige to which their customers aspired. Free entry meant luxury was indeed an experience to which everybody could aspire (Corrigan, 1997).

Department stores are often argued to have particular implications for the female consumer. Bowlby (2000), who argues that a history of shopping is largely a history of women for example, suggests that the department store naturalised the limitlessness of female shopping desires, particularly when the world of abundance represented in the department store compares so favourably with a woman's private life. Bowlby goes as far as to compare the experience of the department store to that of imprisonment. The shopper is imprisoned psychologically in an enclosed, self-contained and yet irresistible environment which allowed middle-class women to take home a world of leisure and luxury 'in fantasy if not in substance' (p. 7). The suggestion here is that the department store flattered female consumers into thinking they belonged in such a luxurious environment. In this dazzling context, anybody could be 'a lady'. An analogous reading would see the department store as offering new public space for women. Women were emancipated by the department store in which men were less prevalent than in the public streets outside. In making this point, Corrigan quotes the work of Gail Reekie (1992) in which she points out that the opening of the McWhirters department store in Brisbane, Australia in the 1930s was very much about constructing a space *for* women, not least given that in segregating space for men and women, women were allocated far more of that space. Reekie goes on to note that by the 1990s the same space is far less clearly demarcated according to gender, the argument being that gendered meanings have been confused (as opposed to having been broken down) and identities are now increasingly playful and non-standard. It is certainly true to say that department stores have always tried to shape women in particular ways by idealising particular body shapes and thereby creating a standard-model female body which actually restricts more than it empowers. For Corrigan, the department store on the one hand met the distribution problems of rapid industrialisation and on the other solved, or at least appeared to solve, the identity problems of the emerging middle classes. The process of democratising luxury was moving on apace and continued to do so with the emergence of the shopping mall.

'The theatre of the street'

There are clear links between the evolution of the arcades, the department store and the shopping mall and the way in which they engage with the 'dream world' of the consumer. Dovey's (1999) argument that spaces of consumption privatised the public imagination highlights the sorts of ambiguities that underpin the relationship between the individual and society in a consumer society. The shopping mall offers a sense of individualised freedom alongside an aura of communal well-being. Dovey goes on to discuss the way in which department stores offer the consumer a world of apparently endless possibility, where the experience becomes more important than the purchase. In effect, the process of consumption starts before the actual purchase of the product. It is experiential and the way in which that experience is conducted is therefore an essential component of both the ideology of a consumer society and its negotiation.

Before we consider the experiential dimensions of shopping in more detail, it would be useful at this stage to mull over the emergence of shopping malls from the perspective of those who designed them. Any discussion of the influence of shopping on both the physical and the mental environment must surely pay homage to Victor Gruen, the architect most responsible for a new building type that he envisaged would re-enliven downtown USA. Gruen's aim was to make the regional shopping centre a vital hub for the local community (Wall, 2005). For Gruen, a shopping centre was far more than a collection of loosely collected stores intent on maximising profit, but could rather fulfil the role of a centre of the community and a place for cultural activities in which the shopping environment became imbued with beauty and entertainment (Satterthwaite, 2002). What is interesting about Gruen, as Wall (2005) notes, is that he sought to link apparently incompatible priorities: the design of shopping malls alongside a broader commitment to an urbanist and environmentalist agenda. Gruen designed 44 million square feet of shopping buildings including 44 shopping malls during his career (Wall, 2005). Gruen is often remembered by his own profession as a villain of shopping centre design, responsible for the so-called 'Gruen transfer', the process by which a visitor to a shopping mall is dazzled by the array of goods available to him or her, to the extent that he or she becomes a critical and pliant consumer losing him or herself in the random act of purchase (Wall, 2005). Gruen himself preferred to describe such a process as being part of the 'theatre of the street' and in this sense his work was the forerunner of many of the spaces for consumption discussed throughout this book. The shop, from this point of view, was about far more than selling but played a key role in constructing a particular kind of ambience. As far as he himself was concerned, Gruen was city-building (Wall, 2005) and as such he saw the shopping mall as a key means of maintaining sociability in the city. For him, the regional shopping centre neither destroyed the city nor was it simply a machine for consumption: rather, it offered a social and cultural centre and effectively a regional sub-centre that had not existed before. For Gruen, the regional shopping centre was an 'agent of recentralization' (Wall, 2005: 58). As well as its broader urban function, the shopping mall reinvented shopping as a potentially pleasurable experience. As Gruen and his colleague Ketchum put it when describing the Harvey park project in Los Angeles:

> It is the aim of our scheme to impress the center's facilities deep into the minds of the people living in a wide surrounding area. The centre shall become to them more than just a place where one may shop – it shall be related in their minds with all the activities of cultural enrichment and relaxation: theatre, outdoor music shell, exhibition hall. (Gruen and Ketchum, 1948)

Thus, in 1956, *Time* magazine described Southdale Mall, Minneapolis, the first climate-controlled shopping mall, as a 'pleasure dome with parking': Gruen's shopping centres offered an 'introverted architecture' in which the facade was well and truly secondary to the content insofar as the street was brought into the building. As far as Wall (2005) is concerned, this represented a collapse between the private shop and the public street that so fascinated Gruen. There is no doubt, as Wall goes on to suggest, that the regional shopping centre became an instrument that nurtured and accelerated post-war consumer culture. The shopping mall constituted 'the community's living room': a community founded on the exchange of goods. To this end, the opportunities that spaces for consumption provide for individual self-expression, for theatrical excess, you might say, are clearly secondary to the economic imperatives of such space.

Controlled space

For other commentators, however, Gruen's version of this evolving community had a more sinister dimension and the sort of motivations outlined by Gruen could, from this point of view, be said to produce the opposite effect. As such, it is worth looking at Dovey's (1999) contribution to these debates in a little more detail. Dovey describes the shopping mall as a highly controlled space where an illusion of happy consumption is busily maintained. This then is the ideal community where poverty is absent and where social divisions or eccentricities are erased. The absent nature of space is further reinforced by the design of the shopping mall: its highly formularised structure with an onus on uniform chain stores, alongside the fact that it often stands in such stark contrast to its external surroundings. This is a space apparently devoid of crime as well as inclement weather and cars. This is or at least aspires to be a pure environment, socially as well as environmentally. In describing the utopia of consumption as expressed by the shopping mall, Crawford (1992) describes the way in which architects manipulate space and light to create a 'fantasy urbanism' devoid of the unseemly side of the city. Free from the expectations of the everyday, the consumer is left to partake of the escapist cocoon of the shopping mall severed from the city which bore it (Dovey, 1999): shopping as theatre and as lifestyle; a world described by Dovey as a kind of 'reverse tourism' in which the world is brought to us and which our role is simply to consume. The shopping mall is ultimately overpoweringly commercial and corporate in nature and, as far as Satterthwaite (2002) is concerned, can never be a genuinely authentic urban place as a result. This brings to mind the visions of Greek civilisation portrayed in the apparently living, breathing, moving fountains of Caesar's Palace hotel shopping mall on the Las Vegas Strip where crowds assemble on the hour to view an imaginary world of fire and water in which the consumer can lose themselves in disorienting hyperspaces so that the mall uses a 'sense of place' to dismantle 'a sense of history'. The historical motif is a common reference point for many shopping malls insofar as it offers a sense of grounding, a historical legitimation if you like, for a world that is actually bereft of the historical authenticity from which it plagiarises.

It is the omnipresence and our tacit acceptance of shopping malls' place in the landscape that makes them so important to our common life. As Sze Tsung Leong (2001a: 129) puts it, shopping is the medium through which the market economy has gripped our urban spaces, cities and life: 'It is the material outcome of the degree to which the market economy has shaped our surroundings, and ultimately ourselves'. Such an influence can be demonstrated quantitatively. For example, 17 per cent of the American workforce are employed in retail, while shops outnumber churches, synagogues and temples by 3.6 times, while in the UK the figure is 8.7 (Sze Tsung Leong, 2001a: 130). Of more interest is the fact that shopping itself constitutes a kind of barometer of social change that adjusts to the changing demands of the market to the extent that, 'In the end, there will be little else for us to do but shop' (Sze Tsung Leong, 2001a: 135). McMorrough (2001) therefore describes shopping as a 'prerequisite to urbanity'. Shopping does not take place within the city; the city takes place within shopping.

The shopping mall offers a festive atmosphere but one devoid of human frailty; shopping offers democracy but gives exclusivity in its place. Thus, Dovey (1999) talks about the ways in which certain forms of behaviour are prohibited in the mall: such as sitting on the floor and distributing political leaflets. Fittingly, the shopping mall can thus be described as what Habermas (1989) might label a 'distorted speech situation' in which free speech (and indeed freedom more generally) becomes illusory. 'While its signifiers are heterotopic the mall embodies the utopian desire for a purified community of social harmony, abundance and classlessness' (Dovey, 1999: 133). The mall uses this illusion of public space (if it is illusory – an issue to which I will return to later) in order to provide a public stage without the impingement of the political. The carefree escapism implied by the mall is in itself suggestive of freedom – its climate-free atmosphere offers consumers a safety blanket within which they can escape (Moss, 2007). As other authors have commented (Featherstone, 1991), the end product is a place and time of fantasy 'exuberant spending without behavioural abandon' (Dovey, 1999: 133).

The public role of the mall

The public role of the shopping mall is further demonstrated by the fact that it often at least attempts to take on many of what we would consider to be public functions: incorporating medical facilities, post offices, museums and the like. But the *actual* communal value of the shopping mall is a matter for debate. Satterthwaite (2001) thus talks about the evolution of US city centres in the 1950s, as the middle classes were leaving the cities, as were city stores as they sought to tap into the suburban middle-class market. Gradually then, the city centre was increasingly characterised by the influx of mega-corporations remote from the locality, thereby creating a more impersonal shopping experience. As far as Satterthwaite is concerned, the communal 'synergy' that local forms of shopping used to bring are yet to return and may never do so. And yet from this point of view, the retail and the sociability of our cities go hand in hand. It is not the fact that retail can no longer provide the sort of civic sociality that we require of it in today's corporate retail culture – what is more important is that, despite this, we still, unwittingly perhaps, depend on it to do so. The retail offer of our cities purports to offer a sense of community based on mutual trust and interaction on 'networks of social exchange': a sense of familiarity and belonging, but it does so in such a way that this belonging is defined not by us, the consumers, but by the process of consumption. Satterthwaite therefore highlights the tug-of-war that exists around consumption between communal interdependence and the desire for self-determination in what is essentially a paradoxical world: a world in which communication and connections to other people are technologically easier and quicker than they have ever been at the same time as us being as isolated and withdrawn from the communal life as ever before.

For Satterthwaite, shopping centres have not succeeded as the new town and city centres primarily because such spaces are private in nature and have not recognised the value of incorporating genuine community functions. In effect then, the recreationalisation of shopping has robbed it of its communal function and replaced it with something that promises community but cannot possibly provide it. Satterthwaite therefore calls for a focus on a sense of local empowerment and thus away from the apparent horrors of homogenisation: ' ... competent retailers realize that the challenges are how to use the new technology to enhance shopping opportunities; how to retain face-to-face retailing; how to increase local store ownership; and how to encourage authenticity' (p. 340). Shopping is primarily a public activity, an activity that brings private desires into the public realm. But the point here, as Dovey suggests, is that this creates a very hazy line between the public and the private in that however public the mall claims to be, it can only be public within the constraints of the privacy from whence it came. Shopping malls offer the image of a community place, but are in actual fact private spaces run by a private set of rules (Satterthwaite, 2001). To this end, Dovey quotes Gottdiener (1995: 89) who argues that the mall is 'instrumental rationality disguised as social communion ... Urban ambience is harnessed to the profit motives of privately controlled space'.

In the above context, Goss (1993) describes the shopping mall as a pseudoplace designed to manufacture the illusion that something else other than shopping is going on whilst maintaining the capitalist status quo: a sort of fantasised dissociation from the act of shopping that ensures the orthodoxy of that very act. From this point of view, we can understand the shopping mall as symptomatic of a broader societal condition 'in which consumption dominates production, the symbolic subverts the material order, and the distinction between

Image 6.1 Public and private: The Met Quarter, Liverpool
(Photo Andy Miah)

illusion and reality has become problematical or entirely collapsed'
(Goss, 1993: 21). Goss therefore considers Debord's (1995) notion
of 'the society of the spectacle' and the way in which individuals are
located in a fabricated world; a world lived indirectly and manifested
more than anything else as a representation of reality. Goss describes
the conceit of the shopping mall which purports to offer an alternative
form of community that it can never produce in reality. Such spaces are
essentially 'anti-community' insofar as their contrived nature actively
works against the possibility of disorder, at the same time as apparently
offering an illusion of endless possibility. In this way, the shopping
mall is a contrived dominated space that self-consciously resembles
a spontaneous social space (p. 30). In interpreting the nature of the

contemporary mall, Goss therefore argues that what we have here is a utopia, an idealised nowhere. In this context, Poynor (2005) describes the Bluewater Mall, Greenhithe, England and the way in which its architects envisaged a city rather than a retail destination. But of more concern is Poynor's allegation that in some respects the mall is patrician and patronising, notably in its efforts to use pseudo-cultural references in order to pretend the mall is something more than it actually is. Interestingly however, although Poynor came expecting to despise Bluewater, he actually ended up enjoying the experience. His suggestion is that it is easy to dismiss the shopping mall at a theoretical level but less easy to do so in practice:

> no wonder we fall for Bluewater. It is secure, tidy, a Pleasantville vision of Utopia – or rather a vision of Utopia for some. To let yourself be lulled by it is to collude with the politicians' rhetoric of classlessness, to forget the ideal of social justice, to pretend that the old class tensions between the haves and have-nots no longer exist in Britain, and having blanked them out of the scene, to abandon the neediest people in society to the town centers we no longer care to visit.' (2005: 98)

Spaces of re-appropriation?

The above arguments might lead us to assume that the shopping mall, or as various authors have described it, the cathedral of consumption, is a hellish arena in which unsuspecting consumers are duped into purchasing products, identity solutions that offer no kind of a solution at all. One author even goes as far as to suggest that the phenomenology of religion and the history of religion actually offer us the most illuminating means of understanding the 'meaning and magnetism' of the mall (Zepp, 1997). Religion, schools and families may not offer the sort of human fulfilment that we require of them and in this situation the mall offers an alternative means of fulfilling basic human needs. Whether or not you accept such a proposition, it is certainly clear that the shopping mall demonstrates the sorts of complexities inherent in contemporary consumer culture that a more rigid Marxist approach to the city is simply not able to accommodate. Consider Nancy Backes' (1997) discussion of the shopping mall as an encoded text of the city. Backes considers it unsurprising that critics condemn shopping malls as a refuge of the duped, but she also asks why it is that such an apparently passive experience is sought so repeatedly and so often. Her thesis then is that shopping malls actually address real needs and desires: 'Malls, for all the calculations of their designs, for all the goals of consumption and profits, are re-appropriated by visitors into resistant and generative practices far different from the intention and the purpose of the space. Visitors, in short, reappropriate the space to satisfy their own purposes in contemporary life' (p. 5). From this point of view, the shifting landscape of the mall offers an escape from boredom and a search for meaning. As Zukin (2005) suggests, shopping is not just about the maintenance of the self: it constitutes a public realm in which consumers struggle to create an objective ideal of value and it is able to act as such insofar as we believe that the arena of shopping allows us to balance creativity and control. In citing Habermas, Zukin argues that mass consumption constructs an alternative space to that of the public sphere which exists between civil society and the state. In the form of shopping, it offers a space between the self and civil society:

> Neither free nor completely democratic, the public sphere of shopping is a space of discussion and debate. It is a space of manipulation and control, but also of discretion and fulfilment. It is, in fact, an ambiguous or a heterotopic space, where we struggle to combine principles of equality and hierarchy, and pleasure and rationality, to create an experience we value. Shopping could in turn be suggested to actively hide the means of exploitation that underpin a market economy, thus shopping offers us a world of commodities that restore, rather than steal, our souls. (p. 265)

In the above context, Backes (1997) points out that malls offer women, in particular, a lack of boundaries that allows a pro-active mediation of the public and the private. This reflects a broader process in which the mall offers a world of possibilities. For Backes, the mall offers an enabling space answerable only to its own existence so that visitors can invent their own realities, histories and cultures. The mall therefore allows the individual to dissolve the boundaries of the self. It offers a richness of experience, a 'surrender alternating with control' (p. 13).

An alternative suggestion might be that the mall represents the temporally displaced nature of the postmodern world: a world of disorder and endless possibility. The suggestion here is that the mall is a strategic space, but one that is closely controlled by an institutional power. Its civic role is thus deemed by Goss (1993) to constitute a pretence. It offers a place to commune but only within the parameters laid down by retail capitalism. It offers solutions to the complex dilemmas of contemporary society but within a framework in which solutions to such dilemmas can only ever be symbolic in nature. In other words, the shopping mall 'is a representation of a space; that is a space conceptualized, planned scientifically and realized through strict technical control, pretending to be a space imaginatively created by its inhabitants' (p. 40). The pretence is allowed to succeed insofar as it constitutes a 'normal' state of affairs. Much like consumer society itself remains unchallenged because it appears to be the only genuine alternative available, shopping malls represent a process of reification in which surface becomes all and whereby the social relations behind the process of exchange are apparently masked. As such, Goss concludes with an interesting thought: the idea that perhaps shopping malls are simply *too* successful. They may be contrived by their designers as a realistic experience of public place, but the consumer takes this one step further and embraces the shopping mall as '*really* real' (p. 43). It is in a sense this experiential realness that underpins the thinking behind this book: how do consumers negotiate a world that suggests a degree of consumer satisfaction that cannot, you would at least, imagine, be realised at a more day-to-day level?

The escapist principles that underpin the shopping mall have profound implications for the nature of the city itself. Although of course many shopping malls contribute to the local economy insofar as they offer local people (albeit largely low-paid) jobs, it is also the case that some of the most successful and most consumer-friendly shopping malls such as San Diego's Horton Plaza have virtually no impact on their immediate surroundings (Crawford, 1992). The shopping mall therefore offers everything but provides very little other than a reinforcement of the status quo: 'The world of the shopping mall – respecting no boundaries, no longer limited even by the imperative of consumption – has become the world' (Crawford, 1992: 30). Such comments need to be considered alongside the somewhat blinkered view of the shopping mall as a kind of 'experience utopia'. Consider Mikunda's (2004) vision of Bluewater: 'The exquisitely styled aisles, atriums and food courts fuse into a never-ending magnet of design experiences. Everyone wants to experience this magnetism, and this is why thousands of buyers crowd to see the "Bluewater experience"' (p. 141). Mikunda talks of consumers being amazed by the world offered to them by Bluewater which itself is in his eyes a kind of design perfection where the architect can stage his or her art whilst the consumer can massage his or her soul.

Perhaps the problem here is that the reason shopping malls hold so much appeal is that there simply is nowhere else to go (Moss, 2007) or at least in a consumer society it feels that way. Shopping malls offer a comforting and yet simultaneously exciting environment in which the hunt for the latest shirt becomes accomplishable and satisfying for the self-respecting consumer. An understanding of shopping can tell us an awful lot about the ways in which consumer society operates and the way in which the individual is obliged to operate within this context. Consumer capitalism is undoubtedly the dominant partner in this relationship, but dominance does not imply complete control for, as McMorrough (2001: 202) suggests, 'To ascribe the effects of the city of shopping purely to the mechanics of late capitalism oversimplifies the situation, as it removes agency and culpability from the equation'.

At this point, it would be prescient to return to the earlier discussion of the history of department stores. Hetherington (2007b) challenges the production-oriented view of nineteenth-century department stores as places of commodity fetishism and phantasmagoria in which consumers' consciousness is falsely manipulated. In fact, the true market of luxury goods as represented by the department store was largely the preserve of the upper classes and it was rather the idea of luxury that the department stores sold to their expanding clientele (Hetherington, 2007b). The democratisation of luxury was about the creation of lavish stage sets that were used to perpetuate a particular ambiance of indulgence. But such an aura need not be understood as a spectacle, a commodity-driven 'dream world' that is more about creating wants than satisfying needs (Hetherington, 2007a). The suggestion here then is that we should not treat consumers as cultural dupes unable to escape the fetishised visions of the consumer society laid out in front of them and that we should, in fact, place more emphasis upon the far more ambiguous nature of the experience of such space. For one, shopping in a department store was always about more than just buying. As Hetherington acknowledges, Rappaport (2000) argues that in its early history the department store was more about providing women with a space to create their own pleasurable activity. The department store provided a space in which a particular female way of looking at the world could develop: a desiring, subjective way of seeing the modern world and indeed herself through the lens of consumption. In developing this idea, Hetherington moves away from an essentialised view of the self to a focus on the self as being constituted through the act of extension into the world of goods:

> In the first case, fetishism creates an illusory world (social space) that obscures reality and presents that illusion as reality; in the second, the fetish facilitates access to a cultural reality that can only exist in the imaginary. But that realm is not an illusory one, it is one where what is seemingly alienated in the first model can be accessed and made real for people – albeit only indirectly. Yet this is not the stuff of individual desires and self-expression that characterizes a postmodern argument about consumption; it is, rather, the stuff of significant social relations. (Hetherington, 2007b: 128–9)

Hetherington therefore attempts to offer a positive model of fetishism, one that sees the consumer as taking possession of, rather than being possessed by, the artefacts on display in the department store. To this end, a case study looking at perhaps one of the most sophisticated examples of a retail experience, namely Universal CityWalk, Los Angeles, will help us to clarify how far the individual is the author of his or her own retail experience.

Universal CityWalk, Los Angeles

As Nelson (1998) suggests, malls are so prevalent these days that we hardly even think about them anymore. They become a natural part of the order of things. Many authors, such as Sorkin (1992a), have described the city as some kind of inauthentic theme park and, in this context, Susan Davis (1999) points out that the urban reshapers are increasingly and literally theme park builders The Walt Disney Company's key role in the redevelopment of 'ground zero' on 42nd Street is an apposite example. Shopping malls are increasingly design-intensive and in order to survive they have to offer an experience, any experience, and in that sense the authenticity of the experience is in itself incidental.

For Davis, this is all about location-based entertainment: the construction of distinctive private spaces for consumption, the consumption of conglomerate culture; the constructing of an awe-inspiring shopping environment with which the individual can construct his or her own identifications.

Jon Jerde's CityWalk in Los Angeles, USA, is a prime example of an urban-themed consumption environment and one that has some pretension to offer something more to the consumer than the hum-drum experience of commodity exchange. For that reason, it is worth closer consideration. In practical terms, Universal CityWalk is a link between two 'anchors': the Universal Studios theme park and a multi-screen cinema complex (Reeve and Simmonds, 2001). Essentially an outdoor shopping mall, CityWalk is designed to 'communicate archi-tectural chaos and unpredictability' (Davis, 1999: 438) or, as Jon Jerde himself put it, to 'break down the walls between cultures and between entertainment and shopping, pleasure and profit, the viewers and the viewed' (Iritani, 1996). The above 'chaos' is constituted in the visually overloaded reconstruction of an apparently 'authentic' combination of snapshots of Los Angles.

A key dilemma for a development such as CityWalk, as Davis sug-gests, is how best to create a sense of place out of what, regardless of its architectural curiosity and superficial appearance, is essentially a standardised commercial space. Place is effectively created through highly coordinated themed space that culminates in 'experiential coherence'. In this way, CityWalk is a parody of Los Angeles itself. It appropriates the imagery of Los Angeles, mass popular culture and constructs a theatrical experience in its own right. In this sense, it is a sort of extreme manifestation of many of the trends discussed earlier in the chapter. What is going on here then, according to Davis, is an acceleration of the management of relationships between people and products: a sculpting of the physical world we move about in in the image of the market which venerates the 'magic of belonging through the corporation ... in these new spaces, the core cultural ideas are not only embodied by products, they *are* products. Citizens are collapsed into consumers and loyalty is a technique that expands the bottom line' (1999: 454).

The argument that urban space is effectively itself a product to be consumed is an important one. This is a product that provides the consumer with a communal experience above and beyond that of the individual consumer. Located within the broader complex of the

Universal City Studio Masterplan, The Jerde Partnership International's official description of Universal CityWalk is as 'a mosaic of small anonymous buildings (not Los Angeles icons), exaggerated and compressed into a pedestrian-scaled terrace of buildings' (Crawford et al., 1999). CityWalk is designed to offer an 'authentic' street quality alongside individually distinctive tenant designs: texture, life and perpetual change. The shopping mall pastiches and redefines the city in which it is located at one and the same time. In analysing Jerde's contribution to the new urban landscape, Klein (1999) describes Jerde's space as a Baroque vision that privileges the visitor's walk and the consumption of the space itself, but which also, crucially, provides well for the corporate client. Klein even refers to Jerde's claim that the new public realm of the city is that of the 'community of consumers'. The disoriented nature of the consuming city gives our lives the order that we crave. From this point of view, the consumer becomes a central character in his or her own movie of illusion or, to put it another way, in his or her own personalised daydream. For Klein:

> The scripted space is a form of predestination, where the consumer 'acts out' the illusion of free will. Each visitor is subject to a different story and it is in the broad nature of its appeal that the beauty of CityWalk lays. It is in effect a movie set onto which the consumer is invited as an active player in a familiar and yet unfamiliar environment in which all the world is a stage. As Klein notes, eight million people visited CityWalk in its first year. All this adds up to 'urban chiaroscuro' for the community of consumers, a condensed narratized substitution for what must be left out. It is designed experience for a world where audiences prefer to eat inside the movie, rather than simply go to the premiere. (Klein, 1999: 121)

This process, according to Klein, reflects a broader one at the end of the 1990s in which the movie set as a city has become a new paradigm for urban planning. In this environment perhaps, Klein's most telling thought is that, in a few more decades, we will find relatively little of the bolder industrial city left, except as zones of neglect. If a street has not been re-scripted as a community for consumers, it may not be able to support itself, and will drift away or be ignored (p. 121). This point is particularly pertinent during a time of recession when retail centres act as a barometer of economic decline; with the number of closed shop fronts offering a graphic reminder of the uncertainties of a market-driven economy.

If you consider Jerde's work from an architectural point of view, it is interesting to note that he has been described as an architect of two architectural pariahs, the shopping centre and the theme park, and in this sense has been excluded from mainstream architecture (Bergen, 1998). He is in a sense, then, 'antiarchitectural' in that his vision for architecture is a broader one – and one apparently determined more explicitly by the market than any conception of what abides by the professional norm. But, if as Bergen suggests, you look at this relationship from Jerde's point of view, he would argue that he is on an architectural mission in which architects more generally have no interest in the building of places, as opposed to one of objects, for the experience of 'communality'. This point is not without irony when you consider that spaces for consumption are most often criticised for the fact that they are supposedly 'placeless'. In fact, Jerde sees the shopping mall as the only place remaining for the creation of communality. He is offering consumers a public space in a society in which such spaces are less and less available to them. But equally interestingly, as Bergen goes on to point out, it is not communality itself that makes Jerde's projects so successful, but rather the pure unadulterated pleasure that they represent. Such pleasure is the product of an attempt to orchestrate a sort of intense hetereogeneity of multiple themes: to construct an environment that feels it is constantly changing and is effectively reinvented by the individual's personal experience of it (Klingmann, 2007). This of course raises questions as to the role of the commodification of space as a means of social control. Bergen (1998) develops this theme further in discussing another Jerde project:

> For Canal City Hakata tells us that if we cannot get rid of the commodity, we can trope it, we can place it beside commonality, the mask it wears as a fetish, and by this 'adjacent attraction', support both as mutually infiltrating vectors of pleasure and need. It is the subversive potential of such architectural punning that should now be the subject of research and debate. (p. 32)

Jerde's Universal CityWalk is a space for consumption which promotes consumption as pleasure and which by doing so compels us to consider the negotiated nature of the commodified city. I want to conclude this chapter by reiterating my concern that it simply isn't possible to understand the role of spaces for consumption in structuring our physical environment without recourse to the role of pleasure in orienting people's relationship to the spaces in which they consume. There is a danger that the momentum generated by effervescence of a sociology of consumption in the 1990s and early 2000s is lost and that, as a result, the complex nature of a society that defines citizenship and belonging through consumption is drowned out by the legacy of the productivist bent outlined by Hetherington (2007a) above. The pleasure to be had by shopping is not something that should be dismissed as evidence of cultural dupery. The significance of pleasure in the shopping experience is that it demonstrates the diversity of pressures that exist in the lives of the modern consumer.

Conclusion

This chapter has focused on the shopping mall as the primary physical form through which consumers enter the world of consumption. Of course, it would be an exaggeration to suggest that the shopping experience is entirely prescribed. Many authors (e.g. Bridge and Watson, 2000) have understood non-Western cities, for instance, as places of the imagination where the senses are actively bombarded. Bridge and Watson (2000) describe the city as represented by the spice markets of Istanbul and the street markets of Hanoi as sites of fantasy. Cities all over the world offer spaces in which sociality is possible and where it does happen. And yet the degree to which such spaces are genuinely liminal, the degree to which they provide an opportunity for transgression and resistance, is highly questionable. In fact, by their very existence, such spaces simply magnify the degree to which corporate spaces for consumption dominate the urban fabric. The consumer society colonises the possibility of resistance for its own ends.

The discussion of Universal CityWalk illustrates the complex nature of spaces for consumption insofar as these spaces, both at the level of the mall, and more broadly as the remaining chapters will go on to testify, do offer freedoms, but the question remains how that freedom is apportioned and understood. Jon Jerde (1998) himself claims that the great attractions of experiential spaces for consumption such as Universal CityWalk is that they are not compelled to be mute and passive in such environments. They are in fact themselves the entertainment. To put it another way, retail spaces of this kind are the theatres of their day: they offer an excitement and a form of escape that challenges the very notion of how active a consumer can be in negotiating his or her relationship with space or place. It could be argued that even if this were true, the experience a consumer gets at Universal CityWalk is very different to the experience he or she will have at the vast majority of the consumer society's more anodyne retail environments. The primary criticism of the powerful influence of retail on our cities is indeed that shopping is the key driver behind an increasingly homogenous urban landscape. Coleman's (2004) contention that contemporary retail is all about opening options in the city is highly contentious. Moreover, the degree of resistance expressed in the shopping mall is a degree of resistance that is inevitably confined to the boundaries laid down by the consumer society in which it operates. To describe the shopping mall as a physical manifestation of an ideology of consumerism should not nonetheless lead us to conclude that ideology constitutes a one-way street. The complexity of contemporary cultural life as expressed through spaces of consumption indicates how the consumer is willing to give up some control for a degree of escape that the consumer society is willing to make available to them in return.

The challenge for the social scientist as he or she continues to emphasise the significance of shopping as an arena that demonstrates the key dilemmas and tensions inherent in what it means to be a citizen of a consumer society is to recognise that it is both constraining and enabling and that the former is protected by the latter, the existence of which is no less significant as a result. This is an issue touched upon by Shields (1992) who describes the shopping mall as a site of social experimentation. Meanwhile, Langman (1992) quotes Kroker and Cook (1989) who describe the shopping mall as the site of possessive individualism *par excellence*. From a political point of view, this may lead us to agree with Zukin's (1993) contention that:

> Shopping centers … are both material and symbolic: they give material form to a symbolic landscape of consumption. Their imagery seduces men and women to believe in the landscape of a homogenous mass consumption by masking centralized economic power in individual choice. (p. 142)

A shopping mall is, however, far more than a site of ideological seduction in which the consumer is subjected to the limited choices of a world defined through consumption. It is partly that, of course, but what is of more sociological interest is the fact that as individuals able to make decisions and judgements about the role consumption might play in their lives, people are more than willing to forsake some of the freedoms implied by a romantic vision of what the city may have been like in the past. They are willing to forsake a degree of control for the pleasure that is offered to them through consumption and by the spaces of consumption that dominate our urban landscapes. The kind of consumption we are talking about here is visual in nature and the emphasis on the visual means that the consumer has at least some kind of an active role to play in determining what it is they want to see and to experience. In this respect, whether such spaces are inauthentic or not is an irrelevance. What matters is whether they are pleasurable. Such spaces respond to the needs of consumers whilst doing so with the framework determined for them by the market. Such spaces ensure the physical and architectural dominance of market forces, despite claims by architects such as Jerde that they are helping to produce a new form of urban communality. Jerde's work is a progression from that of Gruen in the sense that he is providing the very world of entertainment that Gruen dreamt about. But the 'Gruen transfer' is an inevitability at least in some shape or form in such an environment.

The experience of CityWalk and of shopping more generally is such that the sense of well-being engendered by such processes means that the consumer is inevitably dazzled but he or she does not lose his or her critical faculties in the process. As Klingmann (2007: 104) puts it, 'while any staged environment is by definition artificial, the resulting emotion in the audience is real'. This sentiment lies at the very heart of this book. The consumer has had to become more of a partner in the evolution of pleasurable spaces for consumption. This is far from an equal relationship, and it does constitute yet another stage in the pressurised compulsion on the part of the consumer society to reinvent itself in evermore sophisticated guises. This is an issue to which I will return throughout the remainder of this book, as I continue to debate the degree of genuine freedom a consumer can count upon in an urban fabric literally defined by spaces for consumption. As such, in the next chapter, I will turn to the consumption of the spectacular and in particular to the impact of the mega-event which has served to further intensify the nature of emotional investment in the city, but has done so with an economic imperative at its heart.

7

THE SPECTACULAR MEGA-EVENT

The mega-event is an increasingly important indicator of the symbolic impact of consumption on a global consumer society. This chapter looks at the way in which the apparently passive consumption of large-scale events appear to have captured the public imagination and considers what this process means for the redefinition of the consuming city. Despite the high risk nature of urban strategies around mega-events, as exemplified by a number of events that have proven to be onerous on the public purse, many policy-makers see sporting events as a key means of urban regeneration. A core concern here then is the degree to which consumers of mega-events and thus city residents are inevitably passive: that they are simply subjects of ideological processes beyond their control. What then are the implications of the apparent void that exists between the construction of the city based upon conceptions of an abstract space imagined by the state and its planners and the lived experience of consumers who can often do little more than view the mega-event from the outside? By considering the role of the mega-event in the landscape of the twenty-first century and by looking specifically at Beijing's experience as the host of the 2008 Olympic Games, it should be possible to learn a little from the experience of those cities who have gone the furthest to pin themselves to the mast of the commodified city.

Defining the mega-event

This book is founded on the assertion discussed throughout that efforts to stimulate consumer demand increasingly fuel the production (and hence the consumption) of urban space and that this, at least potentially, creates more and more of a homogenised and standardised urban experience. This is an issue taken up by Gotham (2005) in his discussion of New Orleans' Mardi Gras in which he contends that we are living in a society that is increasingly saturated by images. For Gotham who echoes the work of Lefebvre (2005), the city is no longer lived but is an object for the cultural consumption of the spectacular. The mega-event constitutes a kind of spectacle. Moreover, Debord (1995: 12–24) defines the spectacle as 'a social relationship between people that is mediated by images ... The spectacle is capital accumulated to the point where it becomes image'. Such 'unreality' ensures the alienation of the masses through the domination of consumption, in the sense that 'the world we see is the world of the commodity' to the extent that ... social space is continually being blanketed by stratum after stratum of commodities' (p. 29). From this point of view, the world of entertainment and consumption that surrounds us is highly seductive and consumers are arguably passified as a result. In this context, social life is about having rather than living and the images around us are a constant reminder of how to live and the only legitimate way to live is through consumption. Kellner (2003) therefore points out that the culture of the spectacle has been intensified by the 'entertainmentisation' of the economy, politics, society and everyday life.

At its most basic level, a mega-event is a spectacular event self-consciously deployed in a deliberate attempt to portray a city in a particular fashion and to maximise economic advantage on a global stage whilst fostering civic pride in the process. But as Gotham (2005) also points out, and as I will go on to discuss later in this chapter, urban spectacles cannot be analysed in isolation. They are, by their very nature, complex, multi-faceted entities that above all else demonstrate the inherent complexity and apparent contradictions of life in the contemporary city. The emergence of the mega-event on the place-making agenda in recent decades is symptomatic of broader changes going on in the form of the commodification of the city. It demonstrates, specifically, the onus placed by nations and cities intent on reorienting their political identities and the path of development which they are exploring. In this context, Roche (2000: 1) defines mega-events as 'large-scale cultural (including commercial and sporting) events which have a dramatic character, mass popular appeal and international significance'. For Horne and Manzenreiter (2006), a mega-event is deemed 'mega' if it has significant consequences, notably in terms of media exposure, to the host city. Such events have become especially strategically important in light of the sort of post-industrial economic conditions I highlighted in Chapter 2. This reflects a change in the nature of urban governance and an increased emphasis on cities as sites aiming to attract service and high-tech industries, tourism and leisure. Cities aspire to do so through projecting a particular image of themselves to potential investors and audiences in what some authors have described as 'the politics of bread and circuses' in which money and political capital is utilised in pursuit of the discretionary spending of the visitor at the apparent expense of the resident population and their taken-for-granted tax contributions (Eisenger, 2000).

What has emerged then is very much a symbolic process in which mega-events could potentially play a formative role in establishing a city's credentials for a post-industrial future. As Roche (2000: 7) puts it, 'Spatially, mega-events uniquely, if transiently, identify particular urban and national places in the national, international and global spaces of media and tourist markets and the gaze of their consumers. But what is of particular interest for the subject of this book is Roche's (2000: 7) contention in turn that, 'In a world which is arguably becoming culturally homogenised and in which places are becoming interchangeable, they create transitory uniqueness, difference and localisation in space and time. Sociologically they offer concrete, if transient versions of symbolic and participatory community'. Roche's suggestion then is that what mega-events offer, perhaps above all, is a promise of modernity; of momentary charisma in what is otherwise a highly rationalised world. For Roche, the mega-event is of a fluid and ambiguous social character and therefore occupies an intermediary position between aspects of structure and agency. Such events are closely controlled structurally, and yet are founded upon a degree of unpredictable and often agentic action that can serve to transform the nature of that structure.

From the point of view of a book concerned with 'spaces for consumption', mega-events are of interest for what they tell us about the ideological principles that underlie a progressive society. Thus, Roche defines mega-events as modern cultural events which exhibit aspects of both exhibition and performance. In turn, mega-events are national, at times super-national and often international events and as such play a strategic role in the repositioning of place. They are also usually highly localised in space and as such have a potentially significant impact on the physicality of the city. Mega-events consti- tute an important means of promoting 'touristic consumerism' and in doing so play the role of conduits for global consumer culture (Roche, 2000). Their activities are designed through, or at least 'com- plemented' by, opportunities to consume. In order to demonstrate the relationship between consumption and the mega-event, I will now turn my attention to a mega-event that has for several decades played a particular role in the repositioning of cities, namely the EXPO.

The EXPO

Roche (2000) develops the above ideas in the context of the EXPO which he sees as representing the nineteenth-century origin of an emerging consumer culture. As a showcase for the best a city can produce and as a statement for the industrial future of that city, the EXPO self-consciously presents to the world a particularly pow- erful consumer-driven world view. In this sense, the EXPO can be seen to be a key institution (most importantly prior to the emergence of television) in the social diffusion of consumerism. EXPOs offer a particularly consumerist slant on tourism suggesting that tourism could come to you rather than you going to it. For Roche (2000: 70), the EXPO also 'contributed to a popular taste for participation in a cosmopolitan dimension of the public culture of the times'. In many respects then, EXPOs represent a kind of testing ground for con- sumerist institutions such as department stores and museums. There is considerable debate regarding the degree of inclusiveness of such events. From one point of view, EXPOs were historically inclusive, at least for the white, male, working class that is, insofar as they offer a degree of cultural citizenship to the white working class within the emerging frameworks of Fordist capitalism. From another, as Roche (2000) suggests, this attempted inclusiveness backfired insofar as the structures implied by such developments actively tied women to the private sphere and were bounded by the legitimisation of imperial relationships. In this respect, the opening up of cultural institutions and the implied freedoms of consumption were partial in nature, although what is for certain is that huge numbers of consumers were attracted to the EXPOs as expressions of touristic consumption and urban cosmopolitanism (Roche, 2000). This reflects the long-term historical development of World Fairs (as they are referred to in the United States) which Mattie (1998) describes as constituting an idealised version of world peace and trade 'marching hand-in-hand' (p. 8). Such events attracted millions of visitors and despite the high degree of investment involved (and often losses), would usually have considerable long-term benefits through, for example, the design of public spaces and housing, for example. Mattie thus points out that for three cities – Chicago (1893), Paris (1900) and Montreal (1967) – a world exhibition played a vital role in the decision-making process that led to those cities building a metro system. As World Fairs have developed, they have increasingly been defined not so much by their relationship to trade, but necessarily by their industrial prowess and indeed in their potential as consumer utopias (Wood, 2009). Given that these fairs were originally intended to encourage all countries to live in peace through free trade and world peace, it is clearly testament to the power of the market that such values can no longer aspire to be dealt with as complementary ideals.

It is worth briefly considering some of the broader motivations of some of the cities which provided a home for a World Fair on EXPO. We can do so by considering the official documentation and particularly that published around Lisbon's EXPO in 1998. In the foreword to the official architectural accompaniment to the EXPO, Jose Torres Campos waxes lyrical about the 'profound' urban transformation implied by the EXPO, a replacement of an obsolete industrial space with a new metropolitan 'city' on the banks of the Tagus. In describing what makes the Lisbon'98 EXPO unique, Antonio Mega Ferreira (1998) interestingly points out that the EXPO is neither a trade fair nor a fun park, but rather both of those things. It is, in effect, about 'the exchange of experience' (p. 10). Ferreira acknowledges the criticism on the part of many American credits that over time EXPOs have drifted away from presenting the technological vanguard in favour of a strengthening of the commercial dimension of the fair. In a sense, the suggestion here is that the onus on the future is repositioned to focus more closely on the future of the site itself rather than a future implied by the content housed on that site. The site concerned was and is the redevelopment area of the eastern area of Lisbon:

> The decision to locate EXPO '98 in the east of the city, an industrial area crippled by a process of relocation on the part of the great industrial units, created the right conditions for

a controlled reconversion, in form and in time, of a vast area
that was rapidly becoming more run-down and neglected,
with a highly negative environmental impact on the city and
the river... Lisbon followed the example set by Barcelona with
the holding of the 1992 Olympic Games when it decided, and
rightly so, that the holding of international events are not just
media opportunities for political and touristic marketing but also
town planning opportunities par excellence ... Lisbon is using
EXPO '98 as a means and vehicle for transforming East Lisbon
and redeveloping part of its riverfront. (Soares, 1998: 24)

The aim was that the EXPO would provide the means by which the
city of Lisbon could be turned towards its river and be modernised
and internationalised. As far as plans for the public area of the Parque
das Nações (Park of Nations) were concerned, this is demonstrated
by varied spaces that seek to reflect the nomadic nature of contemporary urban life. For Carriere and Demaziere (2002), the Lisbon experience reflects a broader process of urban entrepreneurialism and a
transformation of urban sites by public-private partnerships. In this
respect, EXPO '98, as personified by the Park of Nations, can rightly
claim to be the largest urban regeneration scheme to be carried out
in southern Europe in recent years and a catalyst intended to exploit
the city's Atlantic coastal position. In effect, EXPO '98 represented
an effort to create a new urban centre, an 'Ideal City' that integrated
the derelict land on the riverside more effectively into the core metropolitan area of Lisbon. Perhaps the most important tourist attraction
on the site is that of the Lisbon Oceanarium (I myself can attest to
this. On visiting the site personally, myself and around 30 other tourists were dropped off by bus. My 29 companions walked in unison
towards the Oceanarium, leaving me as the sole survivor walking in
the direction of the main site!). Meanwhile, the Vasco da Gama shopping centre reinforces the urban feel of the site and includes shops,
a supermarket, cinemas, restaurants and leisure activities. In considering the effect of this effort to create a complementary city centre,
it must be recognised that this is a city centre for the chosen few of
25,000 permanent residents, insofar as the residential accommodation on the site is clearly aimed at a consumer of a particular income
bracket. As Carriere and Demaziere (2002: 76) put it, 'One could
argue that a true city centre should be one for everyone in the city,
and not an "island" of higher uses and of very rich social groups'.

Moreover, the site has become a key centre for business in Lisbon and the location for a range of multinational corporations as well as a site that attracts around 18 million visitors annually.

The ideological role of EXPOs as spaces for consumption is further explicated when you consider the way in which such spaces are conceived from a management perspective. Thus, Mikunda (2004) argues that World EXPOs should be the ideal 'experience worlds' or 'Third Places', insofar as they are unforgettable destinations offering true experiences – in short: story-telling for grown-ups. However, Mikunda (2004) goes on to acknowledge that some EXPOs, notably Hanover 2000, have struggled to engage with the public (in Hanover's case, this was in part due to the illegibility of its theme: 'Man – Nature – Technology'). Moreover, the concern here is that World EXPOs suffer the problem of 'uninterrupted over-stimulation', notably given the fact that many such fairs are undermined by the fact that technological innovations are nowadays exhibited on the internet and in trade forums before they even reach a Fair. The role of the EXPO is undoubtedly to provide a grand means of expressing where a city sees itself at a point in time and where it sees itself going in the future. EXPOs, offer, in effect, a means of tying a city's future to the unpredictability of the market.

The economics of the mega-event

Clearly then, the mega-event is more than just an event. Certainly in today's post-industrial climate, there is an expectation that such sites offer a permanent and above all economic legacy. The economic dimensions of the mega-event are discussed in some detail by Gratton et al. (2005) who focus in particular on the role of sport in this process and in doing so recognise that most cities which use investment in the sporting infrastructure are industrial cities as opposed to major tourist destinations. The aim then is to create new foundations for economic prosperity that are dependent on symbolic representations of the city. In his discussion of post-modernity, as I mention in Chapter 3, Scott Lash (1990) once argued that there is no such thing as reality, only 'representations' of reality. Such a sentiment is especially pertinent when you consider the ways in which cities have sought to reinvent themselves through mega-events. The decision to host such events is often the product of a leap of faith in which the bidding city must be prepared to trade the likelihood of significant financial losses on staging an event against the more intangible economic benefits felt by the city as a whole. Thus, the assumption is made that a city will make important economic gains through the additional expenditure generated by the mega-event and the afterglow of that event that, all being well, will help to redefine the city as a tourist destination (Gratton et al., 2005). In this way, mega-events represent a phenomenal marketing opportunity. But decisions to host such events, according to Gratton and Roche (1994), are essentially political in nature given the fact that there is usually so little evidence to prove the economic benefits of such events. Moreover, there is a concern that the economic affects can be negative in nature, particularly as far as the local population, often expected to foot significant proportions of the bill, through taxation, are concerned.

The sports mega-event

Sport has had a long history of reflecting and actively reproducing dimensions of social change, none more so than in the case of the sporting mega-event. In this context, Hill (2002) argues that sport has a long commercial history and that visions of sport being 'of the people' are largely mythical in nature. The emergence of the sports mega-event as a key focus of city development is closely tied up with the remarkable television audiences that world-class sport can command. For example, Madrigal et al. (2005) have noted that for the 2002 World Cup in South Korea and Japan, 213 countries produced a total of 41,000 hours of programming for an audience of 28.8 billion viewers, a figure only likely to increase with future tournaments given the growth of digital and satellite TV channels. Sponsors are clearly attracted by the positive association that sports can bring them and the vast global audiences such events can achieve (Horne and Manzenreiter, 2006).

From the point of view of this book, the key factor behind the growth of sports mega-events has been their role as promotional vehicles, although as Horne and Manzenreiter (2006) point out and as I suggested above, forecasts of their benefits are nearly always wrong. Moreover, the decision-making processes around mega-events are often non-democratic and lack transparency, whilst crucially they tend to be 'in the interests of global flows rather than local communities'

(p. 18). What is important about the process from this point of view is that the focus on global consumers as opposed to local publics implies a shift of public funds into private interests. There is more to the sports mega-event than its superficial allure. Such events actively naturalise social inequalities by the way in which, for example, undesirables are removed from the host venue or through the reassertions of international power relationships through medal tables. What Kellner (2003) describes as the 'sports spectacle' therefore celebrates and reproduces dominant societal values in an 'unholy alliance' between sports, commercialism and the media. Crucial in this respect is the way in which sports help individuals to learn the values and behaviours that are deemed appropriate in a competitive, success-driven society. For Kellner (2003), sport has long been a domain of the spectacle. The more commodified and the more such values are couched in a commodified spectacle, the more consumption is confirmed as the cultural orthodoxy. As Kellner (2003) puts it, 'Postindustrial sports … merge sports into media spectacle, collapse boundaries between professional achievement and commercialization, and attest to the commodification of all aspects of life in the media and consumer society' (p. 66). In a context in which the consumer society has to be reproduced, the appropriation of the spectacle is key. This process is perhaps no more demonstrated, certainly in the UK, than in BSkyB's £1.78 billion deal for Premier League football matches from 2010 to 2013. Look at the spectacle of the playoffs and the fact that the playoff to achieve promotion to the Premier League is considered to be the richest single game in world football. Hull City's success in the Premiership playoff final in 2008 was said to earn the club around £60 million. The transformation of football in the past two decades in the UK is further demonstrated by the impact of the Champions League and the fact that clubs can earn up to around £30 million if they are successful in that competition alone.

But regardless of the financial clout of contemporary sport and its commercial underpinnings, the sporting mega-event tells us more about the role of experiential consumption in the construction of our lived environments. For Silk and Amis (2006), the increasingly high commercial profile of sport is related to the emergence of new relationships between cities and the global economy insofar as sport provides one means of responding to a declining manufacturing base through the construction of 'tourist bubbles' that help to regenerate desolate urban areas. Referring to the work of Saskia Sassen (2006) who is concerned with the way in which the global flows of production, commodities and information constitute a new spatial expression of the logic of accumulation, Silk and Amis (2006) argue that cities have had to engage in a competitive process of economic restructuring in which role as arenas for consumption appear to be key. Silk and Amis also refer to Bélanger's (2000) discussion of the spectacularisation of urban space in which the promotion of the positive service and amenity attributes of a city become a key focus of repositioning as part of a visually seductive, privatised public culture (Zukin, 1995). In this context, Silk and Amis (2006: 152) argue that city spaces are polarised containers of multiple narratives and that such polarity necessitates the cordoning off of specially designed spaces of consumption which protect the consumer from the unknown other: 'In this way, the tourist bubble can provide a sophisticated dream world that belies the structural inequalities in the contemporary cityscape, often becoming manifest in polarized labour markets, extreme economic disparities, and racially differentiated housing and school provision'. For Silk and Amis, as city authorities turned to new forms of entertainment and tourist facilities, sports venues came to play an increasingly important role. Despite the large subsidies often involved, the intention is that such facilities should attract residents, business and tourists stimulating the city economy in the process. Thus, over $2 billion was spent per year in the early 1990s on sports facilities and convention centres in the USA alone (Eisenger, 2000).

In discussing the role of sport in the construction of 'tourist bubbles', Silk and Amis (2006) discuss two pertinent examples of this process in the form of Baltimore and Memphis. The maximisation of the spectacular played a key role in the development of Baltimore as the archetypal late capitalist city of urban renaissance, namely through the unveiling of plans for the construction of a baseball stadium in Camden Yards. With the original Baltimore Orioles stadium descending into a state of disrepair, a new retro-designed stadium provided Baltimore with a very distinctive landmark or space for consumption. The new stadium sits in the 'Westside' area of Baltimore alongside the M&T Bank Stadium (home of the Baltimore Ravens American football team), the Hippodrome Theatre, the Centerpoint retail complex and a range of renovated apartment buildings and hotels. The concern here is that such a development uses spectacle to camouflage the consumer from the realities of inequality in Baltimore.

In this sense, Baltimore's aesthetic rejuvenation is a veneer – quite literally in some run down and deserted neighbourhoods in which city workers are creating an illusion of occupancy... masking the city's deep-rooted structural problems. It is a strategy designed to favour civic image over improved citizen welfare in which the city and the state governments have absorbed most of the financial risk while the private sector has reaped the benefits. (Silk and Amis, 2006: 156)

Similarly, Silk and Amis discuss the $2.3 billion redevelopment of Memphis city centre which includes a 28-block 'Sports and Entertainment District' – a safe and sanitised place of play alongside two brand new sporting arenas, Autozone Park, Home of the AAA Memphis Redbirds which opened in 2000 and the FedExForum home of NBA side the Memphis Grizzles (originally located in Vancouver). Such spaces demonstrate the role of sport as touristic entertainment within a self-consciously global marketplace. In the above context, the Olympics has clearly been the forerunner of the sporting mega-event and in this role it has played a key role in marrying sporting events to a particular ideological intent, as I will go on to illustrate in the next section.

The Olympic Games

The relationship between the Olympic Games and the ideological foundations of social change are perhaps best demonstrated in the work of Anne-Marie Broudehoux (2007a) who looks at the 'making and selling' of Beijing. Broudehoux points out that the image of a city can be conceptualised through two main components: first, the physical image of the city, how it is produced, lived and experienced on an everyday basis and, second, its rhetorical image, the idea or conceptual image of the city as it is imagined in the collective consciousness and through the discourse that emerges from that consciousness. In other words, our image of the city can be both of a visual and a mental nature. The city can mean many different things to many different people. And it is for this reason that the way in which images are actively constructed around, and thereby alter, place constitutes such a sensitive issue (see Chapter 3).

Broudehoux's concern is with the way in which city marketing, in this case through the Olympic Games, serves a strong ideological purpose, not least insofar as it uses the city and its consumption as a focal point for the naturalisation of power. The reinvention of China, a key stage of which was undoubtedly the hosting of the Beijing Olympics, can perhaps be traced back to the Tiananmen Square uprisings of 1989 in and after which anywhere between 1000 and 7000 people are said to have been killed. As a demonstration of the degree of unrest on the part of many Chinese people as regards the pace of reform and as dramatic demonstration that things had to change and fast, the Chinese Communist Party appeared to have little choice but to enter into a social contract with the people of China: a contract in which the freedoms associated with a capitalist system could be exchanged for the continued authority of the party (but not with the sorts of freedoms associated with a more democratic vision of social change). On the basis of this contract, the Chinese state was able to go about presenting Beijing as a modern, entrepreneurial metropolis whilst building national trust in China's stability and prosperity internationally along the way.

For Broudehoux then, Beijing is an example of a city in which urban space becomes a battle for control. In recent years, the Chinese people have become increasingly patriotic about their country. This, as Broudehoux claims, is far from coincidental. The Communist Party has deliberately whipped up a patriotic fervour that promotes their interests both externally and internally. Patriotism is from this point of view the new hegemonic discourse and it's a discourse that is able to predominate at least partly due to the consumer freedoms that it implies. In this context, Beijing's Olympics allowed China to present an image of progress, order and prosperity to the rest of the world. And they managed to do so through the use of the city as a conduit through which such meanings could be established. Above all, Beijing was presented through the Olympics as a valid site of consumption and was thus able to provide manifest evidence of the way in which China was arriving confident and assured in the modern world. To these ends, Broudehoux argues that the mega-event acts as an instrument of popular pacification offering a means of distraction from daily struggle. Having attended the Games myself, an abiding image is indeed of dozens and dozens of local Chinese people gazing over the perimeter fence at the Olympic site and all the wonders that it beheld. The point here is that the Games are more accessible to some consumers than they are to others.

The costs of the above investment are immense but not always immediately obvious in their effect. Broudehoux considers the enormous cost of architectural projects and spectacular urban design which can only be understood in the context of neglected local needs and the exacerbation of local inequalities. The chief concern in that respect being that the costs of the Olympics tend to fall on those who least benefit from them. In quoting the pertinent figures, the Beijing municipal government spent over 10 billion US dollars on transport and infrastructure, for example. Broudehoux argues that such investment blindly disregards local needs, there being no hard evidence that the local population actually benefits from the anticipated economic boom that would result (which in turn has been cut off at the legs by the effects of a world economic downturn). For Broudehoux, the winners in such a scenario are always the multinational businesses involved in sport through sports, tourism and property whilst the locals are left to deal with increased taxation, soaring rents and restricted civil liberties.

I will return to Broudehoux's work and further discussions regarding China's relationship to the Games before the end of the chapter, but before I do so it is worth taking a step back in order to consider the broader nature of the Olympic Games' involvement in the construction of spaces for consumption. Taken at face value, the Olympic Games purports to represent the peak of universal human endeavour in the form of the most prominent recurring global event in the world. Tomlinson (2004) presents a somewhat sceptical interpretation of the Games in his discussion of the process of the Disneyfication of the Olympics. For Tomlinson, this process can be traced back to the award of the 1984 Olympics to Los Angeles, which as the only credible candidate city was able to write its own terms for the Games and in doing so re-set the Olympic mould on the basis of sponsorship deals and marketing. Disneyfication, which I will refer to in greater detail in Chapter 8, refers to the process whereby characteristics associated with the Walt Disney business empire have come to dominate key aspects of cultural production and consumption. Tomlinson discusses the process of Disneyfication in the context of the Sydney Olympics which, he argues, involved the sanitisation of history in the way in which it evoked an Australian multi-culturalism that conveniently smoothed over the injustices and inequalities of Australian racism. Tomlinson (2004: 161) describes the Americanisation of the Olympics not least in terms of its economic infrastructure and its relationship to corporate sponsorship: '... since 1984, and the end of the Cold War in particular across the late 1980s and the early

1990s, [t]he Olympics has endorsed a global consumer culture quite as much as any noble historical ideal of international corporation and universal peace'.

The potential benefits of the Olympics are mixed and many cities have paid heavily for their post-Olympics legacy. The most oft-quoted success in this regard is undoubtedly Barcelona. For many, the great winner of the 1992 Olympics was the city of Barcelona itself. The Olympics played a role in re-imagining Barcelona as one of Europe's foremost tourist cities, partly through the metamorphosis of its urban landscape (Degen, 2004). Barcelona is routinely referred to as an exemplar of post-industrial regeneration, but its reception as a tourist hub, has, according to Degen, as much and if not more to do with the city's view of tourism as a process rather than a product. Thus, Degen refers to the way in which the Olympics played a key role in changing perceptions of Barcelona as a city on the world stage. One of the key dimensions of this process was the way in which the Olympics gave local politicians and planners the opportunity to finance large-scale public works, including the opening up of the city's waterfront as a space for consumption. But the concern here is that an early emphasis on the development of an inclusive model of urban planning was superseded in Barcelona by the raw desire to attract private investment (Degen, 2004). According to Degen, this has involved the 'selling' of the city so that many areas of the city have had to be physically transformed to make them more worthy of consumption. This is an issue discussed in more detail by Miles and Miles (2004) who, as I discuss further in Chapter 8, look at the impact of such developments on the authenticity of cultural production and consumption in Barcelona.

From the above point of view, the re-invention of Barcelona appears to be almost entirely about the commodification of place and the representation of a particularly appealing vision of a Mediterranean lifestyle. As such, Degen (2004) quotes a telling line from the 2002 *Time Out* guide to Barcelona: 'Along with the creation of the new Barcelona in bricks and mortar came a sponsored city promotion of Barcelona-as-concept, a seductive cocktail of architecture, imagination, tradition, style, nightlife and primary colours'. The tourist's experience of Barcelona is very much on the one hand about a process of symbolic consumption (of Gaudi's architecture, for example) and on the other about an embodiment of experience: tourism as cultural practice. Thus, Degen considers the specific dimensions of

Barcelona's relationship to its seafront which was transformed, most markedly around the Maremagnum area, from a functional port into a recreational focal point during the 1980s and 1990s. This area was to begin with a popular location in which consumers could visit stylish bars and restaurants. But over time the lustre of the area has worn away, particularly for the locals, demonstrating a key problem for developments of this kind: namely the need to maintain a balance between a locale clientele and a touristic one (Degen, 2004). Barcelona used the Olympics to catapult it into global stardom, but this is arguably an arena from which its local supporters are very easily alienated.

Earlier I considered some of Broudehoux's work on the potential ideological impact of the Olympic Games in Beijing. It is worth considering such an issue in a little more depth (Broudehoux, 2007). In considering investment amounting to over \$40 billion (more than all the summer games since 1984 combined), Broudehoux discusses the role of mega-projects in the build up to the 2008 Olympics. During this period and able to take advantage of low labour costs, Beijing became a hotspot of iconic building construction in which the public face of the city of Beijing was fundamentally transformed as part of China's efforts to enter the modern world (see my discussion of iconic architecture in Chapter 5). But as Broudehoux (2007) notes, the breakneck speed with which China enters the promised land is inevitably polarising in nature and, for many Beijing residents, such developments simply reinforce the everyday realities of social injustice. Of particular concern in this regard is that the millions of dollars/yuan being spent on such venues will in the longer term be for the benefit of a wealthy elite, as the Olympic park will essentially offer private facilities for those who can afford them whilst those who sacrificed the most are left to imagine what might have been:

> For the most critical, this new delirious Beijing is a city of competing egos, of selfish opportunism, and of betrayed promises. It is a city without urbanity, where megalomaniacal architectural projects are built on the ashes of an organic urban fabric. This new metropolis mirrors the society that builds and inhabits it: an increasingly individualistic society that wilfully sacrifices a more cohesive one, where a predatory elite of private entrepreneurs, technocrats, and party members prey on a disenfranchised and vulnerable populace. A city glittering on the surface but hollow at the core: a truly evil paradise. (Broudehoux, 2007: 101)

As I noted earlier in the chapter, such issues are also closely bound up with ideological concerns and not least as a demonstration of China's national ambitions. For Ren (2008), the building of the Bird's Nest, as it was affectionately labelled by local people, and the broader bid for the Olympics were not simply a key component of an economic strategy for the city, but had a broader ideological significance in representing China's arrival on the global stage. In effect, global architecture has become a form of national expression. Such national expression was built upon the foundations of the needs of corporate sponsors to negotiate a means of entry into the rapidly growing Chinese market, leaving the Olympic movement open to the criticism that the aims of its corporate sponsors are paramount (Close et al., 2007). Meanwhile, the architectural power of the Olympic Stadium creates an experience unique to itself and regardless of the athletic achievements within. By offering an architectural experience that complements a sporting one, alongside a feeling of participating in a global event, the Olympic Games becomes an almost out-of-world experience, something I myself experienced when watching Usain Bolt break the 100-metres world record. My immediate feeling at the time was that I was observing a media event rather than something in the flesh: an event that cannot be consumed and yet was defined by the fact that it could be and would be the world over.

There has of course been limited time to address the impacts of the 2008 Beijing Olympics but one thing is for sure, as de Lisle notes (2009) – architecturally at least, the backdrop for the Games was strikingly and self-consciously cosmopolitan. This reflects a long tradition of architecture being at the centre of Chinese statecraft, in this case mega-public space offering a diversion from protests about human rights issues and a means of reinventing the Communist regime (Marvin, 2008). In discussing the emergence of the new Beijing, Greco and Santoro (2008) argue that the competition for the new National Grand Theatre, an iconic, half-dome, glass construction opened the floodgates for international competition prior to the Olympics. It also opened up debate as to the appropriateness of such iconic buildings, a key criticism being that such a building is an elitist statement and a nonsensical one in a country, which is still, after all, developing. As I suggested in Chapter 5, the Olympic Games allowed Beijing to think big architecturally. The National Swimming Centre is a demonstration of the power of architecture as consumption. It offered the sensation of a magical underwater world and at night a sight to behold as it metamorphosised into a luminescent aquarium (Greco and Santoro, 2008). But, as ever, criticisms of such buildings centre on their long-term use and the fact that use is almost inevitably perhaps socially discriminatory. But what is perhaps most impressive and most scary about all this is the sheer speed of construction and the statement made by that speed as regards China's place as a capitalist technological power that could make things happen.

The Olympic Games was a prime mover in an architectural transformation bigger in scale than even the development of Shanghai in the 1990s. But such developments came at considerable cost. The Olympic site itself was originally a slum district home to tens of thousands of people (Farndon, 2008). A key characteristic of the changing Chinese city is the relentless demolition of traditional housing and thus of Chinese culture. This process is especially graphic in Beijing with the rapid decline of hutong (narrow alleyway) communities formed by lines of quadrangled housing, a distinctive style of Beijing residence (Hom, 2008). The Olympic Games were instrumental in constructing Beijing as a space for consumption and part of this process involved ridding the city of its past. China has never been a country, architecturally at least, to be overly sentimental about its past, and the modern developments sprouting up in Beijing, often as a direct replacement for the hutong, were testament to the fact that the Olympic Games offered a once in a lifetime's opportunity for reinvention. On the positive side, such redevelopment has vastly improved living conditions in the centre of Beijing and although it is very easy to romanticise the hutong, it is also fair to say that a key element of the capital city's historical fabric has effectively been destroyed in the process. In this respect, Beijing can be said to be an increasingly transient city, as are, in a sense, the people that live in it. The key problem here being that those who have been relocated as a result of the redevelopment of the city, and in the name of presenting a vibrant, forward-thinking city to the rest of the world, cannot afford such a move and nor are they culturally prepared for it. In this respect, urban development in Beijing is increasingly determined by a profit motive that by its very nature sits in direct opposition to a traditionally communist welfare approach (see also Chapter 5).

It is in this context that Wu et al. (2006) argue that the establishment of a market situation in the Chinese city has resulted in a process of commodification. In this process, the state has emerged as a market agent with limited controls over often ungovernable disputes over land, an agent that will create increasingly sprawling cities. In this respect, the Chinese city is now primarily envisaged as the entrepreneurial city which commodifies place as a spatial commodity. What is so difficult about this process is that it constitutes a realignment of urban identity for both the city and the people who occupy that city. The big losers in this process are immigrant workers. The rapid speed of development in Beijing is due to the work of an invisible army of migrants who work in unsafe conditions for wages that may or may not be paid. Fong (2008) estimates that in 2004 Beijing construction companies owed around 750,000 workers a staggering $380 million in wages. As Broudehoux (2007) suggests, the reinvention of Beijing constituted a new market-driven spatial logic, but one that is inherently exclusionary not least in how it excludes those very immigrant workers who were responsible for making the image of the re-imagined city a reality in the first place. Officially, 4 million migrant workers live in Beijing, but this seems to be an underestimate given the figure for China as a whole is around 120–140 million (Hom, 2008).

The broader economic concern is that the heavy nature of spending on the Beijing Olympics may in the medium term bring with it an investment downturn of unusually severe proportions. Another concern is that the Olympics has given the Chinese communist party the confidence to 'ride roughshod' over moral condemnation of China's human rights record (Farndon, 2008). Perhaps the most telling demonstration of the Olympics as symbolic consumption on a global scale is the fact that the world's powers are simply not prepared to challenge that record (with the possible exception of the French Premier Sarkozy). The success of the Olympics and of Beijing and hence China is intimately tied up with the success or otherwise of the global economy, and to threaten the growth of China's economy is to threaten the very essence of international economic collaboration. For some authors, such as Hom (2008), the Games are simply a justification for further human rights violations. Meanwhile, Hom suggests that the 'cost' of a single gold medal for China amounts to around $700 million. Is that a cost worth paying and by whom? During and immediately after the Games, the Beijing Olympics helped to foster an atmosphere of national pride that the Chinese Communist Party continued to encourage as part of its plan to stifle internal debate and to promote a vision of a prosperous Chinese future and one in which China was a world, as well as an Olympic, force to be reckoned with. To do anything but support such a vision would of course be unpatriotic.

Image 7.1 The commodified Olympic Green, Beijing 2008
(Photo Andy Miah)

For Tomlinson (2004), Olympic parks are essentially theme parks, Sydney's Homebush Bay site, for example, being a futuristicically reclaimed blighted space. Such spaces offer the illusion of consumption as democracy, and in the process camouflage the realities that lie beneath. So what of the future of the Olympics as the archetypal mega-event? Dayan (2008) suggests that the Olympics is not simply an event, but a media in its own right: a blank slate upon which interested parties can ascribe their messages. This process has significant implications for the global consumption of the Olympic Games beyond that of the actual tourist. Thus, Dayan talks about how events such as the Olympics would in the past have been so powerful and influential as to effectively transform the home into a public space insofar as it invited spectators to assemble into 'viewing communities'. However, new media and in particular mobile phone technology have reintroduced an individualised form of reception that threatens the ability of 'a kind of agreed conspiracy among organizer, broadcaster, and audience: a tacit decision to suspend disbelief, repress cynicism, and enter a "subjunctive" mode of culture' (Dayan, 2008: 397). In this context, the meanings attached to the Olympics are actually highly contested despite efforts to frame the Olympics as a spectacle. Ultimately perhaps, the spectacular mega-event is no more than simulacrum. In other words, the Olympics are simply not as enchanting as they were in the past. Consumers, or some consumers at least, are savvy enough to find a more fulfilling alternative. This process is discussed by Ritzer (2005) whose work I will discuss in more detail in Chapter 8 as a process of 'dematerialisation' in which forms of consumption are actually becoming increasingly ephemeral, as I also pointed out above. They come to us rather than us coming to them: a process that may have significant implications for the reinvention of spaces for consumption.

The opening ceremony of the Beijing Olympics was testimony to the way in which the need for the spectacular underpins the success of collective memory. If people the world over remember one thing about the 2008 games, then it is most likely to be the four-hour opening ceremony, that was critically acclaimed the world over. It was a graphic demonstration of China's concilliation between its past civilisations (and most notably the massive set-piece choreography representing the sheer power of a communist regime and of collective thinking more generally) and the technological future. The opening ceremony of the Beijing Olympics was indeed an awe-inspiring spectacle, and by its nature an exclusive one. The much-derided British contribution (involving a London bus, Leona Lewis and Jimmy Page performing Led Zeppelin's *Whole Lotta Love*, and David Beckham kicking a football) amounted to the 2012 hosts – London – putting their hands up in resignation and saying 'how can we compete?' The mega-event is a demonstration of a market-driven ideology on a world stage. In effect, events such as the Olympic Games idolise the spectacle and displace the role of place in the production of that spectacle. The end result is a global form of consumption in which the unified principles of peace, youth and diversity are usurped by the needs of a media-driven conception of global consumption.

Conclusion

The mega-event is clearly underpinned by the power imperatives that underlie a consumer society. In this sense, it is inherently exclusive. Meanwhile, the 'uniqueness' which mega-event cities trade in is inevitably transient and is in the end more of a media construction than a lived reality. This reality is constructed upon the mythologising impact of a world in which symbolism has such high cultural capital. The main priority for such events is usually a global one and feeds into a broader narrative of globally competitive city-making in which to be 'included' means, more often than not, to be nothing more than an observer.

The danger is that the above process actively takes away from place insofar as it normalises dominant market-driven values and creates an aura around an event that is almost impossible to interpret other than through the dominating discourse of consumption. In a global media age, local impacts are not always as high up the list of priorities as one might imagine. To describe the consumer as inevitably passive as a result would be an exaggeration. But the consumer society operates in such a way that the degree of freedom available to the consumer in experiencing a mega-event is inevitably constrained. The experience of the city is framed through a dominant discourse that promotes a particular image-driven view of the city as a space for consumption and experience. What is less certain is how far that vision is passively consumed by the city's residents. How far is the construction of a city, apparently without urbanity (Degen, 2004), one which is created on the foundations of an imaginary notion of the ideal modern city really all that it is cracked up to be? The mega-event is 'mega' both in the sheer scale of such an event but also in terms of its potential impact upon the individual and not least those actually attending such an event and thereby helps to frame relationships, to social structures. Ultimately, however, the experience of the spectacular perhaps ties the individual to a world in which only the spectacular is good enough and in which the realities of everyday life can never apparently compete.

8

THEMED PARKS

The theme park is arguably the quintessential physical manifestation of the consumer society. It constitutes the ultimate commercial environment and offers escape through experiential homogeneity (Davis, 1996). It offers a non-conflictual environment promoting the riches of a consumer society within what is in actual fact a highly uniform and controlled setting. Many authors have commented on the preponderance of themed environments and their key role in city life. Urry (2002) describes themed environments as, effectively, the inauthentic 'made authentic'. They are hyper-real environments, an idealised version of reality that we carry around in our heads and which we expect to be acted upon and presented to us to be consumed. But the apparent dominance of themed environments has motivated what might be described as an extreme reaction, not least in the work of Michael Sorkin (1992a) who argues that in a themed environment the idea of the city as 'the site of community and human connection' is sacrificed (p. xiii). Of course, theme parks take many forms and will often be located in more rural contexts. The proposition that underpins this chapter is that the ideological impact of such environments is such that these spaces constitute mini-cities of consumption in their own right.

In this chapter, I will consider the significance of the theme park as both an expression of capitalism in perhaps its purest form and as an indicator of the changing relationship between the individual and society that this in turn implies. I will thus discuss the dominant role that themed spaces play in our society, moving on to consider Disney as the ultimate theme park, before widening out the debate again to consider what theming says about the role of spaces for consumption in a changing society.

Themed spaces

Before going on to consider the specific influence of the theme park as a symbol of the consumer society, it is worth thinking about the role of theming in our society more generally. This issue is dealt with in particular depth in the work of Gottdiener (2001) who argues that our daily lives increasingly occur within an environment structured around 'overarching motifs'. The consumer society is from this point of view characterised by the rise of connotative signifiers. In other words, our culture is more and more characterised by fantasy and symbolism. We live in a society in which marketing techniques are having to become increasingly sophisticated and in which consumers are more often than not appealed to on a symbolic or thematic basis. What is interesting about this process is that the environment itself as well as the products, rides or attractions we use or visit, are actively consumed. Entry to the themed environment, according to Gottdiener, allows the individual to actualise their 'consumer self'. But far from this being a passive process, Gottdiener contends that consumers satisfy their desires and seek personal fulfilment through the opportunities that these market-driven spaces provide. Although themed environments are premised on the realisation of capital and of profit-making, this premise must be disguised as far as the consumer is concerned. Hence, 'Theming reduces the product to its image and the consumer experience to its symbolic content' (Gottdiener, 2001: 73).

To the above end, Gottdiener uses the example of the themed restaurant which is often the product of a franchise chain and the best known of which is probably the Hard Rock Cafe (which even boasts its own themed Las Vegas casino). It is particularly important that themed environments are multi-functional. Offering a limited burger-based menu, the success of the Hard Rock Cafe lies in the thematic motifs it deploys, namely its nostalgic representation of the music industry. Its restaurants are decorated with original memorabilia as well as facsimiles, an ambitious programme of merchandising and a predictability reminiscent of Ritzer's (1992) work on McDonaldisation. Gottdiener (2001) also mentions the Planet Hollywood chain of restaurants which runs according to a similar model. In commodifying its founders' (Arnold Schwarzenegger, Sylvester Stallone, Demi Moore and Bruce Willis) connections to the movie industry, Planet Hollywood promotes the symbolic first and the gastronomic a far-away second. As Gottdiener (2001) points out, there are virtually no

Image 8.1   Las Vegas, the ultimate in themed space
(Photo Andy Miah)

differences between the type of food offered by the two restaurants. The difference lies in the theming, or in what I guess you could call the added value provided by that theming. Theming is much more omnipresent than the above discussion suggests insofar as all the key takeaway chains, including McDonalds, KFC, Burger King and Pizza Hut 'abstract their identifying logos into equally pervasive motifs that add to the array of signs and symbols within the built environment' (Gottdiener, 2001: 79). These chains are globally dominant precisely because of the predictability and comfort provided by a brand that is almost exactly the same from one country to another. Meanwhile, such restaurants extend the power of theming by establishing merchandising tie-in deals with major film corporations.

In analysing the above trends, Gottdiener (2001) concludes on a somewhat despondent note in suggesting that in intertwining themes of modernist progress with that of over-used themes of Hollywood Cinema, including the wild west, the legacy of ancient civilisations, and tropical paradises (represented in the UK by Center Parcs, a sort of holiday camp for the aspiring middle classes which has a tropical swimming paradise as its centrepiece), is essentially unimaginative. That, in effect, the motifs deployed are taken from a notably limited pallet. As far as Gottdiener is concerned, commercial imperatives ensure that such themed spaces conform to the lowest common denominator of taste. For Gottdiener, the public/private duality that characterised the early modernist city has been superseded by an environment that privileges consumption/consumer communion. As he puts it, 'These artificial, themed environments are limited substitutes for the rich public places that are nurtured in a healthy society with open cities and a strong public sphere of action. These environments cannot replace the *real* rain forests, tropical paradises, and important local cultures, although they may well contribute to their destruction' (Gottdiener, 2001: 188). Such sentiments reflect a broader trend of cynicism regarding the environmental benefits or otherwise of themed environments in the broadest sense. Such sentiments are evident in the work of Sorkin (1992a) whom I mentioned earlier and who describes an 'ill wind' blowing through our cities 'that has the potential to irretrievably alter the character of cities as the preeminent sites of democracy and pleasure' (p. xv).

The above sentiments reflect an important tranche of work by American cultural commentators, notably through the 1990s, who have criticised the inauthentic nature of the American landscape. Another prominent contributor to this debate is Ada Louise Huxtable (1997) who discusses the emergence of 'unreal' places which have created a fantasy world where the authentic is neither admired nor desired. Huxtable (1997: 2) describes an American state of mind in which illusion is preferred over reality 'to the extent that the replica is accepted as genuine and the simulacrum replaces the source. Surrogate experience and surrogate environments have become the American way of life'. A key concern expressed by Huxtable is the belief that themed spaces, notably those that are involved in the nostalgic romanticisation of history, constitute some kind of democratic and universal *people's* choice. In fact, such environments are made for the moment. They are made for immediate, short-term profit and the mere act of embracing their limited, and by implication exclusionary, intent, means a broader neglect for the needs of place and society (Huxtable, 1997).

Perhaps the key transitional characteristic of themed environments is more fundamental than a consideration of the architectural value of such spaces can provide us. Indeed, it is not so much the physical nature of themed spaces that should be of concern to us, but rather the way in which such spaces involve the enactment of what we can describe as 'the experience economy'. Pine and Gilmore (1999), as I pointed out in Chapter 4, have suggested that experiences represent a crucial genre of economic output in a post-industrial society. In this context, the successful staging of experiences is an essential component of any organisation wishing to develop a successful themed environment. From this point of view, services are the stage and goods are the props used to engage the individual consumer. This reflects a process in which what we used to obtain through non-economic activity, we now pursue through the realm of commerce,

> In the emerging Experience Economy, companies must realize that they make memories, not goods, and create the stage for generating greater economic value, not deliver services. It is time to get your act together, for goods and services are no longer enough. Customers now want experiences, and they're willing to pay admission for them. (Pine and Gilmore, 1999: 100)

In this sense, themed environments must offered layered experiences that compel and captivate the consumer. By doing so, they invite repeat returns and thus the possibility of personal transformation through personal customisation: through the development (or at least the appearance) of a one-to-one relationship between the themed space and the consumer. Another way of putting this is that theming an experience is about scripting a story that would be incomplete without guests' participation (Pine and Gilmore, 1999). Effective theming is about the coherent design of a unified storyline in which the customer feels genuinely involved. But, above all, and from a more critical perspective, themed spaces are all about designing an experience around a particular core, and at that core is ultimately a product to be consumed. It would be very easy to condemn themed environments on this basis (Herwig and Holzherr, 2006). What is more interesting sociologically is that these spaces are under huge demand, and offer consumers safe enjoyable spaces to which they will no doubt continue to gravitate. However fake such spaces appear on the surface, what is interesting is that they command an abiding appeal based upon the apparently endless availability of signs begging to be interpreted.

Theming, alongside shopping (see Chapter 6), was perhaps the most successful commercial architectural strategy of the twentieth century and its influence is still abiding (Herwig and Holzherr, 2006), most graphically in the guise of the theme park. I will now discuss the theme park in more detail before highlighting the powerful ideological impact of Disney as a space for consumption.

The theme park

The modern theme park originated from the World's Fairs held between 1851 and 1939 (see Chapter 7) and Petersen (2007) suggests that given their cultural prevalence, they clearly play a key role in helping to frame people's expectations of the broader social world. These spaces are founded upon approximate pictures. In other words, everything is about the visual and what is constructed is a pronounced visual coherence which offers a symbolically intense representation of space and place. To this end, a particular world view (one that legitimates consumption) holds sway during the visitor's stay in a theme park. He or she enters that park not just with his or her imagination, but with his or her whole being. At that moment, he or she will then experience a 'vigorously sensorial' public life in which one shifts from being part of that experience and a spectator of it.

The theme park is perhaps the most prominent example of a themed environment. It is a physical manifestation of the constant reinvention of consumer capitalism. Characterised by the selling of fantasy for cash, the theme park is so successful as a space for consumption because its childlike exterior is such an effective disguise for the ideology of consumption that lies beneath (Jones and Wills, 2005). Herwig and Holzherr (2006) describe theme parks as self-contained dream worlds bereft of an urban context which constitute the cultural paradigm of our age. One thing for sure is that the theme park represents a strategically important part of a global media system (Davis, 1996) insofar as it offers a new kind of mass medium that synthesises the marketing and advertising activities of the consumer society. From this point of view, the theme park is exhaustively commercial insofar as it offers multinational entertainment companies and their advertising partners a massively profitable opportunity, to the extent that Davis (1996: 403) describes the theme park as 'a machine for the rapid generation of cash'. This is an issue Davis (1997) has explored in more depth in her book on the corporate culture of the Sea World experience. She points out that admissions account for around 50 per cent of theme park revenues with the other 50 per cent coming from food, drink and merchandise of various descriptions. For that reason, the way in which consumers spend their money in theme parks needs to be carefully planned and controlled, coordinated to the last detail to ensure maximum profit. For Davis, this is all about the commodification of space. She sees theme parks as emblematic of contemporary spatial–urban problems and argues that this demonstrates the way in which vernacular and local meanings of place have been transformed into a standardised product. What's distinctive about the theme park, and in particular, Disney, which I will discuss in some detail later, is the way in which it offers an integrated landscape of meaning 'unified around consumption' (Davis, 1997: 3). In other words, the theme park is not just a site of consumption, it is a site of consumption and of cultural production that can be interpreted as being determined from the top down and as such one which deliberately reinforces the status quo. But as Davis notes, such an interpretation was most popular during the 1970s. Since that time and in particular during the 1980s, analysts have preferred to consider theme parks as texts and as part of the broader environment of an accelerated consumer society. The theme park thus became recognised as a physical expression of the outside world, exemplars of capitalist culture 'made up of spectacular privatized spaces' (Davis, 1997: 4). To provide a more straightforward definition, Rojek (1993) describes theme parks as themed leisure parks that incorporate participant attractions and serialised spectacles. Such spectacles are primarily escapist in nature, offering the consumer a world of immersion, ecstasy and excitement.

It would of course be a mistake to dismiss theme parks as superficial forms of culture for, unlike many forms of culture, theme parks are in many respects active in nature, reflecting deep and meaningful emotions and cognitive processes as they do so. Perhaps even more pertinent is the suggestion that theme parks are not merely physical spaces, but emotional spaces that capture the individual imagination (see Lukas, 2008). What is perhaps most interesting about theme parks is the way in which they appear to make the impersonal personal. In other words, they provide an environment in which the consumer can escape, and one that appears to be tailored to their personal needs. Sassatelli (2006: 167) captures this process particularly effectively:

> The animators of theme parks and tourist villages are much like gym trainers in that they have to get consumers to partake in a meaningful experience by furnishing them with a series of practical cognitive and emotional investments to read and enjoy the scene they are entering. Places which could otherwise be too rationalized and standardized may thereby be framed as free, self-gratifying, personalized, amusing and creative.

Theme parks are attractive to consumers in that they offer an enclosed and separated reality, a space that has its own rewards and learning experiences divorced from and yet reflective of the demands of the wider society. For Rojek (1993), this is all bound up with broader issues of velocity and time-space compression. A particular attraction of the theme park is the way in which they propel bodies through great speed, thereby offering a sort of post-modern perpetual motion that inverts the body and challenges reality, as we know it, in the process. The geographical theming of such parks, as Rojek also points out, lends itself to a process in which time and space are compressed or, in effect, dissolved. Disneyland's reconstruction of countries, cultures and magical kingdoms provides a graphic case in point as impossible journeys are presented to the consumer as perfectly natural through the annihilation of temporal and spatial barriers.

Perhaps the most notable recent example of the above is Thames Town, the theme park that isn't a theme park. Thames Town is situated in Songjiang, about 30 kilometres from central Shanghai, China and situated on the Yangtze River. The town was designed to house approximately 10,000 people and cost 5 billion yuan to construct, which as its website states has been compared to a theme park, 'recreating Ye Olde England for homesick expatriates and aspirational, moneyed Chinese'. But this is more than a theme park (see Coonan, 2006). This is the 'real' thing. Thames Town is one of nine planned towns which include German New Town for the car enthusiast, Nordic Town which represents Scandinavian living and Barcelona Town which offers consumers the opportunity to shop along a Chinese

Ramblas (Coonan, 2006). In addition, an Italian town in the suburb of Pujiang is planned to have 100,000 citizens living beside Venetian-style canals. Such developments represent, according to Rojek (1993), a de-differentiation of time and space, a redefinition and relabelling of signs and thus a redeployment of land use for the purpose of recreation.

Branded landscapes

Quite possibly the most important characteristic of the contemporary theme park, as Scott Lukas (2008) has noted, is the transition towards a branded landscape. In other words, theme parks are about more than providing a varied focused diet of amusement, spectacular architecture and the thrill of the ride. They have rather become branded places, intimately bound up with the imagery, ideologies, experiences and myths of the corporate world. Lukas even goes as far as to suggest that theme parks are not simply a source of amusement and thrill, but actually and actively seek to alter society itself. The suggestion here is that brands have evolved with theme parks, notably, for example, in the form of the themed ride. A ride based around Star Wars, for example, will impact upon the consumer's appreciation of the film but also makes him or her potentially receptive to future elaborations of the brand attached to the film; a process akin to 'getting inside a commodity with which they are already familiar' (Lukas, 2008: 185). Lukas goes on to discuss the branding of Harry Potter and in particular 'The Wizardly World of Harry Potter' due to open as part of the Universal Orlando resort in 2010 and which, fascinatingly, has been billed as 'a theme park within a theme park'. Such a park allows the visitor to experience Harry Potter's world in person. This is not about imaging fantasy, but rather about living it:

> All theme parks, even amusement parks that avoid corporatism and theming, emphasize the selling of goods and services that have a larger connection to the world outside the park, but the difference is that the contemporary theme park integrates brands across the park – from rides to shows to gift shops to restaurants – and further naturalizes the patron's roles in consuming the goods and services associated with the theme park … Theme parks have achieved the status of brands but they are much more than this. They are material delivery spaces in which the ideas of the consumer society are instilled in people. (Lukas, 2008: 193–6)

Lukas (2008) discusses the emergence of the lifestyle store including restaurants such as ESPN Zone and Dave & Buster's and retail outlets such as Niketown as an extension of the above process. Crucial here is the way in which such spaces offer the stability of a recognisable and often life-affirming identity in a world which is potentially characterised by the individual's experience of isolation and self-doubt. The themed environment is designed to offer comfort, but also, ironically perhaps, a sense of place. And herein lies a key dilemma for the theme park. Its traditional territory is increasingly being invaded by a broader adoption of the principles of theming throughout our culture to the extent that even so-called 'third spaces' such as Starbucks cafes constitute a new localised form of theming. A particular concern is that the branding associated with theming and theme parks has effectively become naturalised: it is more than a brand but has been vindicated as an essential element of life itself. As far as Lukas (2008: 244) is concerned, we are drawn to theme parks by their recreated facades and by engaging with them: 'We take them, touch them, make them part of us, and we offer something back to them, giving them life'. From this point of view, theme parks offer us more than an escape. They actually provide spaces in which we can symbolically deal with the dilemmas we face on a daily basis: the theme park as a life text, a model for negotiating the world that is about far more than simply maximising the opportunities consumption provides.

What much of the above implies is that theme parks are by their very nature important representations of power in many guises. The role of theme parks in locating nation is particular interesting insofar as it demonstrates the significant power relationships that underpin theming in the urban environment. To this end, the experience of theming in China, a country that almost operates as a test bed for the changes associated with a rapidly developing consumer society, is particularly telling. Ren (2007) looks at the way spatial theming has been appropriated as a powerful means of inscribing and legitimating a new set of social relationships alongside economic reform in China since the late 1970s. Ren goes on to discuss the way in which consumption is used to shape visitors' behaviour in the Chinese Ethnic Culture Park in Beijing. Since 1989, China has experienced a period of theme park fever and these theme parks serve important governmental purposes in the maintenance of everyday life in China (Ren, 2007). Most of all, such parks appear to legitimise neoliberal globalisation and the way in which social relations have in recent decades been reconfigured by the private. The Chinese Ethnic Culture Park includes a group of 16 life-sized villages, each representing a national ethnic group. In this context, consumer facilities such as restaurants and stores are incorporated or hidden as an operational component of the village. The production processes that underpin the villages are camouflaged by the availability of opportunities to consume: 'In this case ... making the backstage invisible to the public does not intend to reduce the impact of imperfect skills or human fallibility, rather, it deliberately separates the sphere of consumption from that of production so that acts of consuming are not seen as productive, or labour intensive' (p. 105). According to Ren (2007), the park offers an enclaved space in which the majority of Han Chinese can maintain their own sense of self whilst consuming the exotic elements of other Chinese ethnic cultures. These cultures are neatly and conveniently packaged for the consumer and the end product is a choreographed vision of a united China driven by an incorporated capitalism. For Ren, the park 'naturalises the visitors' consciousness for consumption', prescribing and organising opportunities to consume so that the visitor is manipulated into spending at appropriate times in appropriate places. From this point of view, the theme park can be described as a landscape of capitalist accumulation, an institution of social engineering: the ethnic costume as commodity. Most importantly, Ren suggests that the company operating the park do so as a de facto government, and visitors to the park thus become subjects of a private authority: citizens who are carefully and perhaps wilfully guided in how to best consume. The sociocultural boundary that the park makes so clear between Han Chinese and the rest is an important element in establishing the air of a proper social order and a necessary one for the social and economic transformation of China.

The above argument attests to theming as an imagineering technology that has significant sociological implications tied up in an ideology of consumption that impacts upon the lives of consumers and their relationship to power way beyond the confines of the immediate spatial context in which it operates. These themed spaces constitute 'dream worlds' in which the good life becomes determined by our relationship with consumption and in which the world becomes a sign to be decoded much more than just a place to be explored (Herwig and Holzherr, 2006). What we are describing here then is very much a symbolic process. Gottdiener (2000) points out that the production of desire in our society depends on symbolic mechanisms to the extent that, in effect, we live in a fully themed society. The exchange of money for goods is no longer the key characteristic of this society – what is more crucial is the way in which the promotion of desire is linked through advertising, and the mass media, to commercial environments including themed spaces where goods can be purchased. In this context, 'Themed environments work not only because they are connected to the universe of commodities and are spaces of consumption but also because they offer consumers a spatial experience that is an attraction by itself, that is they promote the consumption of space. People ... come there to see and be seen' (Gottdiener, 2000: 284). In what follows, I will consider the sociological significance of the ultimate places to see and be seen – Disneyland and Disney World – the most intensely themed spaces and indeed the most visited 'places' in the world (Gottdiener, 2000).

Disney as the ultimate themed space

In considering the spatial and sociological significance of Disney in its myriad forms, it may be useful to start off by considering its architectural manifestations. For Klingmann (2007), Disneyland and Disney World are all about the choreography of scripted experiences which are compounded by the identity of a brand. Disneyland and Disney World are therefore staged events and in this context architecture adopts Disney's cartoon-sensibility in order to create an interactive stage in which visitors become bona fide actors. Disney provides a set that is distorted in order that it feels in perfect proportion to the visitor: through the use of rounded intersections and building edges that make for a more comfortable transition around the site. But the important thing is that the drama of Disney architecture, as opposed to its physical presence, captures the imagination most notably through the activation of images and sensations that are derived from the collective memory. Disney manages to connect with the innermost desires of its customers through a well-constructed narrative and strong visual messages (Klingmann, 2007). As Boyer (1992: 201) suggests, 'Disney expresses the American way of life as a universal sign of progress and consumption is the vehicle upon which progress can be achieved'. Disneyland sparks the visitor's imagination and willingness to buy. Yet it is not the environment that is falsified, for everything in Disneyland is absolutely fantastical, but that fact that

Disneyland is quintessentially a landscape for consumption, not for leisure. The Disney experience is therefore all about putting the subject at the forefront of the planning process as part of a visually persuasive and reassuringly secure consumer experience. The end result of this process is arguably a one-directional form of communication in which consumers inevitably become passive, given the fact that there isn't room in this space for spontaneity and imagination insofar as the spontaneity and imagination come readymade (Klingmann, 2007). By its very nature, this highly programmed world eliminates multiple interpretation and creativity. It is at once the daytime and world of fantasy and of normalcy. As Borrie (1999), quoted by Klingmann (2007), puts it:

> Disney is Hollywood-ized catering to the least offensive denominator. However, the sanitized, romantically familiar is a powerful version that is perhaps more attractive than the original location or event. It is the Disney version that seems more perfect, more possible, and more appropriate. But part of that attractiveness is the loss of the local-based narratives to the commercial, universal whole. (Borrie, 1999: 81)

Disney themes work by immersing the visitor in an alternative world and allow Disney to offer a degree of coherence that they could not otherwise command. This can also be interpreted as a process of McDonaldisation insofar as Disney is highly controlled in the sense that visitors are obliged to follow certain routes between attractions whilst guards are cunningly disguised as 'Disney cast members'. Moreover, as Bryman (1999) points out, visitors to Disney are controlled by a uniquely Disneyfized gaze that promotes a world of progress, often depicted around the white middle-class heterosexual family, and specifically a world in which science and technology can deliver a constant stream of readily available consumer experiences. Given its cultural omnipresence, Disney is also an intensely predictable space in which you know what you will get before you even depart, even if you haven't been there before. But perhaps the key characteristic of theming for Bryman is the fact that the Disney environment softens the commercial nature of the experience for the consumer. The distinction between consumption and fantasy is greatly reduced in a Disney theme park and it is in this sense that theming reaches its logical conclusion.

The manufacture of fantasy is a key of Wasko's (2001) analysis of Disney. For Wasko, the manufacture of fantasy has significant implications for the reinforcement of social values. Much of that fantasy is wrapped up in an almost universal recognition of what the Disney brand represents. Characters such as Mickey Mouse live on in the minds of millions of children and their parents and their parents too. But as Wasko suggests, the universality of Disney is far from natural and is part of a historical process of controlled manufacture. What is concerning about this process is the fact that the theming and the products that Disney promotes are far from innocent, despite the aura of acceptability and safeness that are attached to the Disney brand. The warm family memories of Disney are, in reality, if not in the collective memory, played out through Disney commodities to the extent that 'pleasures and memories have become associated with activities that have lost their connection to their original motivation or their inherent commercial nature' (Wasko, 2001: 223). The Disney world is a conservative, consumer-driven one and it can ultimately be understood as a deeply contradictory organisation whose overcommercialisation is anathema to many of its critics. Disney is about commodifying experiences and memories. In 1998, overall revenues from the Disney theme parks were $6.1 billion and, as suggested, above 50 per cent of that was from entrance fees (Wasko, 2001). Once in the park, further branded consumption opportunities are unavoidable and perhaps the key theme that underpins Disney is that of the family as a unit for consumption.

In his discussion of mega-events in modernity, Maurice Roche (2000) argues that the Disney model of the theme park is innovative in a number of ways – first, in the way in which it implements a form of total environmental control in which everything the consumer does is designed. Second, it provides memorable and most importantly buyable experiences of popular film and TV which in turn provide new media to market the theme parks and vice versa. Third, Disney involves a limited number of key multinationals, such as Coca Cola for example, in delivering the Disney experience so that the site becomes a highly coordinated space for selling and marketing. Disney moved away from the haphazard consumer experience that characterized the first theme parks in favour of a visitor offer in which they have total control over what is offered to the consumer and how. In a sense, this is the very definition of theming: the construction of an apparently varied entertainment landscape that is underpinned by consumerist uniformity. The point here is of course that more and more sectors of society are being infiltrated by the process of Disneyisation (Bryman, 2004). In other words, the principles of the Disney theme parks are increasingly evident elsewhere in society. The effect of Disneyisation, if that's what we want to call it, is to create an urban environment in which theming is becoming the norm; so much so that the brand itself is no longer barely even necessary.

Celebration

The power of the Disney brand is perhaps taken to its logical conclusion in the form of Celebration which itself constitutes the ultimate in Walt Disney's vision of the potential applications of a themed environment: a place in which people could live rather than just visit (Wasko, 2001). Walt Disney's original ambitions in this regard were for the living, breathing, experimental community of EPCOT (the Experimental Prototype Community of Tomorrow), plans for which were shelved after Walt's Disney's death, although EPCOT now plays a non-residential role at Disney World. Located five miles from Disney World, Celebration opened in July 1996 and represents a vivid example of New Urbanism or of urban planning that aims to reassert the traditional values of retro-Main Street USA. According to Klingmann (2007: 77), this idealised (some would say utopic and others dystopic) community demonstrates 'the smooth transition between scripted drama and urban reality'. The physical character of the community is tightly controlled by the Disney corporation, notably in terms of its physical character. To this end, Wasko quotes an article in the *New York Times* which argues that Celebration is run according to a unique model of democracy based on consumerist principles insofar as residents are willing to surrender power over their lives to Disney as long as Disney is responsive to their needs. This is a process of lifestyle branding (Klingmann, 2007) in which a private community masquerades as a public one through the implied family-driven values of the unspoken Disney brand: a brand identity that is in turn manifest socially as a behavioural code. Celebration is brandless in the sense that there is no visible sign of Disney, but as Lukas (2008) points out, this is because Disney is so powerful that it has moved out of the arena of the brand into life itself. In doing so, Disney is effectively naturalised and thus becomes a core ideological dimension of residents' and visitors' everyday lives so that as Bauman (2007: 6) puts it, those residents 'are simultaneously, *promoters of commodities* and *the commodities they promote*' [original emphasis]. Herwig and Holzherr (2006) describe Celebration as 'a town that wants to be a village': a profoundly middle-class and white space (its credentials as a place are debatable), Celebration represents a fleeing from the decay of the city that readily accepts the price to pay that of boredom and control. The validity of Celebration as an 'urban' form is endlessly debated. For some critics, Celebration is no more than a piece of consummate fakery (Huxtable, 1997). Such an analysis reflects how tempting it is to condemn the values that underpin places like Celebration. In practical terms New Urbanist developments offer a lot, as regards their 'walkability' for example and they would certainly be said to engender a considerable degree of community loyalty on the part of their residents. What they achieve in terms of ensuring the diversity of community remains however, highly questionable.

What is perhaps most important about Disney and Celebration is that regardless of how fake or authentic the opportunities to consume they provide may be, as Sharon Zukin (1993) would argue, they can be fundamentally understood as landscapes of power. Disney and Celebration work in this regard insofar as they project a particular idealised image of an harmonious small-time America. Zukin (1993: 222–4) goes as far as to suggest that in doing so Disneyland actually parallels the creation of a mass consumption society in the way in which it projects:

> the collective desires of the powerless into a corporate landscape of power … Just as the real landscape reflected the intensive, unplanned development of the country by subdivision and mass construction, so the imaginary landscape of Disneyland reflected the growth of mass communications built on visual consumption.

In this respect, Disney is a landscape of power which mirrors the creation of a consumption society. Disney grew out of and intensified wider social developments such as expansion of the suburbs and the movement of population to the south-west of the United States. For Zukin, Disney's expertise lies in creating an imaginary landscape based on manipulated memory, the sort of imaginary landscape we can find in many spaces for consumption. And perhaps Disney should take some credit for demonstrating the economic robustness of visual consumption. Zukin acknowledges that in this respect Disney became a model for establishing the economic value of the cultural and thus the cultural value of consumer goods. The end product of this process is a coherent landscape of corporate power: a middle-class nirvana in which social divisions and conflict are designed out and in which 'the guiding corporate hand' gives consumers a sense of control that they perhaps cannot command in other aspects of their lives. In this way, the theme park, as personified by Walt Disney, offers a vision of democracy which concretises that vision in the form of a very particular consumer-determined social future. As a carefully controlled space of consumption then, Disney appears democratic but is deliberately exclusive given that pricing strategies mean the park is accessible to some but not to others. Disney is primarily a space defined for consumers and not everyone is in a position to consume.

Conclusion

The above arguments reflect the concern demonstrated in the work of authors such as Sorkin (1992a) and Davis (1997) that as spaces of high consumption, the boundaries between the theme park and the city are increasingly being eroded. Thus, Davis (1997: 4) raises the concern that urban space is being emptied of memory and history so that 'the potential for meaningful activity in social space, and social space itself' are being redefined. This is particularly demonstrated in the case of Boyer's (1992) discussion of South Street Seaport in New York City. South Street Seaport is a leisure-time zone that offers a combination of shopping and entertainment for the upscale employees of the nearby Wall Street. Previously a derelict space of narrow streets and abandoned piers, South Street Seaport offers a version of a revitalised maritime district similar to those evident at Harbour Place, Baltimore and Quincy Market, Boston. Boyer (1992) describes Seaport as an 'imaginary historical museum'. It skilfully surrounds the visitor (or the spectator) with an artificially constructed historical ambience:

> The aim is theatrical: to represent the certain visual images of the city, to create perspectival views shown through imaginary prosceniums in order to conjure up emotionally satisfying images of bygone times. Architecture and the theatre use similar means

to design places of pleasure and spectacle, manipulating scenery, ornament, and dream worlds, to underscore the sentiment of their play. (Boyer, 1992: 184)

Boyer describes a world of illusion and entertainment; a world of spectacle in which an image of the city is constructed within the city itself, so that the real city disappears from view in favour of a themed version of itself. The concern here is that such spaces deliberately suspend critical judgement. In this sense, the theme park has moved beyond the confines of the park gates. Our cities are full of themed spaces, spaces for consumption often designed merely to recycle historical identities; thus, the reoccurring trend that has seen the regeneration of abandoned industrial wastelands or cultural hotspots for the consumption of the tourist. But this process is not a neutral one and often involves an obscuring of actual history with simulated tradition (Boyer, 1992). This arguably constitutes a stylised appropriation of history in the form of an historic tableau whose rasion d'être is to arrest a sense of non-place:

These tableaux separate pleasure from necessity, escape from reality. They widen the gap between the city on display and the city beyond our view. And in doing so they sever any connection they might have had to the art of building real cities, for after all, these city tableaux only claim to be special places for fun and entertainment, areas of the city to explore during periods of play, which promise not to burden the spectator with the seriousness of reality. (Boyer, 1992: 192)

Boyer's criticism is that through the above the city is reduced to a map of tourist attractions. In South Street Seaport's case, this is demonstrated by the opening of what is effectively an open-air maritime museum alongside the retail opportunities this implies. South Street Seaport is therefore primarily a marketplace that promotes a sense of desire, desire that can (and yet cannot) be fulfilled through the act of consumption. But such opportunities represent an effort to construct a reimagined historical unity that never existed in the first place. And at the heart of the process is the opportunity to consume:

These illusionary environments of simulation provide the decor for our acts of consumption. In contemporary times, commodities are no longer marketed for their utility and efficiency alone, but as a system of values that gives them added meaning. The further away the commodity seems from functional, the useful, and the necessary, the more appealing it appears. (Boyer, 1992: 200)

For Boyer then, this process is all about constructing an environment for consumption that implicates the consumer in a whole series of consumer acts. Such simulated environments privilege consumption by the way in which the seductive power of the commodity becomes unquestionable. Consumption is indeed the only legitimate act: the act of a well-meaning and well-acting citizen. What Boyer is talking about here is the transformation of public experience into the private realm of consumption. The trip to visit a particular area of a city is likely to be just as pleasurable and perhaps more so than it was in the past, but that pleasure is increasingly likely to be framed by the promises fulfilled and otherwise by the opportunity to purchase and consume.

I want to illustrate the above argument further with a brief discussion of two more illustrations of the relationship between theming and history. Of course, it is not the case that all historical tableaux will demonstrate all the characteristics that Boyer describes – regardless of the degree to which they are homogenised, cities are simply too complex for this to be the case. However, the stylised appropriation of history is a common characteristic of a service-driven economy. In this context, in his book *The Anxious City*, Richard Williams (2004) discusses the way in which the city has increasingly been constructed in the form of a visual tableaux to be touristically consumed. As such, Williams argues that the regeneration of the Albert Dock represents an effort to turn what was once an obscure industrial building into a theatrical spectacle for consumption by tourists. Williams considers the role of the Tate Liverpool, part of the national 'chain' of art galleries, which was developed as part of a broader rationale which determined that in order to be fully 'civilised', the people of the north required the benefits of modern art on a regular, easily accessible basis. In opening up his analysis to a broader concern about the state of regeneration in England, Williams describes the English city as existing in a curious state: it appears to be burgeoning and yet it exists in a culture that largely wishes to repress it. The city is left in this perennial state of anxiety as a result. As far as the Albert Dock is concerned, what emerges is nothing more than a symbolic solution to the problems of urban decline. A solution only insofar as it purports to introduce a revitalised landscape, actual in no sense insofar as it has no genuine effect on the problems of a rundown inner city, other than perhaps to reiterate the fact that those excluded simply do not belong there. As such, for Williams, cities are divided along class lines and the urban revolution is a revolution of 'bourgeois taste'. On the surface, the Albert Dock presents to the world a vision of café culture and neoclassical architecture, when in truth it is more easily compared to a less than pristine shopping mall (Williams, 2004).

The addition of Liverpool One, one of the biggest city centre shopping developments in Europe, and the Albert Dock's next-door neighbour, reinforces a sense of consumerist plenty amidst a world of social injustice. Williams describes this as a process of the picturesque: a response to an urban problem through the aestheticisation of that problem. The key questions for him are centred on whether the regenerated city is simply what it appears to be on the surface, a space to be gazed upon by a privileged audience. Perhaps such spaces represent as much a concession of defeat; a recognition that in some senses the barriers inherent in a post-industrial landscape are insurmountable (Williams, 2004). An alternative way of putting all this is that although the Albert Dock represents an effort to regenerate the city, it does so rhetorically. It screams regeneration from the rooftops, but it does not constitute regeneration of place insofar as it symbolically pulls Liverpool up by the boot straps – its effect on the reality of life in that city is marginal.

Another interesting example of urban space that has apparently been aestheticised in a similar way and which in turn can be said to represent a kind of betrayal of place is Barcelona's Bario Chino which is discussed in some detail by Miles and Miles (2004). Miles and Miles consider the development of Barcelona post-1992 Olympics and in discussing the issue of authenticity they argue that the city of Barcelona has deliberately played on its past architectures, and in the process has constructed a vision of a cultural rawness in which tourists can rub shoulders with a diversity of ethnic and cultural groups. Basically, Barcelona rejected the model of mass market tourism in the wake of the Olympics and sought to niche market itself as a cultural destination (see Chapter 7) to the more discerning consumer seeking out 'the real' Barcelona. What emerged in Barcelona was therefore a tourist infrastructure built upon the foundations of local cultural provision. But such provision was in a sense subverted insofar as consumption not production became the priority. The lack of investment in local cultural production and the rising cost of living in the area resulted, perhaps inevitably, in a process of gentrification. As part of this process, the old red light district in Barcelona's Bario Chino was transformed into a new cultural quarter, incorporating the flagship cultural institution, the MACBA. As Miles and Miles (2004) point out, although planning controls required residents to be offered alternative accommodation nearby, not all of them could afford to take up such an offer due to the high service charges involved. Miles and Miles therefore claim that the area has taken on a homogenised and sanitised feel. The area has indeed been aestheticized, with shops catering for local needs having been replaced by art galleries, designer bars, boutiques and hairdressers, arguably resulting in an erosion of the old street life:

> The difficulty, for visitors, is that el Raval seems to be becoming a finished space, its streets set out like the backdrop of a stage for the new cultural and professional elite's performance of their public lives. The evident design of the spaces, their aestheticisation, rather than gradual accumulation of an everyday appearance through everyday occupation and use, renders the stroller's experience ... passive, as if consuming the place but not interacting with it. (Miles and Miles, 2004: 83)

The concern here is that local cultures are being subsumed into a version (an arguably artificial one at that) of high culture. Thus, Miles and Miles (2004) are concerned not with the erosion of cultures in such situations but with the fact that such cultures are subsumed into high culture. What was previously a creative space is effectively standardized in the name of the common good so that the image of the niche being marketed takes precedence over the content of that niche. In other words, consumption drowns out what it is that makes a place special in the first place.

The above discussion should not encourage us to pigeon-hole themed space or indeed theme parks in a particular way. Indeed, any understanding of the way in which meanings are attached to such spaces remains unclear. As I mentioned earlier, it would be very easy to condemn themed spaces as an aberration of the contemporary urban landscape. It is however more worthwhile to consider such spaces as a product of an ideological process in which public space has been transformed.

The public space we associate with themed spaces are typically private in nature and thus constitute a radical reassessment of the individual's relationship to the public sphere. The public sphere is at one and the same time both compromised and energised, the latter being the product of a world in which consumers actively crave the experiences that such a sphere can offer (in contrast to the declining public spaces of the past). What is more interesting then, than a sentimental romanticisation of a past that barely exists, is a recognition that these spaces are hugely popular and that the freedoms consumption offers, authentic or otherwise, are readily taken up regardless of their limitations. The theme park demonstrates the ideological power of a consumer society – what it does not explain in and of itself is why such spaces of consumption are capable of being deplored and yet embraced at one and the same time.

9

CONCLUSION: SPACES *FOR* CONSUMPTION; PLACES *OF* EXPERIENCE

The city is a unit for the effective maximisation of consumption. It constitutes the physical manifestation of an ideology, but of an ideology that is as much relished as it is imposed. In *Spaces for Consumption,* I have critically considered the way in which the recent evolution of cities has been determined, either implicitly or explicitly, by the need or at least the perceived need to reinvent the city as a service-driven entity in which image and perception takes precedence over familiarity and reality. The assertion underlying this book is that the impact of consumption on our experience of cities and of citizenship more broadly is such that our experience of everyday life and of public life in particular is profoundly altered. At least on the surface, spaces for consumption offer the consumer opportunities to satisfy wants and desires. In a world in which basic necessities are more readily satisfied than they were in the past and in which consumption generally exceeds physiological need, the role of consumption as a means of self-actualisation becomes increasingly crucial, as does the city as an arena within which that self-actualisation can be achieved (see Mullins et al., 1999). The irony here however is that the seductive vision of the city that is promoted as a means of reasserting the legitimacy of the post-industrial city is fundamentally incompatible with that city's lived reality. The idealised consumer which a city purports to attract is very different to the consumer of limited resources who accounts for a large proportion of the city's 'indigenous' population. Moreover, what consumption offers and what it conceals are never one and the same thing insofar as Christopherson (1994: 409) suggests that, 'Beneath the surface, the signal qualities of the contemporary urban landscape are not playfulness but control, not spontaneity but manipulation, not interaction but separation'. The impact of consumption on how we relate to the city is of course even more complex than the above quotation suggests. The impact of consumption is profoundly ideological and the city operates as a front stage for an ideology that promotes the constant reproduction of desire. As Sklair (2002: 62) suggests:

> The culture-ideology project of global capitalism is to persuade people to consume not simply to satisfy their biological and other modest needs but in response to artificially created desires in order to perpetuate the accumulation of capital for private profit, in other words, to ensure that the capitalist global system goes on forever.

A key concern here is that the specificities of place are increasingly undermined in a context in which consumption is no longer constrained by time and space. As Sack (1988) suggests, the paradoxes of the consumption experience are the product of a process in which a consumer can enter any context or space to consume, regardless of the public objective space in which they are located. The uniqueness of place is undermined in a situation in which the market obliges places to advertise themselves as having generic qualities so that the post-industrial obligation to offer the city up as a place to be consumed means cities will inevitably lose a degree of their own uniqueness (Sack, 1988). Meanwhile, the image of the city has become an essential element of urban currency, almost as if utopian ideals of an urban future have been rejected once and for all. As Buck-Morris (1995) puts it:

> ... utopian fantasy is quarantined, contained within the boundaries of theme parks and tourist preserves, like some ecologically threatened but nonetheless dangerous zoo animal. When it is allowed expression at all, it takes the look of children's toys – even in the case of sophisticated objects – as if to prove that

>   utopias of social space can no longer be taken seriously; they
>   are commercial ventures, nothing more. (p. 26)

From this point of view, consumption can in effect be recognised as
the stalking horse of contemporary capitalism: it provides the lived
manifestation, the experiential context for, and hence the ideological justification for, a particular way of economic thinking which
can in turn have dire social consequences in terms of promoting
public apathy and urban inequality (see also Mullins et al., 1999).
Crucially, however, I do not mean to imply that the consumer is an
entirely powerless and passive player in this process but rather that
the attractions and appeal of consumerism 'as a way of life' are so
enticing and naturalised that the consumer is inevitably complicit in
a process in which the perception of the city as a space for consumption becomes legitimised. Local governments and councils are compelled to reinvent their cities as commercial entities, and themselves
as a key player in the marketisation of the city alongside a whole
suite of entrepreneurial and public-private relationships. There is no
choice but to compete, but this *choicelessness* creates a city driven by
marketing needs rather than one driven by the needs of its residents.
This in turn creates a conflict of interest between the city as a place
experienced by its residents and the city as a commodity as experienced by the *notional* visitor (Graham and Aurigi, 1997).

Spaces for Consumption has sought to understand a process in
which the apparent disintegration of cities and their redefinition
through consumption has occurred alongside the disintegration of
industry. The city is now a place of rapid and calculated exchange in
which the homogeneity of production and industrial work has been
replaced by an altogether different kind of homogeneity in which
'readymade design solutions' are administrative as well as aesthetic
and in which the tendency is to construct large, highly manageable
commercial and consumption environments (Christopherson, 1994).
Cities act primarily as containers of goods, services and images; as,
in effect, a collection of non-places determined by the mass consumption of goods (Paolucci, 2001). Thus, 'in the global village of
goods, all metropolitan areas share identical dynamics for this sort of
behaviour' (p. 651), creating a situation in which the place where you
consume goods almost becomes incidental compared to the actual
experience of the product or service itself. But a consumer-driven city
is not a city that can be easily understood and certainly should not be

condemned on purely political grounds. The consuming experience is too paradoxical and contradictory for a straightforward political critique to be sufficient (Sack, 1988).

By its very nature, this book constitutes a critique of the consumer society. It has sought to understand the arguably unbreakable nature of the relationship between consumption and the city. For many, it will seem that the thread underpinning this book is one that lacks hope and in which there is very little room for individual agency. Some authors have argued that consumers actively engage with spaces for consumption, opening such spaces up as they do so for an alternative reading in which the ideological nature of their experience is usurped. A broader and yet more sophisticated analysis might prefer to focus on the consumption of the carnivalesque, a world of transgressive consumption where pleasurable excess is pursued as a means of dealing with the oppressive rationality that characterises the society in which we live (Presdee, 2000). From another point of view, consumption is partly irrational; it offers a form of sociality, or even as Shields (1992) suggests, a form of solidarity in which spaces for consumption become tribal in nature. Some authors have gone as far as to suggest that shopping malls verge on being re-enchanted 'utopian islands' where consumers can create their own fantastical worlds:

> ... we can foresee the shopping malls of the future as overcolored and funny 'urban islands' in urban archipelagos, providing the consumer with safe, autonomous (power and air plants, phone networks, etc.) and esthetic substitutes for the everyday life conditions. These 'islands' would be oriented to a prophylactic society of hedonic and spiritual value as well as leisure and friendliness, full of simulacra, where the idea of fear and death will be absent. (Badot and Filser, 2007)

How autonomous can the consumer actually be in the above context? In their discussion of spectacular themed environments, Kozinets et al. (2004) suggest that consumption is negotiated dialectically. From this point of view, consumers are capable of resistance but only to a limited degree. They may not be dominated and to an extent tactics may come into play but the omnipresence of spaces for consumption in our physical environment creates a situation in which the desires of the consumer are privileged so that spaces for consumption captivate the audience through their desire to consume. As Kozinets et al. (2004: 671) put it, 'Refracted through consumer fantasy, consumer agency in an image-driven culture may have become indistinct. It may be indistinct, however, not because consumers are deceived or confined but because they (at least some of them) are inspired and satisfied' (p. 671). It is this sense of satisfaction, however partial in nature, that permeates the consumer's experience of the city. Consumers are not deceived but they are, contrary to Kozinets et al.'s (2004) point above, confined at least in the sense that consumption has a disproportionate influence on how consumers relate to the cities in which they live. Moreover, by the very nature of the consumer society, consumers are effectively excluded from the very existence to which they aspire. In a sense then, all consumers are 'flawed' (Bauman, 1998). Many of us are excluded from the apparent joys of consumerism due to the fairly fundamental problem of a lack of sufficient resources. And yet even those who are capable of partaking fully in a consumer lifestyle never actually reach the point of utter fulfilment. Satisfaction always lies tantalisingly out of reach. Consumption is socially divisive, but that division is ultimately as much a result of the opportunities and choices it provides as those that it cuts off.

The force of consumption upon the city has had a profound impact on urban experience and the nature of such an impact is very much dependent upon the character of specific cities, as authors such as Hayward (2004) have argued. But the suggestion in Hayward's work and here is that the market plays such a fundamental role in the construction of the city and in how consumers engage with the city that it effectively constitutes a physical and emotional manifestation of consumerism as an ideology. This realisation has a profound implication for how we perceive of the city and our interaction with it, as Hayward (2004) notes. The challenge here is how best to understand the individual's relationship with spaces for consumption and thus how to engage with the public realm without descending into a blanket condemnation of the culture that created it.

Consumption and the public realm

The role of spaces for consumption in the reinvention of the public realm are a cause for considerable concern, as I have argued throughout this book. Authors such as Graham and Aurigi (1994) have argued that the public realm has long been in a state of crisis, caught between the privatising and commodifying tendencies of contemporary capitalism, which in turn reinforce notions of a socially segmented and divided city. This issue is also raised in the work of Mitchell (1995: 121) who asks whether or not we have, '… created a society that expects and desires only private interactions, private communications, and private politics that reserve public spaces solely for commodified recreation and spectacle'. The tightly controlled nature of the new public space legislates against uncontrolled social interaction which itself is deemed a threat to exchange value, hence the exclusion of the homeless and the political activist (Mitchell, 1995). This, in turn, creates a vision, an illusion perhaps, of a deeply homogenised public of flawless consumers, an environment in which all is well and in which the reality that the public realm has itself been reduced to a commodity is hidden (Crilley, 1993a; Mitchell, 1995).

The above reflects a broader debate regarding the relationship between the public sphere and public space. One side of the argument suggests that the private has become so exalted that the public has virtually ceased to exist (Boyer, 1993), reflecting Habermas' (1989) concern that the public sphere is limited by the rise of private interests which challenge the power of the state to represent the purposes and interests of the public and Sennett's (1976) contention that the triumph of modern individualism has seen a loss of confidence in what constitutes 'the public'. In this situation, public space effectively becomes emptied of meaning so that the freedoms it offers are only abstract in nature. For Sennett (1977), the urban citizen's pursuit of personal awareness and feeling is a defence against the experience of social relations (see Goheen, 1998) so that any notion of a public personality becomes nothing more than a fantasy:

> To the extent, in sum, that a society mobilizes narcissism, it gives rein to a principle of expression totally contrary to the expressive principle of play. In such a society it is only natural that artifice and convention will seem suspect. The logic of such a society will be the destruction of these tools of culture. It will do so in the name of removing barriers between people, of bringing them closer together, but it will succeed only in transposing the structures of domination in the society into psychological terms. (Sennett, 1977: 336)

The privatisation of the public realm is both symbolic of broader processes of social and economic change and indicative of the complicit nature of the consumer's relationship with a world that limits choice whilst simultaneously claiming to extend it. Meanwhile, as Punter (1990) has argued, privatisation has had a 'pernicious' effect upon the public realm in our cities. The erosion of local government and the increased influence of private property and an onus on short-term profits and long-term returns has created a situation in which 'British cities have become impoverished aesthetically, socially, and culturally and are increasingly distinguished from their European counterparts by their design mediocrity, deadness and public squalor' (p. 9). For Punter, this process is the product of post-war modernist planning and segregation, pedestrianisation and of course the supremacy of the car. But perhaps, in Britain at the end of the twentieth century at least, the real damage was done by the dominance of right-wing politics as manifested in the Conservative government's introduction of Enterprise Zones and a laissez-faire planning regime that served to reinforce, irreparably perhaps, the privatisation of the public realm (Punter, 1990). Such processes in turn reinforced the social logic of capitalism so that the language of markets and politics arguably never quite cohered beyond their rhetorical intent (Couldry, 2004).

Governments have of course latched upon consumption as a liberatory arena. Consumption has been hijacked by politicians of various creeds, parties and ideologies so that consumer freedom has surfaced as a proxy for personal freedom. The powerful ideological appeal of consumption is perhaps best illustrated, as I mentioned in Chapter 7, by social change in China where the atrocities of Tiananmen Square left the Chinese Communist Party in a position where in order to protect their political orthodoxy, they had to offer the people of China a degree of genuine change. They thus entered into a social contract in which the freedoms of consumption were offered in return for the safeguarding of political control on their part. The missing part of the jigsaw is political freedom but the freedoms of consumption appear so seductive to the individual that the desire for deeper human freedoms could almost be put to one side in the name of self-actualisation. At a less dramatic level, political culture in Great Britain has seen a privileging of consumption as a democratic value structure. The effects of leaving so many decisions to the market have come home to roost with the global recession of recent years. This is perhaps no better demonstrated than by the decline of our now battered city centres, characterised by bordered-up shop fronts that provide visible testament to the fact that, regardless of the rhetoric, many less than salubrious cities are simply unable to compete on the global stage. Meanwhile, the flawed logic that underpins the political ideology of consumerism is also evidenced by the idea that league tables offer a democratic means of consumers asserting their own choice, when of course their ability to choose is primarily determined by their access to both economic and cultural capital (Bourdieu, 1979; Miles, 1998). But such processes reflect what Baldock (2003) has described as the 'declining publicness' of public services in which the very essence of what it means to be a member of the public is diluted. The moral primacy given to personal wealth creation has, argues Punter, created a situation in which government has increasingly disinvested in all things public. As Clarke (2004) suggests, neo-liberalism is all about challenging conceptions of private interests by the introduction of private ones through the market. The consequence of this has been an apparent 'disintegration of the public as a collective identity' (Clarke, 2004: 31).

One way of looking at all this is to suggest that the complexities of capitalism allow it to reinvent citizenship through consumption so that consumption is about making active choices rather than being a passive recipient. Thus, for Clarke (2004), the consumer is an economic invention that visualises the world in terms of its responsiveness and adaptability. But the louder proclamations of choice become, the less convincing they are in practice. The logic of capital and thus of consumer choice is increasingly pernicious to the extent that, as Christopherson (1994) puts it, the consumer-citizen is defined by his or her ability to select from a range of goods: to make private choices, apparently without public consequence. In this context, the rights of the individual consumer (and hence his or her experience of the city) is apparently privileged over that of the common good. According to this model, the city must be constructed as a space of exploration for the idealised consumer so that while consumption offers some semblance of common interest, it does so in such a way as to reject claims for a broader social justice (Christopherson, 1994).

The 'individualised' city

If we accept the notion that the public is in a sense in the process of disintegrating, what then of the individual? In Chapter 2, I discussed the impact of individualisation, an apparent increase in social disconnectedness and its relationship to dimensions of the consuming experience. To take this one step further at this stage I would like to consider how relationships to communal forms have had to be re-evaluated in light of the impact of consumption upon our lives. This is an issue addressed in particular depth by Hopper (2003) who argues that the key processes of late modernity are effectively undermining existing social structures in profound ways and in such a way as to encourage greater individualism as a result. For Hopper, a number of characteristics of the consumer society might be said to undermine a sense of civic community. Spaces for consumption, from this point of view, offer limited opportunity for meaningful social intercourse, whilst the sheer act of sustaining levels of consumption means that consumers are actually obliged to spend more and more time in the workplace in order to pay for the goods and services they covert. In this context, Hopper argues that our behaviour becomes increasingly calculating in a market-driven environment where every decision is make or break. An aspirational and thus unequal consumer society is likely to be a divisive society for it is designed to be as such. We are encouraged to believe that fulfilment is an entirely personal project: 'Compared to the citizen, the consumer has no duties and obligations other than to themselves' (Hopper, 2003: 69). Such processes are, according to Hopper, intensified by broader processes associated with transitions in the post-Fordist urban environment that have meant life in the city can often be an alienating and apparently meaningless experience.

The suggestion here then and one that is also ruminated upon by Rifkin (2000) is that there is a profound danger that if the commercial sphere begins to devour the cultural sphere, as I discussed earlier in Chapter 4, then the very social foundations that made commercial relations possible are in danger of being destroyed. In other words, we risk depleting our own culture through the hands of commerce. What Rifkin (2000: 45) calls the commodification of play has been made possible by the deregulation of government functions: 'The great issue at hand, in the coming years, is whether civilization can survive with a greatly reduced government and cultural sphere, and where only the commercial sphere is left as the primary mediator of human life'. Given there is such a potentially significant price to be paid for a market-driven public realm, how do we best deal with such a situation?

Spaces for consumption; places of the future?

Spaces for consumption are worthy of particular attention insofar as they traverse notions of public space and the public sphere and as such offer a new kind of public realm, but one over which the public appear to have less control. The immediate appeal of spaces for consumption lies in the experience they offer the consumer and specifically in the way they stimulate the senses (Mullins et al., 1999). Spaces for consumption constitute what Mullins et al. (1999) have described as a 'third space' other than that of home and work that brings people together for sociability and other forms of social contact. In this context, Punter (1990) argues that retail, office, industry/warehouse and residential constitute the key sectors in which the impact of privatisation has been profoundly felt. The broader impact of a market mentality and the increasingly speculative nature of the city creates a situation in which for developers, elected officials, financial institutions and architectural designers, the only possible response seems to be to merge public and private markets (Zukin, 1993). As such, 'previously bounded institutions', or what I have chosen to refer to as spaces for consumption including hotels, department stores and museums, have morphed into disorienting liminal spaces in which consumption of all kinds can take place (Zukin, 1993). Thus, in considering the power of malls in the late twentieth-century urban landscape, Punter (1990: 10) argues that:

> These new malls are distinguishable by their sheer size, by their almost complete introversion in their minimal external elevations, and in the way in which they turn their back on their contexts, by their almost total exclusion of opportunities for non-consumption and by their resort to complete internal architectural fantasy.

In this way, the mall operates like a city in its own right, a city in which the dreams of consumption are purported to be all, which whilst retaining the ostensible characteristics of city life, simultaneously eliminates the possibility of public expressions and social cohesion (Backes, 1997). One way of understanding the shopping mall then is as a space that fills the gap between the home and public space, so there is, in effect, no need to comprehend of such space as we used to know it. As Backes (1997: 12) puts it, 'The mall, a beautifully imagined and uninhabitable city, satisfies those conflicting desires to build cities and escape them'. In effect then, the mall operates as an enabling space, exuding theatrical excitement and the promise of a consumer-life fulfilled. But the 'liminal' escapism of spaces for consumption can only go so far. Spaces for consumption offer a partial form of belonging insofar as to be a citizen of contemporary society, you need first and foremost to be a consumer. As such, spaces are powerful, but they appear to offer very little beyond this economic imperative in the way of social purpose. Hopper goes on to consider the work of Christopherson (1994) who points out that a commodified city inevitably undermines the public realm. Public sites such as parks, schools and museums are now commonly privatised and as such the city is subjected to an increasingly non-democratic mode of governance. The model of the city that emerges is implicitly distrustful of the street as a public arena. So much so that spaces for consumption are usually divorced from or even provide escapes from the urban environment that surrounds them. The priority here is to occupy the consumer within the arena defined by the walls of the space for consumption concerned.

Flusty (2001) who is particularly concerned with public space in Los Angeles describes the above as 'interdictory space' which he suggests is all about those in control of space excluding not crime, but the avoidance of unsettling social encounters with difference. The product is a city within a city within which excitement is officially sanctioned, but in a riskless environment. According to this argument, the homogenisation of cities is less about the construction of predictable environments and more about an effort to sweep away alternative ways of being in the city (Sorkin, 1992b). The individual therefore primarily identifies with the city through his or her role as consumer. Consumption defines the urban landscape but it also defines the individuals' relationship to that landscape so that he or she can do little more than partake in the escape that it promotes. For Punter, this creates an extraordinarily limited public realm. The building of public, 'mixed-use' spaces of consumption is often at the expense of declining city centres nearby. But most telling of all perhaps is Punter's (1990) quotation of Supreme Court Justice Thurgood Marshall as far back as 1972: 'As governments rely on private enterprise, public property decreases in favour of privately owned property, it becomes harder and harder for citizens to communicate with other citizens. Only the wealthy may find effective communication possible'.

The problem then for many commentators is that the shopping experience has for many people *become* the urban experience (Christopherson, 1994). In a consumer society, public space is increasingly tightly controlled and highly policed. Under such conditions, public space is increasingly subject to private rules of access and as such symbolises the partial nature of the public sphere and the way in which the nominally representative state on the one hand and civil society and the market on the other are differentiated (Low and Smith, 2005). Public space effectively constitutes the spatialisation of the public sphere. It is in this sense that the role of spaces for consumption is so important to how we as citizens relate to the consumer society. As Low and Smith (2005: 15) put it:

> The advent of neoliberalism clearly threatens a return to the exclusionary neoliberalism of the eighteenth-century template, but with the technology of the twenty-first century. It masquerades under the same pretension of universal democratic rights fused with the particular interests of an assertive and nationally rooted yet fundamentally transnational capitalist class ... The control of public space is a central strategy of that neoliberalism.

For Christopherson (1994), the actual practice of citizenship is gradually being reduced to what it means to be a consumer. This emulation of the consumer's world creates a situation in which political interests are fragmented into narrower and narrower communities, thereby undermining the prospect of any kind of a coherent 'social rationality'. The consumer feels like a citizen of public life, but that life is so highly regulated by the corporations of multinational capitalism that the meanings associated with such a citizenship are arguably barely within his or her control.

One way of understanding the impact of consumption on the city may therefore be as a process that undermines the legibility of place. As Boltanski and Chiapello (2005) argue, contemporary capitalism promotes a degree of fragility. As far as the physical layout of the city is concerned, the irony here is that the increasingly efficient, functional and convenient nature of the 'super-functional' city as designed through consumption results in a loss of the very chance encounters and unplanned authenticity that makes our experience of the city what it is (Worthington, 2006). The city of consumption is a city that purports to be able to react to the unstoppable demand on the part of consumers for new experiences by constantly revising their formula so that cities are kept as fresh as possible. The consumer may not be as predictable as such an approach suggests. Thus, Hajer and Reijndorp (2001) argue that consumers of the city have actually developed very sophisticated strategies for using the city of consumption for their own ends, so that, for example, they meet the people they want to meet and avoid the ones they do not. Thus, the city becomes an 'archipelago of enclaves' in which individuals are 'ambivalent towards the homogeneity and predictability of the selection of places from which they can compose their city. After all, they are seeking adventures and experiences that are not consciously pre-programmed' (Hajer and Reijndorp, 2001: 60).

Hajer and Reijndorp argue that urban spaces are nonetheless pre-programmed for certain kinds of behaviour and in doing so they allow no opportunity for the very diversity to which cities, rhetorically at least, aspire. In effect then, public space has been parochialised and stage-managed so that spaces for consumption are merely occupied rather than activated in any animated fashion. The consumer has a degree of freedom, but the nature of that freedom is decided for him or her. What I call spaces for consumption and what Hajer and Reijndorp describe as 'built collective spaces' operate in such a way as to bear no relation to the public realm beyond that defined beyond their four walls. The city of consumption is thus said to be characterised by frictionless public space so that space becomes entirely functional, not creative, and thereby constitutes a serious threat to the public domain. Goss (1993) thus argues that the shopping mall contrives to be a public, civic space even though it is run for profit, whilst it deliberately obscures its own rootedness in capitalism. As the archetypal space for consumption, the shopping mall is inherently paradoxical, a fantastic place that offers so much and yet fulfils so little. The shopping mall therefore operates as the archetypal space of consumption; a space which is highly scientifically controlled and which pretends to be the imaginative and magical product of its inhabitants.

> Ultimately, however, we must realize that the nostalgia we experience for authenticity, commerce, and carnival lies precisely in the loss of our ability to collectively create meaning by occupying and using social spaces for ourselves. While developers may

design the retail built environment in order to satisfy this nostalgia, our real desire ... is for community and space free from instrumental calculus of design. (Goss, 1993: 43)

The paradoxical nature of spaces of consumption appeal to us not purely in our role as consumers, but they also fulfil some kind of emotional appeal. Although they may not provide us with the sense of communal belonging to which we aspire, the sense that these spaces are doing so, even in a partial fashion, is perhaps enough in itself. Another way of understanding these processes is through the lens of Ritzer's (2005) notion of disenchantment and his argument that we have created new cathedrals of consumption to which we make pilgrimages in order to practise our religion. Typically, such spaces for consumption offer a sense of expanse so that the consumer feels he or she is having a different kind of experience to the norm, whilst transcending the limitations of time and space by, for example, dining at a fast food restaurant. A key point here is that the distinctions between the more explicit spaces for consumption and many formerly commercial settings such as the parks, schools and museums mentioned above are becoming increasingly blurred. Moreover, these spaces encourage a situation in which consumers engage less with each other and more with the space itself. This is what I call 'complicit communality', a process which implies a connection with the public realm and yet establishes that connection through individual engagement so that the communal experience is with the ideology of consumption as opposed to with any kind of a discernible complicit. The priority here, particularly during periods of recession, is to stimulate the act of consumption. The social implications of that act are worth, from this point of view, less than an afterthought. Spaces for consumption promote a particular way of being in which consumption pervades our consciousness. Spaces for consumption constitute a further means of reinforcing this process so that 'What sets the new means of consumption apart is that they not only help to create this way of thinking, but they provide the outlets where it can be translated into action, resulting in the purchase of the desired goods and services' (Ritzer, 2004: 188).

In considering the apparent demise of the consuming city, Hopper (2003) advocates the promotion of a more public-spirited culture as a means of invigorating local communities. But such an approach may underestimate the emotional appeal of consumerism as a way of life (Miles, 1998). It is doubtful whether a more public-spirited culture can have any kind of a genuine impact in a society that is so deeply indebted to the market. Other commentators have sought to advocate a more positive notion of citizenship in which cities can take on a far more proactive and less reactive role than is currently the case. As Di Ciccio (2007: 14) rather gloomily suggests:

> The situation is drastic, and the truth startlingly rude. Cities are built by the market, and we stand around with notepads or sullen faces remarking on what could have been done better or what might have been done worse. But the damage has already been done. Cities are travesties of construction, and all we can hope to do is to acquire a civic aesthetic that will resurrect us amongst the tombstones of construction and make the landscape livable by the light of citizenship. If we're lucky, we might even tear things down before we are completely harvested by the scythe of wealth generation.

Di Ciccio contends that the civic heart used to flirt with the economic interest but that more recently this has not been the case. Hence the need for a 'city aesthetic' where the city must be re-aligned to the dreams of citizens and where the building is measured in compliance with, or by transgression of, the civic dream' (Di Ciccio, 2007: 16). For Di Ciccio, the current problem is the fact that the public and the private sphere are oppositional. We seek the protection that our private lives offer us, despite the largely unfulfilled desire to be fulfilled by public encounters so that 'The public sphere is scripted by cynicism in an era of breached trust, in a landscape of discredited institutions, until there is finally a dogged surrender to the global zeitgeist of self-interest' (Di Cicco, 2007: 41). From this point of view, a city must believe in its own uniqueness so 'the artist and the citizen become one, an ethos is created, and art becomes the signature of the ethos … A city's greatness is manifest in a people confident in their ability to take risks, to encounter, share with each other, speak with each other, in the casual grace of citizens who are not self-conscious of norms and predictability' (Di Cicco, 2007: 20–1).

One of the key problems here, as Di Cicco notes, and one that is touched upon throughout this book, is the notion that money predicates vision and the way in which the thirst for competitiveness creates a situation in which the character of that city is undermined. As such, a new mindset is required in which we can look beyond notions of sustainability to see the city as an entity going about the business of human happiness. The city is more than just a functional space, but a space in which human happiness can potentially be fulfilled as Peñalosa (2007: 318) also suggests. The onus should therefore be on the recognition that a successful city is founded upon the fervour and human drama of its citizenship, an environment in which mutual reliance can flourish and one which embraces failure as much as it does success. Whether or not the market is sufficiently tolerant of failure is of course another question altogether.

For Sharon Zukin (1993), the way forward lies in the promotion of 'public value' so there is a concern for a minimum balance to be made in the landscape between natural and social forces in the landscape. According to this approach, the development of the city is controlled democratically, in the sense that the public value responds to market forces and reflects the culture of place. The emphasis here then is on the culturally bounded nature of the urban landscape. According to Zukin, it is absolutely essential to remember that markets are socially constructed. Those responsible for promoting our cities may easily forget the fact that cities are more than just economic entities. As such, conscious actors can play a role in ameliorating the effects of the market. Zukin argues that notions of citizenship have been superseded by that of the consumer (and hence of ownership) and that society can only move forward if it invests in its citizens and in a world in which the citizen has a genuine say in the direction in which market culture is going, a world in which the market is a means to an end rather than an end in itself. In her more recent work, Zukin (1995) has prioritised the way in which the public define for themselves the boundaries between the public and the private. In other words, for Zukin, it is all too easy to over-simplify definitions of the public and the private which are actually the product of contested mediation (see Goheen, 1998).

Given the above concerns and the fact that the process of consumption is itself inevitably mediated, we might ask whether or not consumption offers any kind of grounds for citizenship at all or whether alternatively those grounds are entirely inauthentic in nature. This is an issue raised by Boltanski and Chiapello (2005) who argue that the new spirit of capitalism seeks to satisfy the desire for authentic lifestyles via product diversification, thereby subverting accusations of the inauthenticity of mass production. Thus, consumers can pick and choose the consumer lifestyles of their choice. Lamla (2009) points out that this process is not without its costs. The world of consumption in which we live is a world of choice in the sense that there are more choices out there to be made, even if those choices have to be made within the parameters determined by consumption. As such, many of the old certainties and expectations of long-term careers and life pathways have to be abandoned, given that the world in which we live appears to be defined by the extent to which we are able to maintain an identity in constant flux (Lamla, 2009). Consumption seems to offer identity solutions to such a dilemma but the ways in which consumption appears to unite us are the very same ways in which it manages to achieve quite the opposite. This is something Koolhaas (2001: 416) highlights in his discussion of junkspace which 'creates communities not of shared interest or free association, but of identical statistics and unavoidable demographics, an opportunistic weave of vested interests'.

Concluding thoughts

So what of the future? There certainly seems to be a strong argument for suggesting that the role of the city as a public realm is in some senses threatened by the dominance of consumption in how decision-makers conceive of the city: that spaces for consumption have social power but no social responsibility. The end product of this process appears to be a world in which we consume place rather than interact with it (Miles and Miles, 2004). And yet we must simultaneously acknowledge a broader context in which other alternatives and choices appear to be emerging. In particular, the media has a critical role to play in the construction of public space, especially in its virtual guise (Rees, 2006). On the one hand, as Mitchell (1995) suggests, the migration of the public sphere into electronic media reinforces a situation in which material space is purified of the spectre of democratic politics. On the other, it allegedly compounds a situation of social division in which not everybody can access the sort of networked technologies on offer to the telecommunication consumer. Yet, the emergence of online communities offers the consumer something different, a sense of belonging perhaps that is not available elsewhere at least in the same form: a sense of belonging that at least promotes new forms of interaction and humanness in ways that spaces of consumption cannot. The internet offers the possibility of virtual communities and the hope of a democratic community at that, at a time when cities are becoming increasingly fragmented and are thus themselves unable to integrate a public discourse (see Graham and Aurigi, 1997).

Regardless of the ups and downs of the economy, the roles of consumption and of spaces for consumption are not likely to become less influential in how we relate to the city, certainly in the near future. But technological innovation will nonetheless have a profound impact on the forms of consumption we have available to us. Ritzer (2005) argues that despite the impact of increasingly ephemeral, dematerialised forms of consumption, not least via the internet, we can 'look forward' to a future in which spaces for consumption become evermore elaborate; selling machines that serve to further escalate the world of consumerism. One possibility is that the spectacular becomes so common that it no longer surprises or entertains. And yet the evidence suggests that the consumer society will always find a way and means of reinventing itself and that spaces of consumption will no doubt always play a key role in that reinvention given the consumer's desire to experience consumption in person.

The sorts of swift changes that a consumer society undergoes implies an equally fundamental reassessment of the sociologists' role in understanding such processes. The key here lies in understanding consumption, and indeed the relationship to spaces for consumption, in an emotional context. The important sociological question is not centred around how 'bad' things have become in a society so apparently dependent upon the joys that consumption can or cannot bring, but should rather be concerned with how consumption is able to play on our emotions so effectively. Why is it that consumption is able to appeal to the individual consumer in such a way as to offer a new kind of consumer-driven belonging which seems to operate on the cusp of happiness but without actually achieving it? Various authors have tried to understand how consumption brings consumers together in this way. For example, Arnould and Price (1993) talk about the evolution of *communitas* (Turner, 1969) between consumers; a sense of group devotion in which consumers become emotionally attached over their common experience. The communal appeal of consumption is based on an individualistic impulse and as such appears elusive in the sense that it exists in territory in which sociologists are uncomfortable; an environment in which the comfort zone of 'critical theory', in its broadest sense, no longer holds water given the conflicted experiences of a consumer pulled from pillar to post between the need to assert his or her individuality and the desire to feel that he or she belongs.

Spaces for consumption are then sophisticated entities that appear to maximise an individual's control over the consuming experience (through his or her relationship to technology, for example) whilst arguably simultaneously reducing his or her control over space and place in a more generic sense. The consuming experience is undoubtedly highly staged, but what is of more interest is the degree to which the consumer is complicit in such a staging so that his or her playful engagement with such spaces potentially creates an authenticity on his or her own terms (see discussion of Cohen (1988) whose work is discussed further in Chapter 4). A lack of control should not lead us to conclude that the individual consumer is powerless simply because he or she is escaping into the moment. Rather, the consumer is engaged with a culture that privileges notions of choice and freedom; notions that are undoubtedly more limited than the rhetoric around them suggests, but we are nonetheless obliged as social commentators to engage with the ways in which consumers relate to this world of freedom as it is or maybe isn't manifested in their everyday lives. Celebration, Florida which I discussed in Chapter 8 is an extreme example of this process in action: residents being ready and willing to sacrifice a degree of power over their own lives in order to enjoy the fruits of an environment that, as far as they are concerned, is very responsive to their private needs.

Of course, a political critique of consumption is largely based on the fact that consumption is perceived to be an alienating, individualised experience. The notion that something even vaguely positive may come from such an experience is an uncomfortable one for those who take a 'principled' position on a social experience that is apparently determined for the individual by the 'free' market. The increasingly individualised nature of biographies certainly challenges the way the sociologist understands the social world. The kind of communality that emerges in a world in which the individual is increasingly self-authored is inevitably a partial one and one that is apparently reproduced though the very mechanisms that left-wing critics deplore with such rigourless vigour. As Sack (1992) notes above, the world of consumption is one free of constraint (although perhaps less so in recent years with the gradually higher profile of a public debate around sustainability) and as a result the lines of social responsibility appear increasingly blurred. The individual balances the freedoms of consumption, and the constraints implied by a world in which choice is determined by consumption, with a general sense of uncertainty as to their place in the wider world. Spaces for consumption offer a physically tangible degree of certainty amidst all this uncertainty: a sense of belonging in a society in which being a citizen is achieved through the ability to consume. Moreover, notions of 'post-consumption' have limited value in a context in which what appears to be a progressive change in consumption patterns simply serves to magnify the extent to which the ability to consume vicariously and indeed complicitly is so fundamental to human existence in the developed world.

Spaces for consumption transcend notions of the public and the private and offer the individual a sense of self-authorship and control. As such, however much critics may be uncomfortable with the influence of consumption on contemporary culture, consumption does appear to offer consumers a means, however partial, of crystallising selfhood, as Arnould and Price (1993) suggest. In other words, the experience of consumption is often experienced as a positive one for the individual regardless of the political objections that might be laid at the door of the processes that underpin it. People enjoy visiting spaces for consumption, and they plan their time around the opportunities that such experiences offer. Spaces for consumption provide the post-industrial city with a graphic means of stating its future intent. Spaces for consumption speak to the future whilst offering the individual a foothold in the uncertain present. Moreover, the visual presence of spaces for consumption on the urban landscape reflects a situation in which in the current economic climate, it is entirely incumbent upon cities to *feel* contemporaneous. It is incumbent upon the sociologist, in turn, to understand what this feeling may mean in practice for those individuals who have no choice but to live in the city that they may or may not feel is being taken from under their feet.

It is not apparently fashionable nor perhaps has it ever been at least as far as the discipline of sociology is concerned to put to one side the apparent power imbalances implied by a consumer society in order to understand the meanings that lie behind the consuming experience. It is of course a considerable challenge to even begin to get to grips with why it is people consume and the pleasures they derive from a society that is otherwise apparently characterised by structural constraint. We live in a society that, rhetorically at least, promotes the freedoms of individuality and as such we should aspire to understand the individual's experience as he or she sees it. It is incumbent upon the sociologist to confront the sort of complex psycho-social dimensions of the individual's relationship to the city through consumption that is implied in the work of authors such as Sennett (1977). Of course, consumers are in a sense controlled but how do they engage with the controls that supposedly determine their everyday interaction with the consumer society? Surely spaces of consumption, are meaningful to those people who claim them as their own (Wood, 2009)? As Alain Touraine (1988: 104–5) puts it, 'Let us now change our perspective and place ourselves in the position of those who live in this society, who experience it, and who, especially at the industrial level, behave like consumers rather than producers with respect to it'. The choices evident in what Toffler (1970) called the 'communication society' are real in the sense that they are experienced and attractive to the people that feel they are making them. Indeed:

> The task of sociology is to break through the sewer of dead or perverted ideologies, as much as through the illusion of pure individualism or the fascination of decadence, in order to bring to light the presence of the actors and to help their voices be heard. Sociologists ought then to conduct their analyses far from the discourses that a society holds about itself, and work rather in close proximity to the emotions, dreams, and wounds of all those who assume the lives of actors but are not acknowledged as such because the ideologies and the forms of political organization lag well behind truly contemporary practices, ideas and sensibilities. (Touraine, 1988: 18)

Spaces for consumption do not simply maximise the opportunity to consume; they provide spaces within which we negotiate our own symbolic relationship with the consumer society. Spaces for consumption are effectively the arenas within which the emotions, dreams and wounds of a consumer society are played out. What is of interest about those arenas is not what they tell us about the power imbalances which, no doubt, underpin the consumer society. The fascination of spaces for consumption lies in the fact that they represent a physical manifestation of a way of thinking in which the unfulfilled desires of the consumer have come to define the nature of the relationship between structure and agency in contemporary consumer society. The consumer is complicit. His or her complicity is indeed the very foundation upon which spaces for consumption are built. Spaces for consumption are the stage upon which the ideological dominance of consumption is played out. The actor or indeed the consumer should not however be misjudged for he or she gladly dances in his or her own way to the tune that the consumer society has chosen.

REFERENCES

Aldridge, A. (2005) *The Market*. Cambridge: Polity Press.

Arantes, O., Vainer, C. and Maricato, E. (2000) *A Cidade do Pensamento Unico*. Rio de Janeiro: Vozes.

Arnould, E. and Price, L. (1993) 'River magic: extraordinary experience and the extended service sector', *Journal of Consumer Research*, 20, 24–45.

Augé, M. (1995) *Non-Places: Introduction to an Anthropology of Super-Modernity*. London: Verso Books.

Backes, N. (1997) 'Reading the shopping mall city', *Journal of Popular Culture*, 31 (3): 1–17.

Badot, O. and Filser, M. (2007) 'Re-enchantment of retailing: toward utopian islands', in A. Cari and B. Cova (eds) *Consuming Experience*, pp. 34–47. London: Routledge.

Baldock, J. (2003) 'On being a welfare consumer in a consumer society', *Social Policy and Society*, 2 (1): 65–71.

Balfour, A. (2004) 'Epilogue', in A. Balfour, and Z. Shiling *World Cities: Shanghai*, pp. 360–2. London: Wiley-Academy.

Balfour, A. and Shiling, Z. (2002) *World Cities: Shanghai*. London: Wiley-Academy.

Bauman, Z. (1998) *Work, Consumerism and the New Poor*. Buckingham: Open University Press.

Bauman, Z. (2001) 'Forward', in U. Beck and E. Beck-Gernsheim (eds) *Individualization*, pp. xiv–xix. London: Sage.

Bauman, Z. (2007) *Consuming Life*. Cambridge: Polity Press.

Beck, U. and Beck-Gernsheim, E. (eds) (2001) *Individualization*. London: Sage.

Begout, B. (2003) *Zeropolis: The Experience of Las Vegas*. London: Reaktion.

Bélanger, A. (2000) 'Sport venues and the spectacularization of urban spaces in North America: the case of the Molson Center in Montreal', *International Review for the Sociology of Sport*, 35 (3): 378–97.

Bell, D. and Jayne, M. (2004a) 'Afterword: thinking in quarters', in D. Bell and M. Jayne (eds) *City of Quarters: Urban Villages in the Contemporary City*, pp. 249–55. Aldershot: Ashgate.

Bell, D. and Jayne, M. (2004b) 'Conceptualizing the city of quarters' in D. Bell and M. Jayne (eds) *City of Quarters: Urban Villages in the Contemporary City*, pp. 1–15. Aldershot: Ashgate.

Benedikt, M. (2007) 'Less for less yet: on architecture's vale(s) in the marketplace', in W.S. Saunders (ed.) *Commodification and Spectacle in Architecture*, pp. 8–21. London: University of Minnesota Press.

Benjamin, W. (1970) *Illuminations*. London: Fontana.

Benjamin, W. (2002) *The Arcades Project*. Harvard: Harvard University Press.

Bergen, A. (1998) 'Jon Jerde and the architecture of pleasure', *Assemblage*, 37: 8–35.

Blum, A. (2003) *The Imaginative Structure of the City*. London: McGill Queen's University Press.

Boltanski, L. and Chiapello, E. (2005) *The New Spirit of Capitalism*. London: Verso.

Boorstin, D.J. (1987) *The Image: A Guide to Pseudo-Events in America*. New York: Vintage.

Borrie, W.T. (1999) 'Disneyland and Disney World: constructing the environment, designing the visitor experience', *Society and Leisure*, 22 (1): 71–82.

Bourdieu, P. (1979) *Distinction: A Social Critique of the Judgement of Taste*. London: Routledge, Kegan and Paul.

Bowlby, R. (2000) *Carried Away: The Invention of Modern Shopping*. London: Faber and Faber.

Boyer, M. (1992) 'Cities for sale: merchandising history at South Street Seaport', in M. Sorokin (ed.) *Variations on a Theme Park: The New American City and the End of Public Space*, pp. 181–204. New York: Hill and Wang.

Boyer, M. (1993) 'The city of illusion: New York's public places', in P. Knox (ed.) *The Restless Urban Landscape*, pp. 111–126. Englewood Cliffs, NJ: Prentice Hall.

Bradley, A., Hall, T. and Harrison, M. (2002) 'Selling cities: promoting new images for meeting tourism', *Cities*, 19 (1): 61–70.

Braudel, H. (1974) *Capitalism and Material Life, 1400–1800*. New York: Harper & Row.

Bridge, G. and Watson, S. (2000) 'City imaginaries', in G. Bridge and S. Watson (eds) *A Companion to the City*, pp. 7–18. Oxford: Blackwell.

Brill, M. (2001) 'Problems with mistaking community life for public life', *Place*, 14 (2): 48–55.

Broudehoux, A.-M. (2004) *The Making and Selling of Post-Mao Beijing*. London: Routledge.

Broudehoux, A.-M. (2007) 'Delirious Beijing: euphoria and despair in the Olympic metropolis', in M. Davis and D.B. Monk (eds) *Evil Paradises: Dreamworlds of Neoliberalism*, pp. 87–101. London: New Press.

Bryman, A. (1999) 'Theme parks and McDonaldization', in B. Smart (ed.) *Resisting McDonaldization*, pp. 101–15. London: Sage.

Bryman, A. (2004) *The Disneyization of Society*. London: Sage.

Buck-Morris, S. (1989) *The Dialectics of Seeing: Walter Benjamin and the Arcades Project*. Cambridge, MA: MIT Press.

Buck-Morris, S. (1995) 'The city as dreamworld and catastrophe', *October* 73 (Summer): 3–26.

Campbell, C. (1987) *The Romantic Ethic and the Spirit of Modern Consumerism*. London: WileyBlackwell.

Carriere, J.-P. and Demaziere, C. (2002) 'Urban planning and flagship development projects: lessons from EXPO 98, Lisbon', *Planning, Practice and Research*, 17 (1): 69–79.

Castells, M. (1994) 'European cities, the informational society and the global economy', *New Left Review*, 29–30: 204.

Chaplin, S. and Holding, E. (1998) 'Consuming architecture', *Architectural Design Profile* No. 131: 7–9.

Chatterton, P. and Hollands, R. (2003) *Urban Nightscapes: Youth Cultures, Pleasure Spaces and Corporate Power*. London: Routledge.

Christopherson, S. (1994) 'The fortress city: privatized spaces, consumer citizenship', in A. Amin (ed.) *Post-Fordism: A Reader*, pp. 409–27. Oxford: Blackwell.

Chtcheglov, I. (2006) *Formulary for a New Urbanism*, Available at: http://library.nothingness.org/articles/SI/en/display/1 [accessed 1 July 2009].

Clarke, J. (2004) 'Dissolving the public realm? The logics and limits of neo-liberalism', *Journal of Social Policy*, 33 (1): 27–48.

Close, P., Askew, O. and Xu, X. (2007) *The Beijing Olympiad: The Political Economy of a Sporting Mega-Event*. London: Routledge.

Cohen, E. (1988) 'Authenticity and commoditization in tourism', *Annals of Tourism Research*, 15: 371–86.

Cohen, E. (1989) 'Primitive and remote: hill tribe trekking in Thailand', *Annals of Tourism Research*, 16: 30–61.

Coleman, P. (2004) *Shopping Environments: Evolution, Planning and Design*. London: Architectural Press.

Coonan, C. (2006) 'Welcome to China's Thames Town', Monday 14 August, Available at: www.independent.co.uk/news/world/asia/welcome-to-chinas-thames-town-411856.html [accessed 28 July 2009].

Corrigan, P. (1997) *The Sociology of Consumption*. London: Sage.

Couldry, N. (2004) 'The productive "consumer" and the dispersed "citizen"', *International Journal of Cultural Studies*, 7 (1): 21–32.

Craik, J. (1997) 'The culture of tourism', in C. Rojek and J. Urry (eds) *Touring Cultures: Transformations of Travel and Theory*, pp. 113–36. London: Routledge.

Crawford, M. (1992) 'The world in a shopping mall', in M. Sorokin (ed.) *Variations on a Theme Park*, pp. 3–30. New York: Hill and Wang.

Crawford, M., Klein, N.M. and Hodgett, C. (1999) *You Are Here: The Jerde Partnership International*. London: Phaidon Press.

Crilley, D. (1993a) 'Architecture as advertising; constructing the image of advertising', in G. Kearns and C. Phillo (eds) *Selling Places: The City as Cultural Capital, Past and Present*, pp. 231–52. Oxford: Pergamon Press.

Crilley, D. (1993b) 'Megastructures and urban change: aesthetics, ideology and design', in P. Knox (ed.) *The Restless Urban Landscape*, pp. 127–63. Englewood Cliffs, NJ: Prentice Hall.

Damer, S. (1990) *Glasgow for a Song*. London: Lawrence and Wishart.

Davis, M. (2007 'Sand, fear and money in Dubai', in M. Davis and D.B. Monk (eds) *Evil Paradises: Dreamworlds of Neoliberalism*, pp. 48–68. London: New Press.

Davis, M. and Monk, D.B. (2007) 'Introduction', in M. Davis and D.B. Monk (eds) *Evil Paradises: Dreamworlds of Neoliberalism*, pp. ix–xvi. London: New Press.

Davis, S. (1996) 'The theme park: global industry and cultural form', *Media, Culture and Society*, 18 (3): 399–422.

Davis, S. (1997) *Spectacular Nature: Corporate Culture and the Sea World Experience*. London: University of California Press.

Davis, S. (1999) 'Space jam: media conglomerates build the entertainment city', *European Journal of Communication*, 14: 435–59.

Dayan, D. (2008) 'Beyond media events: disenchantment, derailment, disruption', in M.E. Price and D. Dayan (eds) *Owning the Olympics: Narratives of the New China*, pp. 391–409. Ann Arbor, MI: University of Michigan Press.

Debord, G. (1995) *Society of the Spectacle*. New York: Zone Books.

Degen, M. (2004) 'Barcelona's games: the Olympics, urban design, and global tourism', in M. Sheller and J. Urry (eds) *Tourism Mobilities, Places to Play, Places in Play*, pp. 131–42. London: Routledge.

De Lisle, J. (2009) 'After the gold rush: the Beijing Olympics and China's evolving international roles', *Orbis*, 53 (2): 279–304.

De Tocqueville, A. [1850] (1988) *Democracy in America*, 13th edition. New York: Harper Row.

Di Ciccio, P.G. (2007) *Municipal Mind: Manifestos for the Creative City*. Toronto: Mansfield Press.

Donald, J. (1999) *Imagining the Modern City*. London: Athlone.

Dovey, K. (1999) *Framing Places: Mediating Power in Built Form*. London: Routledge.

Dungey, J. (2004) 'Overview: arts, culture and the local economy', *Local Economy*, 19 (4): 411–13.

Eisenger, P. (2000) 'The politics of bread and circuses: building the city for the visitor class', *Urban Affairs Review*, 35: 316–33.

Evans, G. (2001) *Cultural Planning: An Urban Renaissance*. London: Routledge.

Evans, G. (2003) 'Hard-branding the cultural city – from Prado to Prada', *International Journal of Urban and Regional Research*, 27/2 (June): 417–40.

Farndon, J. (2008) *China Rises*. London: Virgin.

Featherstone, M. (1991) *Consumer Culture and Postmodernism*. London: Sage.

Ferreira, A.M. (1998) 'World Expo's', in L. Trigueiros and C. Sat with C. Oliveira (eds) *Architecture Lisboa EXPO'98*, pp. 9–12. Lisbon: Blau.

Firat, A. and Venkatesh, A. (1993) 'Postmodernity: the age of marketing', *International Journal of Research in Marketing*, 10 (3): 227–49.

Florida, R. (2002) *The Rise of the Creative Class*. New York: Basic Books.

Flusty, S. (2001) 'The banality of interdiction: surveillance, control and the displacement of diversity', *International Journal of Urban and Regional Research*, 23 (3): 658–64.

Fong, M. (2008) 'Building the new Beijing: so much work, so little time', in M. Worden (ed.) *China's Great Leap: The Beijing Games and Olympian Human Rights Challenges*, pp. 171–79. London: Seven Stories Press.

Frieden, B. and Sagalyn, L. (1990) *Downtown Inc.: How America Rebuilds Cities*. London: MIT Press.

Fuller, G. and Harley, R. (2005) *Aviopolis: A Book About Airports*. London: Black Dog.

Garcia, B. (2005) 'Cultural policy and urban regeneration in Western European cities: lessons from experience, prospects for the future', *Local Economy*, 19 (4): 312–26.

Gibson, C. and Klocker, N. (2005) 'The "cultural turn" in Australian regional economic development discourse: neoliberalising creativity?', *Geographical Research*, 43 (1): 93–102.

Goheen, P.G. (1998) 'Public space and the geography of the modern city', *Progress in Human Geography*, 22 (4): 79–96.

Gomez, M.V. (1998) 'Reflective images: the case of urban regeneration in Glasgow and Bilbao', *International Journal of Urban and Regional Research*, 22 (1): 106–21.

Goodwin, M. (1997) 'The city as commodity: the contested spaces of urban development', in G. Kearns and C. Philo (eds) *Selling Places: The City as Cultural Capital, Past and Present*, pp. 145–62. Oxford: Pergamon Press.

Gordon, A. (2008) *Naked Airport: A Cultural History of the World's Most Revolutionary Structure*. Chicago: Chicago University Press.

Goss, J. (1993) 'The "magic of the mall": an analysis of form, function, and meaning in the contemporary retail environment', *Annals of the Association of American Geographers*, 83 (1): 18–47.

Gotham, K.F. (2005) 'Theorizing urban spectacles: festivals, tourism and the transformation of urban space', *City*, 9 (2): 225–46.

Gottdiener, M. (1995) *Postmodern Semiotics*. Oxford: Blackwell.

Gottdiener, M. (2001) 'The consumption of spaces and the spaces of consumption', in M. Gottdiener, *New Forms of Consumption: Consumer, Culture and Commodification*, pp. 265–86. Lanham, MD: Rowman and Littlefield.

Gottdiener, M. (2001) *The Theming of America*, 2nd edition. Boulder, CO: Westview.

Goulding, C. (1999) 'Contemporary museum culture and consumer behaviour', *Journal of Marketing Management*, 15 (7): 647–71.

Graham, A. and Aurigi, S. (1997) 'Virtual cities, social polarization, and the crisis in urban public space', *Journal of Urban Technology*, 4 (1): 19–52.

Graham, B. (2002) 'Heritage as knowledge: capital or culture?', *Urban Studies*, 39 (5–6): 1003–17.

Gratton, C. and Roche, M. (1994) 'Mega-events and urban policy', *Annals of Tourism Research*, 21 (1): 1–19.

Gratton, C., Shibli, S. and Coleman, R. (2005) 'Sport and economic regeneration in cities', *Urban Studies*, 42 (5/6): 985–99.

Greco, C. and Santoro, C. (2008) *Beijing: The New City*. Milan: SKIRA.

Gruen, V. and Ketchum, M. (1948) *Chain Store Age*. July, LoCVGP.

Habermas, J. (1989) *The Structural Transformation of the Public Sphere: An Inquiry into a Category of Bourgeois Society*. Cambridge, MA: MIT Press.

Hajer, M. and Reijndorp, A. (2001) *In Search of New Public Domain*. Rotterdam: NAi.

Hall, C.M. (1997) 'Geography, marketing and the selling of places', *Journal of Travel and Tourism Marketing*, 6 (3/4): 61–84.

Hall, T. and Hubbard, P. (1998) *The Entrepreneurial City: Geographies of Politics Regime and Representation*. Chichester: John Wiley.

Hannigan, J. (2003) 'Symposium on branding, the entertainment economy and urban place building: Introduction', *International Journal of Urban and Regional Research* 27(2): 352–60.

Hannigan, J. (2005) *Fantasy City: Pleasure and Profit in the Postmodern Metropolis*. London: Routledge.

Harvey, D. (1989) *The Condition of Postmodernity: An Enquiry into the Origins of Social Change*. Cambridge, MA: Blackwell.

Harvey, D. (2008) 'The right to the city', *New Left Review*, 53: 23–40.

Hayward, K. (2004) *City Limits: Crime, Consumer Culture and the Urban Experience*. London: Glasshhouse Press.

Herman, D. (2001a) 'High architecture', in *Harvard Design School Guide to Shopping*, pp. 390–401. London: Taschen.

Herman, D. (2001b) 'Three-ring circus: the double-life of the shopping architect', in *Harvard Design School Guide to Shopping*, pp. 737–47. London: Taschen.

Herwig, O. and Holzherr, F. (2006) *Dream Worlds: Architecture and Entertainment*. London: Prestel.

Hetherington, K. (2007a) 'Manchester's urbis: urban regeneration, museums and symbolic economies', *Cultural Studies* 4/5: 630–49.

Hetherington, K. (2007b) *Capitalism's Eye: Cultural Spaces of the Commodity*. London: Routledge.

Hill, J. (2002) *Sport, Leisure and Culture in Twentieth Century Britain*. Basingstoke: Palgrave.

Hobbs, D., Lister, S. Hadfield, P., Winslow, S. and Hall, S. (2000) 'Receiving shadows: governance and liminality in the night-time economy', *British Journal of Sociology*, 51: 701–17.

Hochschild, A.R. (2003) *The Commercialization of Intimate Life: Notes from Home and Work*. Berkeley: University of California Press.

Hom, S. (2008) 'The promise of a "people's Olympics"', in M. Worden (ed.) *China's Great Leap: The Beijing Games and Olympian Human Rights Challenges*, pp. 59–72. London: Seven Stories Press.

Hopper, P. (2003) *Rebuilding Communities in an Age of Individualism.* Aldershot: Ashgate.

Horkheimer, M. and Adorno, T. (1973) *The Dialectic of Enlightenment.* London: Verso.

Horne, J. and Manzenreiter, W. (2006) 'An introduction to the sociology of mega-events', in J. Horne and W. Manzenreiter (eds) *Sports Mega-Events: Social Scientific Analysis of a Global Phenomenon*, pp. 10–24. Oxford: Blackwell.

Huang, T.-Y.M. (2004) *Walking Between Slums and Skyscrapers: Illusions of Open Space in Hong Kong, Tokyo and Shanghai.* Hong Kong: Hong Kong University Press.

Hubbard, P. (2006) *City.* London: Routledge.

Hubbard, P. and Hall, T. (1998) 'The entrepreneurial city and the "new urban politics"', in T. Hall and P. Hubbard *The Entrepreneurial City: Geographies of Politics, Regime and Representation*, pp. 1–23. Chichester: John Wiley.

Huxtable, A.L. (1997) *The Unreal America: Architecture and Illusion.* New York: The New Press.

Iritani, E. (1996) 'A mall master takes over the world', *Los Angeles Times*, 5 July: A-1–A-17.

Isin, E. and Wood, P. (1999) *Citizenship and Identity.* London: Sage.

Iyer, P. (2001) *The Global Soul: Jet-Lag, Shopping Malls and the Search for Home.* London: Bloomsbury.

Jacobs, J. (1961) *The Death and Life of Great American Cities.* New York: Random House.

Jayne, M. (2004) 'Culture that works?', *Capital and Class*, 84: 199–210.

Jencks, C. (2006) 'The iconic building is here to stay', *City*, 10 (1): 3–20.

Jerde, J. (1998) 'Capturing the leisure zeitgeist: creating places to be', in *Consuming Architecture*, pp. 68–71. London: Architectural Design.

Jones, P. (2009) 'Putting architecture in its social place: A cultural political economy of architecture', *Urban Studies* 46 (12): 2519–36.

Jones, P. (2010) *The Sociology of Architecture.* Liverpool: Liverpool University Press.

Jones, K.R. and Wills, J. (2005) *The Invention of the Park: From the Garden of Eden to Disney's Magic Kingdom.* Cambridge: Polity Press.

Jones, P. and Evans, J. (2006) *Urban Regeneration in the UK.* London: Sage.

Jones, P. and Wilks-Heeg, S. (2004) 'Capitalising culture: Liverpool 2008', *Local Economy*, 19 (4): 341–60.

Judd, D.R. (2003) 'Building the tourist city: editor's introduction', in D.R. Judd (ed.) *The Infrastructure of Play: Building the Tourist City*, pp. 3–16. Armonk, NY: M.E. Sharpe.

Judd, D.R and Fainstein, S.S. (1999) *The Tourist City.* New Haven, CT: Yale University Press.

Kavaratzis, M. (2004) 'From city marketing to city branding: towards a theoretical framework for developing city brands', *Place Branding*, 1 (1): 58–73.

Kellner, D. (2003) *Media Spectacle*. London: Routledge.

Kirshenblatt-Gimblett, B. (1998) *Destination Culture: Tourism, Museums and Heritage*. London: University of California Press.

Klein, M. (1999) 'Electronic baroque: Jerde cities', in M. Crawford, M. Klein and C. Hodgett (eds) *You Are Here: The Jerde Partnership International*, pp. 112–21. London: Phaidon Press.

Klingmann, A. (2007) *Brandscapes: Architecture in the Experience Economy*. London: MIT Press.

Koolhaas, R. (2001) 'Junkspace', in *The Harvard Design School Guide to Shopping*, pp. 408–21. London: Taschen.

Koolhaas, R. (2008) 'In search of authenticity', in R. Burdett and D. Sudjic (eds) *The Endless City*, pp. 320–3. London: Phaidon.

Kotler, P. (1993) *Marketing Places: Attracting Investment, Industry and Tourism to Cities, States and Nations*. New York: Free Press.

Kozinets, R., Sherry, J., Storm, S., Duhachek, A., Nuttavuthisit, K. and Deberry-Spence, B. (2004) 'Ludic agency and retail spectacle', *Journal of Consumer Research*, 31 (3): 658–72.

Kracauer, F. (1994) *Uber Arbeitsnachweise: Knostruktion eines Raumes* [1930]. Reprinted in *Die Tageszeitung* (Berlin) 30 April: 37.

Kracauer, S. (1995) *The Mass Ornament*. Harvard: Harvard University Press.

Kroker, A. and Cook, D. (1989) *The Postmodern Scene*. New York: St. Martin's Press.

Krugman, P.R. (1996) 'Making sense of the competitiveness debate', *Oxford Review of Economic Policy*, 12: 17–25.

Kunstler, J.H. (1993) *The Geography of Nowhere*. London: Simon and Schuster.

Laenen, M. (1989) 'Looking for the future through the past', in E.D. Uzzell (ed.) *Heritage Interpretation, Vol. 1*, p. 329. London: Belhaven Press.

Lamla, J. (2009) 'Consuming authenticity: a paradoxical dynamic in contemporary capitalism', in P. Vannini and J.P. Williams (eds) *Authenticity in Culture, Self and Society*, pp. 172–85. Aldershot: Ashgate.

Landry, C. (2006) *The Art of City Making*. London: Earthscan.

Langman, L. (1992) 'Neon cages: shopping for subjectivity', in R. Shields. *Lifestyle Shopping: The Subject of Consumption*, pp. 40–82. London: Routledge.

Lasch, C. (1984) *The Minimal Self: Psychic Survival in Troubled Times*. London: W.C. Norton.

Lash, S. (1990) *Sociology of Postmodernism*. London: Routledge.

Lash, S. and Urry, J. (1994) *Economies of Signs and Space*. London: Sage.

Laurier, E. (1993) '"Tackintosh": Glasgow's supplementary glass', in G. Kearns and C. Philo (eds) *Selling Places: The City as Cultural Capital, Past, Present and Future*, pp. 267–90. London: Pergamon Press.

Lefebvre, H. (2005) *Writing on Cities*. London: WileyBlackwell.

Leiss, W., Kline, S. and Jhally, S. (1990) *Social Communication in Advertising: Persons, Products and Images of Well-Being*. London: Methuen.

Levin, T. (1995) 'Introduction', in S. Kracauer, *The Mass Ornament*, pp. 1–30. Harvard: Harvard University Press.

Lin, N. (2001) 'Architecture: Shenzen', in *The Great Leap Forward, Harvard Design School Project on the City*, pp. 156–253. London: Taschen.

Lipovetsky, G. (2005) *Hypermodern Times*. Cambridge: Polity Press.

Lloyd, J. (2003) 'Airport technology, travel, and consumption', *Space and Culture* 6 (2): 93–109.

Lofland, L.H. (1998) *The Public Realm: Exploring the City's Quintessential Social Territory*. New York: Aldine de Gruyter.

Low, S. and Smith, N. (2005) 'Introduction: the imperative of public space', in S. Low and N. Smith (eds) *The Politics of Public Space*, pp. 1–16. London: Routledge.

Lukas, S.A. (2008) *Theme Park*. London: Reaktion.

MacCannell, D. (1976) *The Tourist: A New Theory of the Leisure Class*. London: St. Martin's Press.

MacLeod, G. (2002) 'From urban entrepreneurialism to a "revanchist city"? On the spatial injustices of Glasgow's renaissance', *Antipode*, 34: 602–24.

McCarthy, J. (1998) 'Dublin's Temple Bar: a case study of culture-led regeneration', *European Planning Studies* 6 (3): 271–81.

McCarthy, J. (2006a) 'Regeneration of cultural quarters: public art for place image or place identity?', *Journal of Urban Design*, 11 (2): 243–63.

McCarthy, J. (2006b) 'Cultural quarters and regeneration: the case of Wolverhampton', *Planning Practice and Research*, 20 (3): 297–311.

McCracken, G. (2005) *Culture and Consumption II: Markets, Meanings and Brand Management*. Bloomington: Indiana University Press.

McGuigan, J. (1996) *Culture and the Public Sphere*. London: Routledge.

McGuigan (2004) *Rethinking Cultural Policy*. Buckingham: Open University Press.

McKendrick, N., Brewer, J. and Plumb, J.H. (1984) *The Birth of a Consumer Society: Commercialization of Eighteenth Century England*. London: HarperCollins.

McMorrough, J. (2001) 'City of shopping', in *Harvard Design School Guide to Shopping*, pp. 183–202. London: Taschen.

Madrigal, R., Bee, C. and Labarge, M. (2005) 'Using the Olympics and FIFA World Cup to enhance global brand equity', in J. Amis and T.B. Cornwell (eds) *Global Sport Sponsorship*, pp. 179–90. Oxford: Berg.

Maitland, R. and Newman, P. (2009) 'Conclusions', in R. Maitland and P. Newman (eds) *World Tourism Cities: Developing Tourism off the Beaten Track*, pp. 134–40. London: Routledge.

Mansvelt, J. (2005) *Geographies of Consumption*. London: Sage.

Mars, N. and Hornsby, A. (2008) *The Chinese Dream: A Society Under Construction*. Rotterdam: 010 Publishers.

Marshall, R. (2001) *Waterfronts in Post-Industrial Cities*. London: Spon Press.

Marvin, C. (2008) '"All under heaven" – megaspace in Beijing', in M.E. Price and D. Dayan (eds) *Owning the Olympics: Narratives of the New China*, pp. 229–59. Ann Arbor, MI: University of Michigan Press.

Mattie, E. (1998) *World's Fairs*. New York: Princeton University Press.

Meethan, K. (2001) *Tourism in Global Society: Place, Culture, Consumption*. Basingstoke: Palgrave.

Mikunda, C. (2004) *Brand Lands, Hot Spots and Cool Spaces*. London: Kogan Page.

Miles, M. (2004) 'Drawn and quartered: El Raval and the Hausmannization of Barcelona'. in D. Bell and M. Jayne (eds) *City of Quarters: Urban Villages in the Contemporary City*, pp. 397–408. Aldershot: Ashgate.

Miles, S. (1998) *Consumerism as a Way of Life*. London: Sage.

Miles, S. (2000) *Youth Lifestyles in a Changing World*. Buckingham: Open University Press.

Miles, S. and Miles, M. (2004) *Consuming Cities*. Basingstoke: Palgrave Macmillan.

Millington, S. (1995) *City marketing strategies in the UK*, Unpublished typescript, Manchester Metropolitan University.

Mitchell, D. (1995) 'The end of public space? People's park, definitions of the public, and democracy', *Annals of the Association of American Geographers*, 85 (1): 108–33.

Mitchell, D. (2000) *Cultural Geography: A Critical Introduction*. Oxford: Blackwell.

Montgomery, J. (1995) 'The story of Temple Bar: creating Dublin's cultural quarter', *Planning, Practice and Research*, 10 (2): 135–72.

Montgomery, J. (2003) 'Cultural quarters as mechanism for urban regeneration. Part 1: conceptualising cultural quarters', *Planning, Practice and Research*, 18 (4): 293–306.

Montgomery, J. (2004) 'Cultural quarters as mechanisms for urban regeneration. Part 2: a review of four cultural quarters in the UK, Ireland and Australia', *Planning, Practice and Research*, 19 (1): 3–31.

Montgomery, J. (2007) *The New Wealth of Cities: City Dynamics and the Fifth Way*. Aldershot: Ashgate.

Moss, M. (2007) *Shopping as an Entertainment Experience*. Plymouth: Rowman and Littlefield.

Mullins, P. Natalier, K., Smith, P. and Smeaton, B. (1999) 'Cities and consumption spaces', *Urban Affairs Review*, 35 (1): 44–71.

Murray, C. (2001) *Making Sense of Place: New Approaches to Place Marketing*. London: DEMOS.

Nelson, E. (1998) *Mall of America: Reflections on a Virtual Community*. Lakeville: Galde.

Omar, O. and Kent, A. (2002) 'International airport influences on impulse shopping: trait and normative approach', *International Journal of Retail and Distribution Management*, 29 (5): 226–35.

Paddison, R. (1993) 'City marketing, image reconstruction and urban regeneration', *Urban Studies*, 30 (2): 339–50.

Paolucci, G. (2001) 'The city's continuous cycle of consumption: towards a new definition of the power over time?', *Antipode*, 33, 647–59.

Paterson, M. (2006) *Consumption and Everyday Life*. London: Routledge.

Pawley, M. (1998) *Terminal Architecture*. London: Reaktion Books.

Peck, J. (2005) 'Struggling with the creative class', *International Journal of Urban and Regional Research*, 29 (4): 740–70.

Peñalosa, E. (2007) 'Politics, power, cities', in R. Burdett and D. Sudjic (eds) *The Endless City*, pp. 307–19. London: Phaidon Press.

Perry, D. (2003) 'Urban tourism and the privatizing discourses of public infrastructure', in D.R. Judd (ed.) *The Infrastructures of Play: Building the Tourist City*, pp. 19–49. Armonk, NY: M.E. Sharpe.

Peter, B. (2007) *Form Follows Fun: Modernism and Modernity in British Pleasure Architecture 1925–1940*. London: Routledge.

Petersen, A.R. (2007) 'The work of art in the age of commercial funscapes', in G. Marling and M. Zerlang (eds) *Fun City*, pp. 235–58. Copenhagen: Danish Architectural Press.

Philo, C. and Kearns, G. (1993) 'Culture, history, capital: a critical introduction to the selling of places', in G. Kearns and C. Philo (eds.), *Selling Places: The City as Cultural Capital, Past and Present*, pp. 1–32. Oxford: Pergamon Press.

Pimlott, M. (2007) *Without and Within: Essays on Territory and the Interior*. Rotterdam: Episode.

Pine, J. and Gilmore, J. (1999) *The Experience Economy*. Boston: Harvard Business School.

Podesta, S. and Addis, M. (2007) 'Converging industries through experience', in A. Caru and B. Cova (eds) *Consuming Experience*, pp. 139–53. London: Routledge.

Poynor, R. (2005) 'Inside the Blue Whale: a day at the Bluewater Mall', in W.S. Saunders (ed.) *Commodification and Spectacle in Architecture*, pp. 88–99. Minnesota: Harvard Design Magazine Reader.

Prentice, R. (2001) 'Experiential cultural tourism: museums and the marketing of the new romanticism of evoked authenticity', *Museum Management and Curatorship* 19 (1): 5–26.

Presdee, M. (2000) *Cultural Criminology and the Carnival of Crime*. London: Routledge.

Prior, D., Stewart, J. and Walsh, K. (1995) *Citizenship: Rights, Community and Participation*. London: Pearson.

Pryce, W. (2007) *Big Shed*. London: Thames and Hudson.

Punter, V.P. (1990) 'The privatisation of the public realm', *Planning, Practice and Research*, 5 (2): 9–16.

Putnam, R. (1995) 'Bowling alone: America's declining social capital', *Journal of Democracy*, 6 (1): 65–78.

Putnam, R. (2001) *Bowling Alone: The Collapse and Revival of American Community*. New York: Simon and Schuster.

Rains, S. (1999) 'Touring Temple Bar: cultural tourism in Dublin's "cultural quarter"', *International Journal of Cultural Policy*, 6 (1): 225–67.

Rappaport, E. (2000) *Shopping for Pleasure: Women in the Making of London's West End*. Princeton, NJ: Princeton University Press.

Reekie, G. (1992) 'Changes in the Adamless Eden: the spatial and sexual transformation of a Brisbane department store 1930–1990', in R. Shields (ed.) *Lifestyle Shopping: The Subject of Consumption*, pp. 170–84. London: Routledge.

Rees, R. (2006) 'The brand new authentic retail experience: the commercialization of urban design', in M. Moor and J. Rowland (eds), *Urban Design Futures*, pp. 142–8. London: Routledge.

Reeve, A. and Simmonds, R. (2001) '"public realm" as theatre: Bicester village and universal city walk', *Urban Design International*, 6: 173–90.

Ren, H. (2007) 'The landscape of power: imagineering consumer behaviour at China's theme parks', in S.A. Lukas (ed.) *The Themed Space: Locating Culture, Nation and Self*, pp. 97–112. Lanham, MD: Lexington.

Ren, X. (2008) 'Architecture and nation building in the age of globalization: construction of the national stadium of Beijing for the 2008 Olympics', *Journal of Urban Affairs*, 30 (2): 175–90.

Richards, G. (1996) 'Production and consumption of European cultural tourism', *Annals of Tourism Research*, 23 (2): 261–83.

Richards, G. and Wilson, J. (2006) 'Developing creativity in tourist experiences: a solution to the serial reproduction of culture?', *Tourism Management*, 27: 1209–23.

Rifkin, J. (2000) *The Age of Access: How the Shift from Ownership is Transforming Capitalism*. London: Penguin.

Ritzer, G. (1992) *The McDonaldization of Society: An Investigation into the Changing Character of Contemporary Social Life*. London: Pine Forge.

Ritzer, G. (2004) *Enchanting a Disenchanted World: Revolutionizing the Means of Consumption*, Second edition. London: Pine Forge Press.

Ritzer, G. (2005) *Enchanting a Disenchanted World*. London: Pine Forge.

Robins, K. (1993) 'Prisoners of the city: whatever could a postmodern city be?' in C. Carter, J. Donald and J. Squires (eds) *Space and Place: Theories, Identity and Location*, pp. 303–30. London: Lawrence & Wishart.

Roche, M. (2000) *Mega-Events: Olympics and EXPOs in the Growth of Global Culture*. London: Routledge.

Rojek, C. (1993) *Ways of Escape*. London: Macmillan.

Rojek, C. (2000) 'Mass tourism or the re-enchantment of the world? Issues and contradictions in the study of travel', in M. Gottdiener (ed.) *New Forms of Consumption, Consumers, Culture and Commodification*, pp. 51–70. London: Rowman and Littlefield.

Ryan, N. (2007) 'Vegas at the tipping point?', *Urban Transformations: Regeneration and Renewal Through Leisure and Tourism*, Brighton: Leisure Studies Association, 1: 141–59.

Sack, R.D. (1988) 'The consumer's world: place as context', *Annals of the Association of American Geographers*, 78 (4): 642–64.

Sack, R.D. (1992) *Place, Modernity and the Consumer's World*. New York: John Hopkins University Press.

Sassen, S. (2006) *Cities in a World Economy*. Thousand Oaks, CA: Pine Forge.

Sassatelli, R. (2006) *Consumer Culture: History, Theory and Politics*. London: Sage.

Satterthwaite, A. (2001) *Going Shopping: Consumer Choices and Community Consequences*. London: Harvard University Press.

Saunders, P. (1993) 'Citizenship in a liberal society', in B. Turner (ed.) *Citizenship and Social Theory*, pp. 57–90. London: Sage.

Savitch, H.V. and Kantor, P. (2002) *Cities in the International Marketplace: The Political Economy of Urban Development in North America and Western Europe*. Oxford: Princeton University Press.

Scott, A.J. (2000) *The Cultural Economy of Cities*. London: Sage.

Sennett, R. (1970) *The Uses of Disorder: Personal Identity and City Life*. New York: Knopf.

Sennett, R. (1977) *The Fall of Public Man*. New York: Vintage.

Shields, R. (1992) *Lifestyle Shopping: The Subject of Consumption*. London: Routledge.

Short, J.R. (2006) *Urban Theory: A Critical Assessment*. Basingstoke: Palgrave Macmillan.

Short, J.R. and Kim, J.H. (1999) *Globalization and the City*. Harlow: Addison Wesley.

Shoval, N. (2000) 'Commodification and theming of the sacred: changing patterns of tourist consumption in the "Holy land"', in M. Gottdiener (ed.) *New Forms of Consumption: Consumers, Culture and Commodification*, pp. 251–64. Oxford: Rowman and Littlefield.

Silk, M. and Amis, J. (2006) 'Sport tourism, cityscapes and cultural politics', in H. Gibson (ed.) *Sport Tourism: Concepts and Theories*, pp. 148–69. London: Routledge.

Simmel, G. (1950) 'The Metropolis and mental life', in K. Wolff (ed.) *The Sociology of Georg Simmel*, pp. 324–39. London: Collier-Macmillan.

Sklair, L. (2002) *Globalization; Capitalism and its Alternatives*. Oxford: Blackwell.

Soares, L.J.B. (1998) 'EXPO '98 and Lisbon's return to the river', in L. Trigueiros and C. Sat with C. Oliveira (eds) *Architecture Lisboa EXPO'98*, pp. 21–5. Lisbon: Blau.

Sorkin, M. (1992a) 'Introduction: variations on a theme park', in M. Sorkin (ed.) *Variations on a Theme Park*, pp. xi–xv. New York: Hill and Wang.

Sorkin, M. (1992b) 'See you in Disneyland', in M. Sorokin (ed.) *Variations on a Theme Park*, pp. 205–32. New York: Hill and Wang.

Stevenson, D. (2003) *Cities and Urban Culture*. Maidenhead: Open University Press.

Sze Tsung Leong (2001a) 'The last remaining form of public life', in *Project on the City 2: Harvard Design School Guide to Shopping*, pp. 128–55. London: Taschen.

Sze Tsung Leong (2001b) 'Captive', in *Project on the City 2: Harvard Design School Guide to Shopping*, pp. 174–92. London: Taschen.

Thomas, D. (1997) 'Retail and leisure developments at London Gatwick Airport', *Commercial Airport*. British Airport Authority, August: 38–41.

Toderian, B. (2008) *Does Vancouver Need (or Want) Iconic Architecture?* Available at: www.planetizen.com/node/29385 [accessed 30 October 2009].

Toffler, A. (1970) *Future Shock*. New York: Random House.

Tomlinson, A. (2004) 'The Disneyfication of the Olympics: theme parks and freak-shows of the body', in J. Bale and M.K. Christensen (eds) *Post-Olympism?: Questioning Sport in the Twenty-first Century*, pp. 147–63. Oxford: Berg.

Touraine, A. (1988) *Return of the Actor: Social Theory in Postindustrial Society*. Minneapolis: University of Minnesota Press.

Tucker, M. (2008) 'The cultural production of cities: rhetoric or reality? Lessons from Glasgow', *Journal of Retail and Leisure Property*, 7 (1): 21–33.

Turner, V.W. (1969) *The Ritual Process*. Chicago: Aldine.

Urry, J. (2002) *The Tourist Gaze: Leisure and Travel in Contemporary Societies*, 2nd edition. London: Sage.

Vaz, P.B. and Jacques, L.F. (2006) 'Contemporary urban spectacularisation', in J. Monclus and M. Guarida (eds) *Culture, Urbanism and Planning*, pp.241–53. Aldershot: Ashgate.

Wall, A. (2005) *Victor Gruen: From Urban Shop to New City*. New York: Actar.

Ward, S. (2006) '"Cities are fun!": inventing and spreading the Baltimore model of cultural urbanism', in J. Monclus and M. Guardia (eds) *Culture, Urbanism and Planning*, pp. 271–86. Aldershot: Ashgate.

Ward, V. (1998) *Selling Places: The Marketing and Promotion of Towns and Cities*. London: Spon.

Wasko, J. (2001) *Understanding Disney*. Cambridge: Polity.

Watson, G. and Kopachevsky, J. (1994) 'Interpretations of tourism as a commodity', *Annals of Tourism Research*, 21: 643–60.

Williams, R. (2004) *The Anxious City: English Urbanism in the Late Twentieth Century*. London: Routledge.

Wishart, R. (1991) 'Fashioning the future: Glasgow', in M. Fisher and U. Owen (eds) *Whose Cities?*, pp. 43–52. London: Penguin.

Wood, A. (2009) *City Ubiquitous: Place, Communication and the Rise of Omnitopia*. Cresskill, NJ: Hampton Press.

Worthington, J. (2006) 'Giving meaning to the experience economy', in M. Moor and J. Rowland (eds) *Urban Design Futures*, pp. 159–69. London: Routledge.

Wu, F. (2000) 'Place promotion in Shanghai: PRC', *Cities*, 17 (5): 349–61.

Wu, F., Xu, J. and Gar-On Yeh, A. (2006) *Urban Development in Post-Reform China: State, Market, and Space*. London: Routledge.

Yeoh, B. (2005) 'The global cultural city? Spatial imagineering and politics in the multi(cultural) marketplaces of south-east Asia', *Urban Studies*, 42 (5/6): 945–58.

Young, C. and Lever, J. (1997) 'Place promotion, economic location and the consumption of city image', *Tijdschrift voor Economische en Sociale Geografie*, 88 (4): 332–41.

Zepp, I.G. (1997) *The New Religious Image of Urban America*. Niwot: University Press of Colorado.

Zukin, S. (1993) *Landscapes of Power: From Detroit to Disney World*. London: University of California Press.

Zukin, S. (1995) *The Cultures of Cities*. Oxford: Blackwell.

Zukin, S. (1998) 'Urban lifestyles: diversity and standardisation in spaces of consumption', *Urban Studies*, 35 (5/6): 825–40.

Zukin, S. (2005) *Point of Purchase: How Shopping Changed American Culture*. London: Routledge.

INDEX

Research Methods
Books from SAGE

Read sample chapters online now!

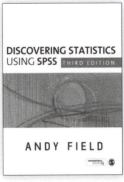

DISCOVERING STATISTICS USING SPSS THIRD EDITION

ANDY FIELD

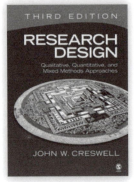

THIRD EDITION

RESEARCH DESIGN

Qualitative, Quantitative, and Mixed Methods Approaches

JOHN W. CRESWELL

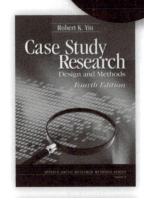

Robert K. Yin

Case Study Research

Design and Methods

Fourth Edition

APPLIED SOCIAL RESEARCH METHODS SERIES Volume 5

Second Edition

QUALITATIVE INQUIRY & RESEARCH DESIGN

Choosing Among Five Approaches

John W. Creswell

Doing a Literature Review

Chris Hart

STATISTICS for People Who (Think They) HATE STATISTICS

3rd EDITION

NEIL J. SALKIND

SECOND EDITION

INTERVIEWS

Learning the Craft of Qualitative Research Interviewing

Steinar Kvale
Svend Brinkmann

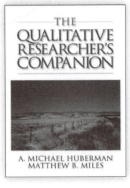

THE **QUALITATIVE RESEARCHER'S COMPANION**

A. MICHAEL HUBERMAN
MATTHEW B. MILES

Basics of **QUALITATIVE RESEARCH** 3e

Juliet Corbin
Anselm Strauss

www.sagepub.co.uk

SAGE